I0569553

SAILING WITH FARRAGUT

SAILING WITH FARRAGUT

THE CIVIL WAR RECOLLECTIONS
OF BARTHOLOMEW DIGGINS

Edited by George S. Burkhardt

Voices of the Civil War
Michael P. Gray, Series Editor

Knoxville / The University of Tennessee Press

The Voices of the Civil War series makes available a variety of primary source materials that illuminate issues on the battlefield, the home front, and the western front, as well as other aspects of this historic era. The series contextualizes the personal accounts within the framework of the latest scholarship and expands established knowledge by offering new perspectives, new materials, and new voices.

LIBRARY OF CONGRESS CATALOGING-IN-PUBLICATION DATA

Names: Diggins, Bartholomew, 1844-1917, author. | Burkhardt, George S., 1927- editor.
Title: Sailing with Farragut : the Civil War recollections of Bartholomew Diggins / edited by George S. Burkhardt.
Description: Knoxville : The University of Tennessee Press, 2016. | Series: Voices of the Civil War | Includes bibliographical references and index.
Identifiers: LCCN 2015048911 (print) | LCCN 2015049518 (ebook) | ISBN 9781621902089 (hardcover : alk. paper) | ISBN 9798895270844 (paperback) | ISBN 9781621902096 (PDF)
Subjects: LCSH: Diggins, Bartholomew, 1844-1917. | United States—History—Civil War, 1861-1865—Personal narratives. | Hartford (Ship)—Biography. | United States—History—Civil War, 1861-1865—Naval operations. | Mississippi River Valley—History—Civil War, 1861-1865. | Gulf Coast (U.S.)—History, Naval—19th century. | Farragut, David Glasgow, 1801-1870. | Mobile Bay, Battle of, Ala., 1864. | United States. Navy—Biography. | Medal of Honor—Biography.
Classification: LCC E595.H2 D54 2016 (print) | LCC E595.H2 (ebook) | DDC 973.7/83092—dc23
LC record available at http://lccn.loc.gov/2015048911

For the sailors of both sides:
May you always have fair winds and following seas

CONTENTS

ILLUSTRATIONS

FIGURES

Confederate "Torpedoes" or Mines
Tunis A. M. Craven
USS *Tecumseh*
Quartermaster John H. Knowles
Rear Admiral Franklin Buchanan, CSN
CSS *Tennessee*

Maps

FOREWORD

New York City's wharves were thronged with people in the fall of 1899, as onlookers awaited the triumphant return of George Dewey and a celebratory procession of warships in the lower Hudson River. Dewey's newfound fame came from his victory at Manila Bay, bringing him a congressional commission as admiral of the U.S. Navy. At his side, among the dignitaries, was Bartholomew Diggins. Diggins, who had served with Dewey during the inland water campaigns in the Civil War, had in his possession a memento from his old sloop, the USS *Hartford*, the flagship of the navy's first ever admiral, David Glasgow Farragut. Diggins had kept the flag for nearly twenty years, claiming it after he helped dedicate a large bronze statue of his old commander in downtown Washington, D.C., in a large square that now bears Farragut's name. The guardian of the venerable flag, the nostalgic Diggins recognized the value in this piece of posterity, as well as the parallels in Dewey and Farragut's achievements as admirals. The gesture in bringing back the *Hartford's* flag bridged these two great maritime commanders; the "Hero of Manila Bay" and the "Hero of Mobile Bay" were connected by a common sailor, Bartholomew Diggins.

Today, not far from where these festivities took place, the neoclassical architecture of the New York Public Library conspicuously stands out among the cluttered modern buildings in midtown Manhattan. The marble structure is accentuated with long columns, rising steps, and two large statuesque lions that seemingly guard its entrance. Inside the building is just as impressive, with powerful artwork, ornate chandeliers hanging from high ceilings, and arched hallways, which are generally filled with visitors. While the library serves as worldwide tourist attraction, it is also an attractive destination for scholars due its immense published and unpublished holdings. Perhaps it is appropriate that Bartholomew Diggins's memoir found its way here, in the same city the *Hartford's* flag was handed over to the highest-ranking naval commander. Since then, Diggins's recollections had only been referenced by a few writers, virtually passed over and never published in its entirety for its full value—until George S. Burkhardt, newspaper proprietor and seasoned editor, recognized its worth. Burkhardt skillfully plies his craft by weaving his subject's narrative together with vigilant editorial commentary, correcting Diggins's rare lapses or departures when needed. The *Voices of the Civil War* series is proud to offer its readership its first complete Union naval primary account, punctuated by a comprehensive Civil War sailor's perspective in coastal "salt water" and inland "brown water" endeavors.

A dearth in Civil War naval primary accounts from sailors, marines, or other seamen might leave scholars and enthusiasts of seafarers frustrated with the Civil War sources. As Burkhardt elaborates, the navy had fewer numbers compared to that of the army, and that fact, compounded by particularly low literacy rates among many foreign-born seamen, makes this volume all the more indispensable. Furthermore, the large diversity among the crew on the USS *Hartford* makes it a very unique vessel and affords a special perspective. The *Hartford* crew comprised some twenty-five different nationalities, or two thirds of its seaman; one was the teenaged Diggins, who hailed from Ireland. Burkhardt visits questions of what motivated him to enlist, as well as other seamen who came from different corners of the world with their own beliefs, prejudices, and incentives to join the Union cause. Motivation to fight has long been a vexing question in the historiography of Civil War soldiers serving in the field, but it also serves historians well to explore similar questions for those who served on water.

Dealing with currents, tides, and storms, along with fire from enemy ships, forts, or from ashore near hostile communities, led water warfare to be dangerous duty on confined ships. Diggins writes about gun boats, iron clads, supply ships, monitors, submarines, and semi-submarines on rivers, bays, and oceans. He also explains weaponry, tactics, and strategy. For example, the Confederate usage of torpedoes or mines struck fear into many a seaman, and it was crucial that they be avoided at all costs. Running aground also caused much distress in many of the "brown water" navies, leaving one vulnerable to attack and the perils of sinking. Diggins reports many examples of vessels that had sunk during his tours. Recent archeological discoveries, like the CSS *Georgia* in the Savannah River, among other wrecks, bring more of an interdisciplinary approach in our field, documented by Diggins, as he details the loss of ships. The close confines onboard ships made daily life interesting; Diggins spoke to what distinguished navy life, such as drill, masting, fuel, sails, losing contact with loves ones, and coming in contact with strangers of all sorts, including animal mascots brought aboard, preparation for combat, and finally battle. Civil War historians, military historians, maritime historians, social historians, environmental historians, and archeologists, among others, will see much merit in this work.

Readers of the *Voices of the Civil War* series may be aware of our volume *Loss of the Sultana and Reminiscences of Survivors* (2005) by Chester D. Berry, which speaks to the tragic events that took place on the Mississippi River. The *Sultana* currently holds the ignominious record of being the worst maritime disaster in our history, with more than 1,700 passengers, most released Union prisoners confined in the South, having perished. A more recent release, *The Memoirs of Winfield Scott* (2015), edited by Timothy D. Johnson, offers contextualization on Diggins's story. The reader gains better understanding of Old Fuss and Feathers's military mind in embracing combined soldier and sailor operations, something practiced in the Mexican War, and further cultivated in the Civil War with his Anaconda Plan; indeed, Sailor Diggins proved to be one of the cogs in a very large wheel in helping carry out Scott's plan of strangling the Confederacy. Diggins not only describes the naval actions in Scott's strategy and tactics of blockading coastlines and controlling the Mississippi, which helped turned the war, but he also elaborates on a slew of Union and Confederate maritime leaders and warships. Bartholomew Diggins fleshes out characters during his service, listing members on the *Hartford's* crew and describing the many he came in contact with, from lower ranking to the highest order—the latter including Farragut, David Dixon Porter, George Dewey, Benjamin Butler, Nathaniel Banks, and Ulysses S. Grant. Perhaps the highlight is a conversation Diggins chronicled between Grant and Farragut about Vicksburg, as he intently listened to their dialogue as he was working near the two.

The young Irishman describes the filling out of crewmembers at the Philadelphia Navy Yard in early 1862, the outfitting of weapons in Hampton Roads, and their final departure in carrying out the far reaches of Scott's Anaconda Plan. There were stops at Key West, Havana, and Ship Island—the latter port was where Farragut officially took over command of the *Hartford*. Fighting finally came when the *Hartford* headed for the protected entry into New Orleans, yet Forts Jackson and St. Philip could do little to keep the Union flotilla from capturing the city. Diggins describes the atmosphere in a hostile New Orleans as the restless citizenry complied little with the Union occupation, elaborated by Benjamin Butler's policies, especially Orders No. 28, which earned him the sobriquet "Beast Butler." Diggins writes about the incited citizens, chamber pots and all, as well as mob-violence, murders, and the Union's attempt to quell disturbances with Butler's policing in the uneasy city.

The reader steams up the Mississippi toward Vicksburg, with excellent descriptions of the environs; here Diggins received a perilous injury from Confederate cavalry fire from the shore. The sailor suggests that the dangerous passing of the well-fortified city was a futile mission to begin with as well-planted batteries overlooking the river made for a too risky voyage. Besides military operations, the Union army was not alone in being exposed to other by-products of war. The sailor elucidates on how naval forces dealt with the dilemma of runaway slaves, as contrabands flocked to Union vessels in hopes that they might serve as a safeguard during their turbulent transition to freedom. He also makes reference to "refugees," Confederates who abandoned their cause and also looked to these roaming vehicles for protection. After Vicksburg, Farragut moved back toward New Orleans. Diggins mentions it was the first time the men were given a much-needed respite with twenty-hour leave, something they had not enjoyed since they had left Philadelphia a year before.

Farragut's flagship next set its course upriver for Port Hudson, an operation that brought many trials and tribulations. There is excellent elaboration on the coordination between the navy and army, headed by General Nathaniel Banks. Diggins also details the many vessels involved and their captains, techniques in lashing, civilian interaction, the taking in of more African American contrabands as they, some African Americans provided information about Confederate positions for advance warning to the Union vanguard. Diggins tells of a special mission in going ashore, cutting down telegraph lines, dangerous work in enemy territory that came with his marine duty. The sailor takes the reader to the blockading of the mouth of the Red River, tormenting duty as heavy rains and light rations led the sailors to eat weevils and worms, which found their way into food. They had to be resourceful, so they devised fishing equipment and caught catfish in helping stave off their "starving time." News of the surrender of Vicksburg arrived, and finally, when the last stronghold on the Mississippi, Port Hudson, raised the surrender flag, the *Hartford's* spirits were lifted. They shipped back to New York for the Brooklyn Navy Yard so the battered sloop might make the necessary repairs to fight again.

The mended *Hartford* headed south for Mobile Bay, where it would claim its place in maritime history. Of particular interest, Diggins participated in two night raids that targeted the blockade-runner *Ivanhoe* prior to the great battle. They were not recorded in the official reports, yet Diggins includes the perilous events, which culminated in hand-to-hand fighting. His strength as a chronicler shows in his Mobile account, listing the Union ships involved as well as their captains, recounting the formation of the ships, recalling Farragut's exploits, including the admiration he won from his crew for his resilience in his famous passing of forts into the bay; Diggins, in the meantime calls it a "fluid battle." Diggins contrasts Farragut's character with that of Confederate commander Franklin Buchanan, at the helm of the Confederate ram CSS *Tennessee,* and former commander of the CSS *Virginia.* Diggins recounts their rise in the U.S. Navy together before the Civil War, and he observes that Farragut (born near Knoxville, Tennessee) and the Baltimorean Buchanan chose their respective sides as they came up through the ranks. The climax of their already battled-tested careers came at Mobile Bay. Diggins elucidates the battle and its aftermath, as the *Hartford* was again being battered, with a section of the ship termed the "Slaughter House." He had helped in the bloody clean up, where arms, legs, and bodies were gathered—bagged up, two at a time, undoubtedly some appendages not properly placed with proper trunks—and buried at sea. Diggins also lists the casualties, including Admiral Buchanan. Finally, Burkhardt gives the particulars about Farragut's spoils of war and lays the framework for Diggins's return home—itself a still very venturous, if not dangerous voyage. If Buchanan could not sink the *Hartford*, Mother Nature did her best to do so. As they moved around Key West and up the coast, they hit heavy gales off Cape Hatteras. They managed to maintain their set course, however, and ended back at a familiar place in the Diggins story: New York Harbor. As they approached, the *Hartford* was greeted with cheers and cannon fire from nearby forts in celebration of Farragut and of those, like Diggins, who sailed with him.

Michael P. Gray
East Stroudsburg University
of Pennsylvania

ACKNOWLEDGMENTS

While I am solely responsible for editing decisions, commentary, and endnotes in this work, many people helped to make this project possible.

First and foremost, Bartholomew Diggins deserves primary gratitude. It is he who compiled this account of the USS *Hartford* during the Civil War, a sustained and self-effacing effort. His labor has added to the scant store of personal narratives by sailors of both sides. Perhaps it was a purgative exercise for Diggins, a release of sorts from the burden of his experiences. Certainly it is not a self-serving account, a heroic self-portrayal. On the contrary, he relates how he thought to abandon the *Hartford* during a fighting passage to New Orleans, and when he was shot and wounded by Confederates, he was almost a hapless bystander. Yet he was always there, for three years, through the fire and thundering cannonades and he won the Medal of Honor for his actions during the battle of Mobile Bay. Whatever his motives in carefully writing his recollections, he deserves the lion's share of credit. Then, the librarians and curators at the New York Public Library next deserve credit. They preserved his recollections, given to them in a large ledger book. They arranged for the photocopying to microfilm of the whole, which permitted the editing and presentation of Diggins's work. Special thanks go to librarians Thomas Lannon, for his research and help with this project, and Laura Ruttum, for her assistance.

Much gratitude is due William H. Boswell of Alexandria, Va., a direct descendant of Diggins. Besides providing a detailed, exhaustive family genealogy report, Boswell also conveyed what he had learned about the manuscript's history.

Repeatedly, arcane information about wooden sailing and steam ships cheerfully came from Michael J. Crawford, head of the Early History Branch, Naval History and Heritage Command, Washington, D.C. For instance, Crawford supplied explanations about how sailors stripped the ships for battle, a puzzling question.

Many curators, librarians, editors, and other specialists at a variety of institutions assisted with requests for photographs, records, sketches, letters, diaries, and journals. Eileen Sullivan, rights and permissions,

New York Metropolitan Museum of Art, went out of her way to obtain permission for the use of a photograph on exhibition there from the private owner and to supply a copy of that photo. Kim Y. McKeithan, archives specialist at the National Archives in Washington, D.C., also exerted herself in furnishing Diggins's muster roll and other information about him.

David D'Onofrio, special collections librarian, Nimitz Library at the U.S. Naval Academy, Annapolis, Md., quickly provided photographs, including one of old salt John H. Knowles wielding a cutlass. Museum curator Deborah S. Wood, Wilson's Creek National Battlefield in Missouri, not only copied a requested photo but also sent several others of interest and a list of all available at her museum. Evelyn M. Cherpak, Ph.D., head of the Naval Historical Collection at the Naval War College in Newport, R.I., promptly sent copies of David G. Farragut letters, and Bonnie Coles and Patrick Kerwin helped considerably with requests.

Once again, thanks go to John T. Magill, curator and head of research services, Historic New Orleans Collection, for his advice about Civil War New Orleans. The same appreciation is owed Thomas Knoles, curator of manuscripts, and Jaclyn Penny, rights and reproductions, American Antiquarian Society, Worcester, Mass., who once more allowed the use of a map-diagram.

George Skoch, a first-rate mapmaker, again used his expertise to contribute a map showing Diggins's voyages on the USS *Hartford*.

Much appreciated is the unwavering support and encouragement from great friends John Gabriel, Noreen Cavanaugh, and Ann Parkinson. Always in mind are the strict standards and guidance of former editor Sylvia Frank Rodrigue.

Lastly, thank goodness for the Internet, which makes any researcher's task so much easier these days.

INTRODUCTION

A National Archives writer declared, "Given the wealth of available information about Civil War soldiers, the comparative poverty of such knowledge about Civil War sailors borders on the astonishing."

Joseph P. Reidy, the writer, concluded that this resulted from an emphasis on the land battles in the popular media and a similar emphasis on the navy's strategic roles, its commanders and technical innovations during the war. What Reidy says is true enough as far as it goes. But other reasons also exist for that poverty and the paucity of naval narratives and accounts.[1]

Mainly, the naval forces of both sides were tiny compared to the millions who served in the armies. So there are hundreds of accounts of land battles and more hundreds of personal narratives by soldiers, but far fewer by sailors or of naval life and actions.

Still another practical reason exists for the comparative dearth of personal narratives: illiteracy. African-Americans, mostly illiterate, constituted from 8 to 23 percent of the navy's strength. Foreign-born men provided a "whopping" 45 percent of enlistments at recruiting stations, and in March 1863, USS *Hartford's* complement of 324 had 216 foreign-born members of 25 different nationalities, more than two-thirds of the crew. While some, such as the Irish-born Bartholomew Diggins, knew English, many others understood only basic commands. This lack of literacy in English further constricted sailor writing.[2]

Total wartime enlistments in the U.S. Navy were 118,000. As an indicator of strength, this figure is misleading. That number includes reenlistments, bounty-men who jumped ship at the first opportunity, and ordinary deserters. On August 1, 1862, one ship's captain complained, "We lost a hundred men who overstayed their leave," and, in these recollections, Diggins wrote that at one point "the number of desertions greatly increased, so much so that we sailed for Pensacola to stop it."[3]

At peak strength in 1865, the Federal navy floated 671 ships, a tremendous expansion from the 89 at the war's start. To man those ships and shore installations, naval personnel surged from a total of 11,412 in 1861 to a high of 61,965 officers and men, including 3,850 marines, at the war's end in 1865.[4]

With those ships and sailors, the navy blockaded southern ports from Virginia to the Texas border with Mexico in the gulf; engaged in combined or amphibious operations with the army, such as at Port Royal, S.C., in November 1861, and the Fort Fisher, N.C., attack in late 1864; transported troops, sometimes in conjunction with army ships; carried out independent operations, such as the capture of New Orleans in 1862 or closing Mobile in 1864; hunted Confederate commerce raiders (a largely unsuccessful mission, except for the CSS *Alabama's* destruction in June and the capture of the CSS *Florida* in October 1864, though raiders did cause shipping insurance rates to soar and inflicted longlasting damage to the American merchant marine); and fought Confederate warships like the CSS *Albemarle* in April and May 1864.[5]

In addition, the navy operated supply ships, which carried provisions, water, ice, mail, munitions, and spare parts, as well as replacement sailors; the navy's first hospital ship, the USS *Red Rover*; tugs; dispatch steamers; receiving ships; and ice boats.[6]

Recruiting sailors for all these ships proved a persistent problem for the navy, and commanders chronically lamented the shortage of men. Even a lowly sailor on the western rivers noted the shortage. He wrote home, "They are building so many gunboats that they cannot get men enough to man them."[7]

Both tangible and intangible considerations pushed military-age men away from the navy, causing shortfalls in recruiting after the first rush to arms in 1861. Army volunteers got bounties, while it was not until 1864 that Congress voted a bonus for navy recruits. Men joining the army usually did so with friends and neighbors from their towns or counties, or sometimes as ethnic groups, thus enjoying a cohesive, supportive framework from the start; sailors enlisted alone, usually without friends or fanfare. Many people saw serving in the navy as a dodge to escape a man's duty of meeting the southern rebels face to face on the field of battle.[8]

In addition, many viewed seafaring as an alien life and sailors as a brutish, drunken underclass. Motivation also played a large role; patriotism often propelled citizen-soldiers, while sailors often cited other motives.

One Ohio youth, who first enlisted in a 100-day infantry regiment, said he did not know quite why he next joined the navy. A Massachusetts lad shipped as a paymaster's clerk in May 1861 for the adventure, but said that patriotism drove many men from his town who came aboard in a late draft from the receiving ship Joseph T. Collins, who enlisted in 1862 as a seventeen-year-old New York landlubber, admitted six months later that he had acted in headstrong fashion against his mother's wishes when he joined the navy.[9]

Yet an older married man with children who enlisted in 1862 for three years and sailed away on the high seas aboard USS *Kearsarge* said that "it was incumbent upon all Loyal Subjects . . . to give their Aid in doing all they could to suppress [the rebellion]." On the western rivers, on the USS *Rattler,* William N. Bock donned navy blue "in defense of the old flag." Very unusual for both soldiers and sailors were the abolitionist sentiments of a crewman aboard the USS *Albatross* off Mobile. W. H. Price aimed to crush slavery, Copperheads, and the rebellion.[10]

Diggins never gives his reason for enlisting at age seventeen. As a recent Irish immigrant it is unlikely that patriotic fervor prompted him. To speculate, perhaps the need for employment and income spurred him, especially since he apparently lacked a trade or any special skills. The lure of prize money may have influenced him, as it did many. Then, the prospect of regular meals, sheltered sleeping quarters (rather than a soldier's cold or muddy ground), and a home always under his feet was attractive. There was also the popular perception that the navy provided safer service than soldiering.[11]

This last belief rested on fact.

Killed in action rates were one in nine for soldiers but just one in sixty-five for sailors. Deaths from disease rates were also higher in the army—about one in fifteen soldier recruits died of disease, while that loss was but one in forty for the navy. In total numbers, the army, with more than two million men, counted 389,000 deaths; the navy, with a top strength of almost 62,000, listed 1,804 killed and 2,226 wounded.[12]

These statistics, however accurate, admit of no nuances and so do not tell the full story. Sailors served on a confined, self-contained, isolated space, their ship. Accordingly, a disaster could engulf almost the entire crew. James E. Campbell, a volunteer master's mate on the tinclad USS *Naiad,* candidly voiced the sailor's worry. He said that "worst of all was the fact that you could not run away . . . there was no place else to go."[13]

So when the buttoned-up monitor USS *Tecumseh* hit a mine in Mobile Bay and disappeared "like an arrow twanged from the bow," the one in sixty-five killed statistic did not apply. Of the 115 men aboard, only 21 escaped entombment at the bottom. Neither did it apply when enemy fire hit a boiler, sending searing steam throughout a ship, killing or scalding most of the crew. That happened to the USS *Mound City* on a western river. A single ship might bear the brunt of Confederate fire during an engagement, which occurred when the CSS *Arkansas* pounded the USS *Tyler,* resulting in fifty-seven of her small crew killed, wounded and missing. More than half the USS *Cricket's* crew became casualties on the Red River when eighteen artillery pieces shredded her, hitting the sidewheel steamer thirty-eight times in April 1864. Confederates boarders surprised the anchored small sidewheel gunboat *Underwriter* at New Berne, N.C., in February 1864. Those boarders, freely using the cutlass, captured the two-gun ship, inflicting forty-eight casualties on the Federal crew in the process.[14]

Shipboard duties also exposed sailors to a variety of accidents, most peculiar to the navy. Personal narratives by Civil War sailors often mention such mishaps, which occurred throughout the fleet. With no safety harness, men plunged to their deaths from masts, yards, and rigging or fell overboard to drown. Capstans whirled, their bars injuring twenty-four men in one incident. Objects dropped from above, as when a heavy block-and-tackle came down, just missing the head of Farragut's chief surgeon, or when a big block of ice went over a hatchway's edge, bruising a yeoman's side. Perhaps amusing to others, but not to the victim, was the severe gash Wiliam F. Keeler suffered when a cutlass slipped from its scabbord hanging above his bed when the ship's cannon fired.[15]

Although not unique to the navy, there were more heavy cannon aboard ships than in many army artillery units. These huge muzzle-loaders exploded with dismaying frequency, killing or wounding their crews. Repeatedly, sailors noted such lethal blasts. They also reported less common mishaps such as bolts failing, hawsers parting and snapping back to kill and injure, a sailor disappearing in a small boat, or the mortar fleet sailor who lost his head while carrying a powder container over his shoulder and smoking a cigar at the same time.[16]

Prize money proved a chimera for many or even most sailors, though the navy trumpeted the possibility as a fact, sometimes in exaggerated terms. Prize money derived from the capture and sale of ships and their cargo and equipments, as well as seized contraband goods, mainly cotton. Sale proceeds went to captains and crews on a prorated basis, depending upon participation in the capture and rank. Ship captains got the biggest share and the lowest rated enlisted men, the least. Some officers and captains fared very well under the prize money program, which Congress abolished in 1900. Judging from Civil War sailors' accounts, chicanery attended some captures, including the seizure and sale of cotton and in cash distributions.[17]

Still, the crew of one Union ship salvaged bales of cotton tossed overboard by a blockade runner, and each sailor collected about three months' pay in prize money. Paymaster's clerk Frank R. Butts was happy when his ship caught a blockade runner and he received $49.97 as his share. But Quartermaster John H. Knowles, an old salt aboard the *Hart-*

ford, complained that "we had not much chance to get prize money but we had plenty of fighting all the prize money I got . . . was $80 for Mobile and $150 from Washington and I think they cut us rather short."[18]

However, regular meals and sheltered sleeping quarters, a home afloat, did bless naval service. Moreover, sometimes ships in hot climates received a supply of ice, "What is to us an inestimable luxury," as one sailor exulted.[19]

Yet often ships lacked fresh provisions, generating complaints from high and low. On one occasion, Farragut wrote the Navy Department, "Our supply vessels do not bring half provisions enough for the fleet . . . potatoes ought to be cheap & yet no vessel gets a tithe of what they want. . . ." On New Year's Day of 1862, a sailor on the USS *Essex* said that he dreamed of chicken and roast beef but he knew full well that all he would get for dinner was salt meat and hard bread. Even more plaintively, a fireman on the USS *Nansemond* wrote, "I am near starved . . . if I get much thinner it will take two of us to make one shader."[20]

Even if fresh provisions came, they were not always very fresh, particularly meats, which sometimes arrived in near-putrid condition. Aboard the *Hartford* at Pensacola in early 1864, a sailor reported a supply boat had brought some beef. He wrote, "*Such* beef, a look and a sniff was all we wanted." In October 1864, a nineteen-year-old USS *Hindman* sailor on the Mississippi reported that sometimes the beef is "purple" but that now and then they got sweet potatoes "sliced and fried in flavored grease and frequently seasoned with roaches, red ants, nigger wool and dust from everything but a man can get accustomed to all these little things."[21]

Predictably, scurvy, that mariners' ancient bane, appeared in ships' crews. That affliction, which can lead to death, results from a lack of vitamin C, found in fresh fruits and vegetables. Most navy medical officers knew the cause and the remedy, but the cure was not always available. But when scurvy appeared on a blockader off the Texas coast, the ship's captain sailed to Matamoros, Mexico, where they bought a "generous supply" of fresh fruits and vegetables to avert a serious outbreak.[22]

Other captains, usually upon the advice of their surgeons, also took direct action to secure fresh food. A fireman on the USS *Hastings* said their captain did not hesitate when they spotted a flock of geese near the bank of a western river. He loaded a cannon with canister, fired and nine geese became the ship's dinner fare. The fireman thought that was wonderful, a great change from the customary menu. On the tinclad USS *Silver Cloud*, the crew benefited from Sanitary Commission supplies of onions, potatoes, and cabbage, but they also went hunting for raccoons, wild swan, and squirrels. Approaching an island in the Tennessee River, the crew of the USS *Silver Lake* saw cattle and potato pits, so they got fresh meat and potatoes, messily butchering cattle right on the ship's deck. When possible or permitted, sailors also augmented their diet with the sea's bounty, catching fish and harvesting oysters.[23]

Even so, many sailors found shipboard life extremely monotonous. This was especially true of those serving on blockading ships. Though an essential part of northern war strategy and increasingly effective as the conflict wore on, both officers and men considered it "dreary" duty, "dreadful monotony," and "a dreadfully dull business." To keep crews occupied and the ship shipshape, captains and officers ordered constant repetitive drills and housekeeping. A sailor on the Texan blockade thought of several ways to escape the prison atmosphere: an accidental machinery breakdown, an epidemic of some deadly disease like yellow fever, or, more sure, sabotage of the machinery by the crew. Aboard the USS *Ossipee* off Mobile, a crewman wrote home, "How happy we shall be when this blockade duty is finished! You, at home, can hardly realize the dull, monotonous life on the Blockade."[24]

With the exception of national holidays and Sunday church services, sailors had to rely upon themselves to break the monotony. So sailors wrote letters, fished, swam, practiced fencing, skylarked in rough-and-tumble contests, played dominoes, cards, backgammon until the boards and dies became worn, spun teetotum tops, gambled on the sly, danced, heard and played musical instruments, listened to singers, and watched minstrel shows. Many ships also hosted pets, sometimes a regular menagerie, including foxes, raccoons, dogs, squirrels, cats, goats, pigs, and bears. An assistant paymaster on the USS *Florida* wrote, "They aid in passing away a good many leisure hours at sea." Officers had a wider variety of entertainments available to them, including balls and more liquor.[25]

Soon enlisted men no longer enjoyed a daily tot of grog, a mixture of water and whisky or rum. Temperance groups, navy doctors, ranking officers, and officials had increasingly pressed for the grog ration's abolishment. Assistant Secretary of the Navy Gustavus Vasa Fox insisted, "All insubordination, all misery, every deviltry on board ships can be traced to *rum*." With the approval of Congress, the navy on July 14, 1862, ordered that "the spirit ration . . . shall forever cease," effective September 1, 1862.[26]

As the *New York Times* reported, the end of the grog ration excited the "most intense commotion" in naval circles. Indeed, when the USS *Brooklyn*'s captain read the order ending the ration, his crew become so indignant that he immediately spliced the main brace, restoring the ration for that day at least. Many sailors took the stoppage as a personal affront. Charles K. Mervine, a second class boy on USS *Powhatan*, protested, "If you want a sailor to work, give him his whisky." George A. Bright, an assistant surgeon on the USS *South Carolina*, offered a clinical assessment. He wrote his father, "I'm sorry the grog was abolished in the Navy in such an absolute way by our sober legislators. There are many times when it would be a good thing to give Jack a glass to fortify him against the weather."[27]

However, some volunteer sailors welcomed the stoppage. George S. Geer, a fireman on the USS *Monitor*, ranted about grog and told his wife that there were three great evils abroad: "whiskey, whiskey and whiskey." And when a former merchant mariner downed his first grog ration, he said it was his first and last time. He added that "if hot lead had been poured down my throat, I should have suffered no more."[28]

For many volunteer sailors, mail from home or the lack of it, loomed just as large as good food or its lack. Throughout the blockading squadrons, mail arrived and went out about every two weeks on the average. But that was not true for every one or every ship, and some sailors complained bitterly about the lack of mail from home.[29]

Not once does Diggins speak of either writing or receiving letters. Though his mother had settled in Baltimore when they first arrived in the United States, possibly she was illiterate and perhaps Diggins himself was not handy with pen or pencil at the time. Additionally, Diggins often wrote his later recollections as a detached observer. While he mentions bad food, miserable living conditions, unrelieved exposure to rain, tedium, and danger, his reaction to these conditions require a bit of deduction: he was there, so he also must have felt the adversities, the danger, perhaps some fear.

Good sailor that he is, Diggins largely keeps his concerns and worries to himself, voicing few complaints. In the extreme, when he suffers two bad wounds at the hands of mounted irregulars or guerrillas, he bemoans neither pain nor treatment. It is almost as if it all happened to somebody else. Yet he will speak of "provisions . . . unfit for human food" while the *Hartford* is river-locked for months on the Mississippi between Port Hudson and Vicksburg.

Some readers may find Diggins's approach more credible and a better way to recount dramatic events; others may regard it as wanting.

Eventually his manuscript ended up in the New York Public Library, but curators there do not know how or when that accession occurred.

PART 1
OFF TO WAR

TO THE MISSISSIPPI

With legions of other Federal sailors and soldiers, Diggins helped advance the Union's plan to squeeze the life out of the Confederacy. In essence, this was a modified version of General-in-Chief Winfield Scott's "Anaconda Plan," a design to strangle the southern states into submission.[1]

A blockade of southern ports, ordered by President Lincoln early on, sought to prevent the Confederacy from receiving needed supplies from abroad or shipping cotton and other goods overseas to earn money to conduct the war. A second vital aspect of Scott's Anaconda Plan was to control the Mississippi River, driving southward from the North to achieve that goal.[2]

Union domination of that vital north-south artery would split the Confederacy into two unequal parts. Texas, parts of Louisiana, Arkansas, and Missouri would be isolated in the Trans-Mississippi. This would deny the eastern sections the troops, supplies, foodstuffs, horses, and revenue that came from across the river. Conversely, success would give Federal ships and troops free movement on the vital waterway, enabling the Union to make gains in the West. This strategy required the capture of New Orleans, the South's largest city, and the reduction of fortified Vicksburg, the upstream bastion that allowed Confederates to control the river. Although the blockade took a long time to become effective and never stopped all blockade runners, interdicting southern ports indisputably contributed to the Confederacy's defeat. While the Union followed Scott's basic plan to clear the Mississippi, the navy and the army first moved up from the south, rather than down from the north.

According to David D. Porter, then a new commander in rank, it was he who first proposed to begin retaking the Mississippi River by capturing New Orleans. When that idea won approval, it was he who chose Captain David G. Farragut to lead the attack from the Gulf.[3]

Porter's contemporaries all gladly credited him with organizing a flotilla of 13-inch mortar boats to pound New Orleans's guardian forts into submission, a goal the mortars failed to achieve. But as one naval officer wrote, "It has astonished a great many people to learn . . . that he was the first man to propose the opening of the Mississippi." Their surprise was well-founded because Lincoln, Secretary of the Navy Gideon Welles, and other ranking officials had discussed and prepared for the attack in the summer of 1861, long before Porter appeared on the scene. Further, Porter was not instrumental in Farragut's selection, though perhaps he could have killed the appointment. Successfully passing New Orleans's guardian forts and taking the city were the initial objectives. It was in this effort that Diggins played his part.[4]

Beginning his "Recollections," Diggins describes the *Hartford*, her history, lists her officers, and recounts the preparations for war.

Throughout his narrative, Diggins is fairly accurate, erring only occasionally. In his description of the *Hartford*, for instance, he describes her as a 2,000-ton propeller sloop, when in reality she was 2,900 tons. He relates that she was "built" in 1857, while the Naval Historical Center lists her as launched in November 1858 and commissioned in the spring of 1859. Sometimes, too, he repeats suspect tales retailed by old sailors. Often, it is impossible to either verify or disprove such yarns. But for events within his purview, Diggins usually provides a reliable account, one supported by others who were also eyewitnesses to those momentous events. Here he begins his recollections.[5]

The *Hartford* was built in Boston in 1857. Rated as second class, she was a spar deck Sloop of War of about 2000 tons and drawing about 18 feet of water. She was full ship-rigged and had port holes for 24 broad side guns, but carried only 16 in time of peace. She was considered the handsomest ship in the Navy in the water and was one of the best sea boats.[6]

She made her first cruise to China and carried the first battery of nine inch Dahlgren guns to those waters, which were the astonishment of the people and officers of other navys who thought them too large for ship board and predicted that in action they would tear the ship's side from

4

her. The guns chiefly in use by other navys up to this time being 12 to 32 pounder, or from 3 to 6 inch.[7] At the breaking out of the war the *Hartford* was ordered home. She arrived at Philadelphia where she was hurriedly repaired and by the middle of January 1862 she was ready for sea. A crew of nearly 400 men were selected from the Receiving Ship *Princeton* at the Philadelphia Navy Yard and put on board at the same time.[8]

The following is a list of her officers[:]

Richard Wainwright, Captain; James S. Thornton, Lieut. and executive officer; [Lieut.] Albert Kautz; Lieut. J. Crittenden Watson, Master; Albert Cook, act[ing] master;

H. J. Draper, act. master; Ezra S. Goodwin, act. master; Daniel S. Murphy, act. master; Herbert B. Tyson, act. midshipman; Edward C. Haseltine, act. mid[shipman]; John H. Read, act. mid.; E. J. Allen, act. m[aster's] mate; Thos Mason, act. m. M[ate]; Lewis [S.] Locke, act. m. m; James Walker, boatswain; John Duncan, gun[n]er; James H. Conley, carpenter; and John Hallbrook, sail M[aster];

Geo [H.] Loundsberry, act. m. mate; John M. Foltz, fleet surgeon; Stewart Kennedy, surg; James Hogg, asst. surg; Geo Plunkett, paymaster; J. B. Kimball, chief engineer; John Purdy, second asst. eng.; E. B. Latch, second asst. eng.; F. A. Wilson, second asst. eng.; C. J. Cooper, third eng.; Chas M. Burchard, third asst. eng.; J. De Graff, third asst. eng.; A. H. Fulton, third asst.; A. V. Heurel, flag officers secretary; A[lbert] D. Bache, capt[ain's] clerk; B. S. Osbon, f[lag] o[fficer's] clerk.

The morning after our arrival on board all hand[s] were called aft where we were addressed by Captain Wainwright in a short speech in which he assumed command. The men now received their stations to the different parts of the ship. I was stationed in main top. Men and officers now went to work with [a] will, getting the ship in order and cleaning her up ready for sea.

We dropped down the Delaware River to the Powder Magazine and got our ammunition on board. At New Castle, Delaware, Flag Officer Farragut came on board for the first time. We had heard that our ship was to be flagship and every body was anxious to see the new commandant. We had heard of him and opinions of him among the crew was less favorable than otherwise. He had the reputation of a strict desciplinarian. I, like the rest, wanted a good look at him and stationed myself at the poop ladder near the entrance to his cabin door when he was reported coming along side. He came hurriedly over the starboard gangway, hastily shook hands with the officers on deck and, with Captain Wainwright, entered his cabin. He was slightly less than medium size, about 5 ft 7 or 8 in high, of square full build and would weigh about 160 pounds. He wore no beard, the color of his hair was a medium between dark and light and in loose curls below his ears, clear hazel eyes well covered with heavy eyebrows. He was very bald which he tried to cover by combing the side hair across the top of his head.[9]

The expression of his face was earnest and agreeable. He was very plain and unassuming in his manner, he was very quick and active in his movements. He wore the undress uniform of a Captain, his coat buttoned by a single button at the throat which was his style of wearing it afterwards on the ship, except on ocasions of ceromony when he would button an odd button down the breast. At his own request there was none of the ceromony usual on such occasions at his reception on the ship.

He came out of his cabin soon after entering it and called to me, I being the nearest of any of the men, to bring a small nail. When I brought the nail, I saw the picture of a Lady in his hand (his wife's). He drove the nail himself and hung the picture on the front wall of the cabin where one could not miss seeing it at the left of the door coming out.

He did not assume any authority on the ship. Things went on as before he come on the ship.

This ended our business in the Delaware and we sailed for Hampton Roads, arriving about the 25th of January 1862. Here we commenced our preparations for war. Our crew, though a fine ablebodied set of men, but few of them had ever been in the navy before and needed much drilling and other instruction to fit them for their several stations. Here we received our stations at the heavy guns and in the ship's boats. I was stationed at No. 5 gun and, being one of the youngest on the ship (17 years old), with four other boys I was stationed in the dinghey, the smallest boat to a ship.[10]

The continued drill at something, together with the wild rumors floating about Fortress Monroe, made us feel that there was work ahead for us. On the 3rd of Feb we sailed for Key West.

This Island has a fine harbor and at this time was used as a depot for coal and other stores and a randevues for the Western Gulf Squadron. From here we soon sailed for Havana.

Here I experienced for the first time the strange sensation of being in a city full of people where no one could understand me, where my tongue was of no use, and was compelled to make my wants known by signs or any other way I could.

From here we sailed for Ship Island where we arrived about the 20th of Feb. This is a small island near the mouth of the Mississippi River and

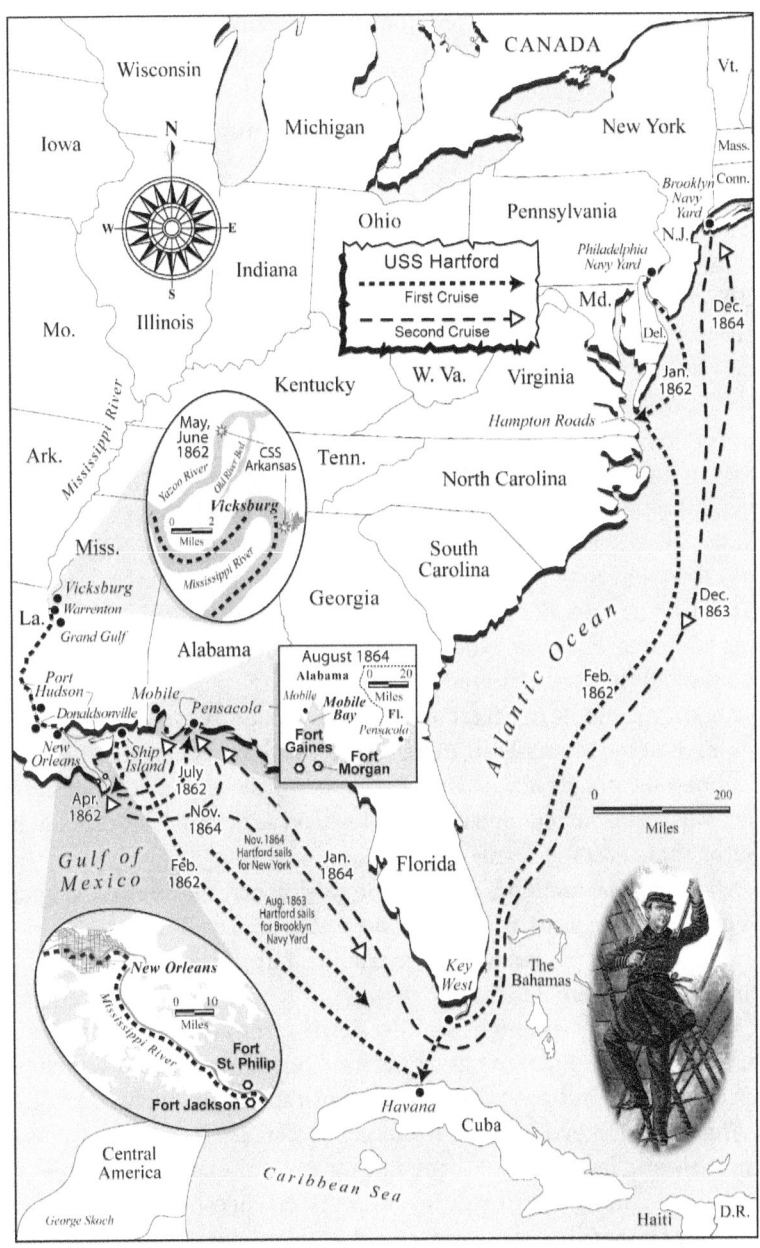

The USS *Hartford* and Diggins made two separate voyages from Philadelphia and New York to the Gulf battle waters, as shown here. The first, by way of Havana, Cuba, and Ship Island, took ship and sailors to and up the Mississippi River; the second aimed at Mobile Bay and its closure as a blockade runners' port. Map by George Skoch.

is now used as the headquarters for the army and navy forces to attack New Orleans.[11]

Here Farragut relieved Flag Officer [William W.] McKean in command of the West Gulf [Blockading] Squadron, who emmediately left for the North with his Flag Ship, the U. S. Ship *Niagara*.[12]

Here Captain [Henry H.] Bell came on board of the *Hartford* as chief of Staff or fleet Captain or, as the men called him, "fighting captain." It was said among the men that he had fought several duels with Englesh and French officers and had allways killed his man and that he was the best swordsman in America. He certainly looked all that was said of him. He was over six foot high, straight and wirey, well proportioned with a quick active movement. He was about 55 years old, grey hair, a heavy coarse mustache which was perfectly white and kept cropped strait across in line with the mouth. He had a stern commanding appearance which disappeared in conversation when he was gentle and courteous to all alike. He was soon a great favorate with the men.[13]

Vessels were arriving every day so that we soon had a large fleet gethered. Large numbers of troops were also arriving from the North and being landed on Ship Island under command of Gen. B. F. Butler who was to command the attack by land.

About the middle of March our fleet was made up and we started for the mouth of the Mississippi. There are no less than six entrances, caused by numerous islands formed from the sediment and drift that come down with [the] current and deposited when the current slacks about its mouth. These entrances are called passes.

After an examination by a Coast Survey officer, the South West pass was decided upon as carrying the most water, 15 feet. Through this pass the smaller vesels passed with little trouble, but the larger vesels had to be lightened up from 2 to 3 feet.

We worked day and night sending down yards and masts and taking every spare article out of the ships and landing them at Pilot Town where, with much hope and great cheering, we hoisted the United States flag.[14]

The few old Man of Wars man among us were the greatest growlers at so much work, few, if any of them, having any war experience, while the newer hands thought it all natural and work on cheerfully.

When all spare articles were landed at Pilot Town, the *Brooklyn* was the first large ship to go over the bar, succeeding after much trouble. The *Hartford* followed the *Brooklyn* with about the same trouble, plowing through two feet of mud. The *Pensacola* and frigate *Mississippi* had a time of it, all the small gun boats were used as tugs and it required all their powers to pull those noble ships through the mud [and] over the bar. It was found impossible to get the frigate *Colorado* over the bar which lost to us the largest and best ship of the fleet, but her officers and men were distributed, with her guns, where they were most needed among the other vesels. Captain [Theodorus] Bailey, her commander, [was] placed in command of the second division of the fleet.[15]

When our fleet were over the bar and anchored above Pilot Town, we could draw a breath and look about us. The number and variety of vesels that had gathered here in course of ten days was astonishing. Coal schooners, beef boats (as the sailors called transports), and many others, such as tug boats, peddling vesels, etc., at least one third of them in continual motion, making it a lively and busy scene.

After establishing an hospital at Pilot Town, supplying it with surgeons, nurses and medicine from the ships, we moved grandly up the River, our noncombative tribe following in our rear.

There was nothing to be seen along the swampy banks except swamp grass and wild cane untill about five miles below the forts, when we come [upon] a few dilapidated houses which we found abandoned like those at Pilot Town. The solid ground, which was well wooded, commenced about four miles below the forts. When between three and four miles below the forts, our fleet come to anchor about 70 miles below New Orleans & 30 miles from the mouth of the river. We found that the enemy had cut down many of the trees [so] that the forts might have a clear range for their guns down the river against our approach.

Capt. David D. Porter (who commanded the Mortar Flotilla) on his flag ship the *Harriet Lane* was working hard putting the mortar schooners in position to commence the emediate bombardment of the forts. There were about nine schooners, each with a thirteen inch mortar placed amidships between the fore and main masts. Four was placed on the east and five on the west bank of the river.[16]

On the 16th of April, every thing being in readiness, the mortars opened fire on the forts. The forts returned the fire with vigor and soon drove the mortar vessels from the east bank to the shelter of the trees on the other side of the river. There was little time lost by the change, the mortars all the time keeping a continual fire on the forts. The forts also opened a heavy fire on the fleet, causing the vessels to drop down the river farther untill out of range of their guns. About three P.M. on the first day, large volumes of smoke were seen in the direction of Fort Jackson [and] the smoke continued through the night.

On the 19th, a deserter from Fort Jackson come on board. He said the smoke of the 16th was caused by the burning of the Citadel and did other damage and that one of our shell had dismounted one of their largest

9

guns. He also said that many in the fort were Union men and anxious for a chance to get away.[17]

On the first night they introduced us to a new weapon of war by sending a large fire raft down upon us. It consisted of a Mississippi flat boat, 100 by 150 feet square and three feet deep, filled with pine knots and other combustible matter, this all in flames 30 to 50 feet high. [This] was sent down with the current among our vessels. This one, like those they sent down afterward, give our vessels a deal of trouble trying to avoid them. Our ships fouled each other, often carrying away masts, rigging, and doing much other damage.[18]

In a scrape of this kind, the gun boat *Sciota* lost her mainmast. Not having one to replace it, it was decided to take the other mast out of her. This so improved her, reducing her liability to fouling and giving her a snug, tidy appearance, that it was decided to take the masts out of all of her class which was done to some ten of them. Those vessels were about 600 tons and so much alike that it was nessesery to number them by painting a large white number near the top of the smokestack of each to distinguish them.[19]

On the second day the enemy somewhat slackened their fire. They, however, succeeded in sinking one of our mortar boats and their fire was becoming so accurate that it was found nessesery to change their position. There was also a deception adopted by Admiral Porter by lashing green branches to the masts and rigging, making it hard for the enemy to distinguish the schooners from the trees on the bank of the river where they were moored. This was a great success, throwing the enemy off their range. The forts did them little harm afterwards.[20]

In the mean time, the large vessels were making preperations for the grand attack. The ships were stripped to the topmasts, lower and topsail yards and bowsprit. All spare boats, rigging and other articles were sent to Pilot Town. Heavy guns taken from the *Colorado*, which had failed to get over the bar, were distributed on other ships where there was room for them. The ships were taking full supplys of coal, provisions, and ammunitions.[21]

One great source of trouble while below the forts was trying to hold our anchorage in the strong current of the river which ran at the rate of 7 or 8 miles an hour. Our anchors and chains were being continually lost. A whirling eddy would ketch a ship and swing her to one side. She would then come back to her old place with a surge that was almost certain to carry away the anchor or something els. We lay at all times with our chains around the capstan, the [capstan] bars shipped, ready at a moments notice to heave up anchor.

While laying in this condition, the ship come back with one of her usual surges about midnight of April 20, carrying away the pawlls [pawls] of [the] capstan causing it to fly around with lightning rapidity. The bars flew in all directions, injuring many of the men who slept around the capstan on the berth deck, three of whom were sent to the hospital at Pilot Town.[22]

Our other great trouble, the fire rafts, were becoming more numerous, the[y] being sent down on us at all times from dark to day light. To combat them there was a fire raft brigade organized, composed of one or two boats from each ship. These boats were supplyed with grapelines [grappling lines], axes, buckets and other aplyances for putting out fire and distroying the rafts.

This little but numerous fleet would start off from the shipping about sun set and report to the gun boat doing picket duty and form a long line from her stern. The whole then would take position well in advance of the fleet and await the appearance of fire rafts. As soon as a fire raft made its appearance around the point, the boats would cast of[f] and pull for it, throw their grapelines on board and tow it so as to avoid the shipping, then let it go with the current to consume itself at its leasure.

On the night of the 21st of April, Captain H. H. Bell, with a number of firemen from our ship provided with hack saws, chisels and other aplyances for cutting chain, went up to cut the chain that was across the river at the forts. There was a Frenchman went with them who claimed the invention of a Petard that would blow up all obstructions to our passage up the river. The Frenchman's invention was a failure, but our firemen, under a heavy fire from the forts, succeeded in cutting an opening sufficient for our vessels to get through and pass up by the forts.[23]

At this time the captain of an Englesh carvett [corvette], the *Rinaldo*, who by mutual consent was permitted to pass through the lines up to New Orleans to look after English interest there, returned. He give a terrible account of the preperations the enemy was making and had made to drive us out of the river. He said it was desperate folly and certain distruction to our fleet if it was attemted to pass the forts. He said the Rebel fleet was superior to ours and if we were successfull in an engagement with the forts and fleet, there was enough guns between the forts and city to distroy our fleet.[24]

Notwithstanding the Engleshman's warning, the fleet was making hurried preperation for an attack on the enemy. Extra guns were put where there was room for them, under the topgallant forecastle was being filled with bags of sand to prevent our decks being [illegible], the chain locker was emptied and the chains bolted to the outside of the ships, hanging down in bites [bights, i.e. loops] where it would protect the boilers and machinery, a boat howitzer was placed in the fore and main tops of larger ships.[25]

Through the exertions of the following named gentlemen of the Coast Survey Steamer *Sachem* (which was alway[s] present on active duty): F. H. Gerdes, T. C. Bowie, J. G. Oltmanns and others who surveyed the river under great disadvantages and most of the time under heavy fire of the forts. [They] succeeded in placing the mortars at accurately known distences from the forts so that though the forts was intirely hidden behind the trees between them, every shell from the mortars entered the forts and made it safe for our own fleet when in front of the forts.[26]

Soon after our arrival below the forts, the Admiral issued the following instructions to the Commander[s] of vessels[:]

[Omitted here, Diggins copied Farragut's General Order of preparation for battle with Confederate forts and warships. Farragut's original lengthy, very detailed order is found at *Official Records of the . . . Navies* (ORN), vol. 18:48–49. In his order, Farragut called for "stout hearts and quick hands" to fight fires and repair damage. He also ordered, "No vessel must with draw from battle under any circumstances without the consent of the flag officer."]

The Flag Officer now visited all the vessels of the fleet to see that his instructions were carried out and every ship prepared for action.

On the night of the 23rd of April it was rumored we were to attack the following morning. The rumor was made a certainty at 12 oclock that night when the few men that had turned in were quietly notified to stow their hammocks and the cooks ordered to have coffee ready at 1 a.m. We were all anxious that it come off as we knew we had to go through with it and the sooner it was over, the better. While waiting further orders, the men gethered in little knots about the ship talking quietly of our chances and fixing their little affairs in case the worst should happen.

One thing had a depressing effect on the men. Their favorate officer, Captain H. H. Bell, had left the ship to take command of a division of the fleet. Except [for] Lieut. Thornton, the executive officer, the men knew little of the officers as fighters. Farragut had no intercourse with the men. He seemed more like a passenger, spending most of his time seated on the propeller block on the poop deck where he received and conversed with the other officers of the fleet.[27]

The captain of the ship, Wainwright, was as little known as the other officers at this time, he seldom having anything to say and spending most of his time with Farragut on the poop deck or in his cabin.

12

During this evening and night the mortars were at their best, keeping a continual stream of shell in the air. It was a grand sight but fearful in effect. The shell could be plainly seen as they left the mortars, each following the other through [the] heavens like large stars in a half circle like path and dealing death and distruction at the end of their mission.[28]

A little before 1 a.m., the men were served with hot coffee and hard tack. Many thought that grog ought to be served, but the flag Officer was opposed to it. After that, those that had any remaining preperation for the battle commenced to make them; the carpenters gang commenced preparing their plugs and patches to stop shot holes. The carpenters mate had a canvas overhauls with leaden shoes suspended from long lines, [so] that he might be suspended at any place over the ship's side where a hole would occur. The gunners mate was busy looking after the lock strings, filling the division tubs with water for use in case of fire, or to drink and suplying buckets of sand which were placed in the rear of the guns to be scattered on the bloody deck to keep the men from slipping.[29]

The doctors and nurses were placing swinging cats at the main hatch for lowering the killed and wounded to a newly constructed hospital in the main hold. These and many other preperations were going on through the ship while we were waiting for the signal from the gunboat *Itasca*, Lieut. [Charles H. B.] Caldwell, which had been sent up to the forts to find if the opening made in the obstructions a few nights previous by Capt. Bell and our firemen still remained clear. If all was clear, she was to display a light at her masthead and all eyes were now anxiously watching for that light.[30]

We saw the forts open fire on the *Itasca* and could see that gallant little vessel, regardless of their fire, held her course up the river.

The enemy now started fires along the river shore which was good evidence that they now expected us. They now sent one of their largest fire rafts down, the last effort they will ever make to us below the forts. It, like its numerous predecessors, passes us without injury.

At 2 a.m., the *Itasca* showed the wished for signal that all was clear. In a moment after our ship gives the signal to the fleet to get underway and take their places in line. At the same time, all hands were called on board of us to up anchor. There was little necessity for ordering [as] the men were all ready at the capstan bars.

Nothing will better illustrate the feeling of the men than that the anchor was secured at the cathead in seven minutes from the time the order was given.[31]

The whole fleet was soon underway and taking their places in line. All this was done quietly without bustle or nois. All seem anxious to conceal our intentions from the enemy. As soon as the ship began moving ahead, the men [went] quiet[l]y to their places at the guns, a solom stillness prevailed. All that could be heard between the thundering of our mortars, was the revolutions of our own engine. It was a relief from the stillness to see the lively movements of our vessels as they quietly took their assigned places in the line of battle, and, at the same time, all heading for the forts.[32]

FIGHTING THE FORTS: "THE NOIS WAS TEROBLE"

Steaming upstream toward the "Paris of America," the fleet would first pass in front of Fort Jackson on the left, the stronger of the two lower forts, then confront Fort St. Philip, slightly higher on the river's right or eastern bank. To bombard the forts during the passage, the 17 wooden Federal warships had 192 guns, though only some would bear upon the forts at any given time.[1]

Between them, the forts mounted 126 guns, with Jackson boasting 74 large and small cannon, including 8 in a water battery, or a position near water level. Confederates had another forty guns aboard the fourteen fighting ships that they had assembled to defend New Orleans. However, as one observer noted, 70 percent of Confederate guns were 32-pounders or lighter, while only 37 percent of the Federal guns were of such small calibers. Further, that observer thought the usual advantage of shore-based cannon over ships' guns did not apply, as Farragut sought only to pass the forts, not reduce them.[2]

Also ready and waiting were the many primed fire rafts and the Confederate fleet. That naval force presented a real threat, since many of those fourteen ships were rams. Even a small but skillfully handled ram could sink a much larger ship with one iron-fisted blow.[3]

While the Federals knew about the ram danger, they did not know until later that the Confederate fleet was a mélange of three separate commands—Confederate States Navy, Louisiana State Navy, and the River Defense Force. This disorganized, sometimes hapless conglomerate lacked a central command, a cohesive strategy, a desire to cooperate or, among some, a will to fight the Yankees. Many Confederate officers lamented these crucial defects but could do nothing to remedy the situation in time to confront Farragut. They blamed the central and state governments and some individual naval officers, including the commanders of the stationary ironclad *Louisiana* and the River Defense Force.[4]

As Diggins and other Federal sailors soon learned, some intrepid Confederate ship captains acted vigorously to cause them woe and distress. As it turned out, only the water-borne defenders sank or seriously damaged any of Farragut's ships. So the Confederate naval force threat lent some creditability to Porter's assertion that "the odds were strongly in favor" of the defenders and to a USS *Brooklyn* seaman's declaration that the ensuing battle was "one of the greatest naval fights on record."[5]

Our progress up the river was very slow owing to the very strong current, but good order prevailed. As soon as the head of the lines was discovered by the enemy, they opened fire on us.[6]

Our men were all at the guns ready for action but our broadside guns could not bear on them. This is the most depressing experience of a warriors life, waiting to be engaged and under a heavy fire from the enemy. One has nothing to do to occupy the mind [and] the mind runs on the great uncertainty about to take place untill it is a relief when the battle opens.[7]

The mortars now redoubled their fire, averaging a shell a minute from each mortar vessel. As we neared the forts the position of the half circle of boms [bombs] in the air so changed [that] to us it seemed they would soon be falling on our decks. The little gunboat *Cayuga*, comd [commanded] by Lieutenant N. B. Harrison and the flag ship of Capt. Bailey, 2nd in comd of the fleet, reached abreast of the forts about 3:30 a.m. She, being a little in advance of the rest of the fleet, received their full fire and noblely held her course up the river. She was soon followed by the *Varuna* and *Oneida*.[8]

This much could be seen from our ship as we were only firing our bow guns, our place in line was about the center of the fleet. The vessels ahead, together with the smoke from the forts, added to an already dark night, cut off from our view much of what was going on ahead. As we rounded the point and ranged up between the forts, there was little to be seen but a great deal to be heard. The boms from the mortar fleet now appeared to be coming down straight upon us and really fell but a few feet distant. The action was now general, the fleet and the forts were at their best. We

16

had little to guide us but the flashing guns of the forts and batterys and those could not always be seen, the smoke was so thick.[9]

Our broadside guns were now in full action and every man had all he could attend to.

(Many suppose that a broadside means the discharge of all the guns on one side at the same time. Such is not the case. The most foreward gun is brought to bear first, then the next after one and so on untill the whole broadside is in action, thus keeping up a continual di[s]charge.)

When we reached abreast of Fort Jackson, our deck was a scene of the greatest activity, some guns running out to the ports loaded, some being loaded, and others flying back from the ports, recoiling from their discharge, and the men working as if the issue depended on each individual exursion [exertion]. The smoke now became so thick we eather fired at the enemy's flashes or by the reports of their guns. One could scarcely distinguish the man standing next to him. We now began loading with grape and canister. This indicated that we were at very close range.[10]

The nois and roar at this time was teroble and cannot be discribed. But to help the emagination, there was over three hundred guns and mortars of the largest calabre in full blast. Double this by the explosion of shell fired by them, then add to this the hissing and crashing through the air and shifring [shivering]. Confine this in a half mile square [and] it may give some idea of the nois and uproar that was taking place.[11]

We now discovered on our front bow and coming straight for us a large fire raft. It looked like the whole river surface was on fire ahead, the flames rising ten or fifteen feet untill they lost their fiery tongues in the thick smoke. As it came nearer, we discovered what appeared to be the ironclad *Manassas* alongside of it and towing it upon us. Our helm was put quickly to port to avoid it. This run us hard aground with our bowsprit over Fort St. Philip. Luckily the enemy thought we were going to land men and ran from their guns, intirely deserting a powerful water battery. If this battery had been bravely fought at this time, it would have easily ended the career of the *Hartford*.[12]

But we did not escape the fire raft and the guns of Fort Jackson. As soon as grounded, the fire raft struct us under the port fore rigging and swung her lenth along side. The *Manassas* then cast off from her and left us, as they thought, to distruction, turned and went up the river to soon meet the fate she [had] prepared for us.

Up to this time, being over an hour at our terrible work, the men [had] stood bravely to their guns. As portions of the guns crews were killed and wounded, others would quickly fill their places. All the appliances of naval warfare was in full operation. The swinging cat at the main hatch was in active service lowering the killed and wounded to the temporary hospital in the main hold.

Sand was scattered on the bloody deck [and] the great tubs of water located in each division was in great demand, the work and smoke creating thirst. The carpenters mate in his overalls swinging over the side, assisted by his men, stopping shot holes, the men's faces darkened and smeared from the smoke and blood, the murderous smell of burned powder, together with the smell of fresh blood, the screaming nois of shot and shell in the air, the lightning crash of those that struck us, altogether made up a scene and created a feeling that can never be forgotten and never known but by experience.[13]

The hot weather since our arrival in the river had softened the pitch in the ships seams, causing it to run in long drips down the ship's side. The tar in the rigging was of the same inflamible charecter, so that we were an easy prey to the flames of the fire raft. In a minute after it struck our side, the pitch from our seams was on fire. The fire spread rapidly up the fore and main rigging on the port side. This was the side we were fighting, [but] the flames and heat drove the men from the guns as powder could no longer [be] handled on deck. The men found themselves without occupation. This threw the men and most of the officers into the greatest confusion. For a few moments it looked like every one [was] for himself. My youthfull emagination of hell did not equel the scene about us at this moment. The terrific roar of cannon, the thick smoke and unnatural smell, the flames from the fire to the masthead & hissing and leaping along one sides and lapping their firey tongues in through the ports, making a lurid light about us in which one could scarcely distingesh another at an arms lenth. The men were moving about the deck excitedly without object.[14]

I was standing near the main hatch wondering what next when a masters mate came along and, grabbing up one of the main hatch gratings, he started for the forecastle with it. The ship seemed lost and thinking the mate knew more about those things than me, I grabbed up a grating and followed him, intending, when the ship got too hot, to jump over board. I had made but a few steps forward through the confused and excited men when through all the nois and din I heard a voice. I turned and could just distingesh through the thick smoke the tall form of Captain Wainwright.[15]

He was moving slowly forward through the excited people, calling through a speaking trumpet, "Take your places at fire quarters," then tapping one and calling another by name, always repeating, "Fire quarters," his calm fearless manner and dignified bearing had a quick effect on the

18

men, calmed the tumult and restoring confidence, almost making one ashamed of his fears. Farragut was walking at his side and Lieut Comd. Thornton was industresly placing the men and directing their work. The captain's order was quickly taken up by the men and passed through the ship so that in a few moments every man was at his station and doing his best to combat the flames.

At the first sight of Captain Wainwright I dropped my grating and started for the fire room hose. At this time also a shell exploded in the cabin, setting it on fire which made considerable headway before it was discovered, the smoke and flames bursting through the windows being the first notice of it.

Misfortunes seemed to crowd the old ship and it looked that only a miracle could save her. We were hard aground, the engines backing with all their power and could not relieve her, in flames from the water to the masthead from the fire raft, the cabin ablaze from an exploded shell, and the ship the center of a terrible storm of shot and shell, the crew in a death struggle with the flames, heat and smoke, the latter at times so thick that we were compelled to grope our way. While connecting the hose at the engine room hatch, I heard this conversation occur[:]

Captain Wainwright hailed the engine room and inquired, "Where is the chief engineer?"

Someone answered, "I don't know, Sir."

The capt: "Who is in charge of the engine?"

Answer, "Mr. Purdy, Sir."

Capt: "Tell Mr. Purdy I want to see him."

Capt: "Mr. Purdy, are you doing all you can with the engines? You know we are in a very bad way if she dont back off."

Purdy: "The throttle is wide opened on the engines, Sir."

Capt: "Is there any way you can increase her power?"

Mr. Purdy: "[Yes,] by reducing her water which would endanger her boilers."

Capt: "Well, try anything to get her a float."

Mr. Purdy: "All right, Sir."

Mr. Purdy then went down in the fire room that he might better execute the captain's order reducing the water and superintending the management of the fires. In a few minutes the ship commenced jumping. The vibration was so great from the revolutions of the engines that one could scarcely hold his feet.[16]

She came off and cleared the fire raft at the same time, calling forth a spontaneous cheer from every man aboard. The cheering was an outburst of relief experienced by all as we backed out in deep water, for notwithstanding the great exertions of all on board we could make little headway against the fire while the fire raft remained alongside. The men now fought the fire with renewed vigor and soon had it extinguished and were again at their places at the guns.

We all felt that the safety of the ship and crew was wholly due to Captain Wainwright. His powerful voice claimed the attention of the men, his tall form and commanding presence, and his cool, fearless manner inspired all who saw or heard him with his own courage and made men feel that with such a leader there was nothing to fear. From this time till his death, he was the idol of his crew.

(This incident, I believe, passed intirely without record or farther notice. Yet it was one of the most daring and recless acts of bravery that I knew of through out the war. It was a choice between giving up the ship or blowing up the ship and Capt. Wainwright chose the latter. Few of the ship's company knew what was going on. The captain still stood near the engine room hatch, while Mr. Purdy remained in the fire room. Some of the firemen told me afterwards that they expected every moment to be their last and the danger was increasing every moment untill she came off. Nor was Mr Purdy less brave than his captain. He left the throttle opened on the engine and remained in the fire room, forcing the fires on almost empty boilers. If anything had happened to the boilers, the people taking part in this effort to get the ship afloat, not one of them would live to tell the tale.) As we headed up stream, we came close upon the *Brooklyn*, just passing Fort Jackson. The flashing guns from her sides brought a hearty cheer from the *Hartford*. We soon after emerged from the smoke and carnage between the forts to find ourselfs in the center of the enemy's fleet. The [CSS] *McRae* passed close aboard of us and give us a broadside. She so nearly resembled our own gunboats that we were undecided weather to fire and gave her the benefit of the doubt. This same cause deceived others of our fleet and the *McRae* escaped the general distruction of the enemy's fleet.[17]

It was warm work still, but seemed only fun compared with what we had just been through. We continued to fire just the same at anything and everything that did not fly our flag. Our attention was particularly claimed by a large river steamer crowded with soldiers. She was approaching us apparently with the intention to board us. Captain Wainwright hailed her and demanded her surrender. We delayed our fire for an answer and when it came, "No, never," a full broadside was our reply. It sent her drifting towards the shore in flames.[18]

As we turned the bend on the Fort St. Philip side, we ran close upon the monster ironclad *Louisiana*. She was lying under the shadow of the bank. We would not have noticed her, but for the heavy broadside she gave us. We returned her broadsides and kept the fire on her untill we past up out of range, with no more effect, however, than to dent her iron sides.[19]

The gunboat *Cayuga* held the lead untill she reached the center of the enemy's fleet above the forts when she was attacked on all sides. The *Varuna*, comd. C. S. Boggs, was next to arrive and then the *Oneida*, Comd S. P. Lee. Those three gunboats bore the brunt of the fight with the enemy's fleet. The *Varuna*, bring the fastest, got some distance ahead of the others when she was engaged by four of the enemys gunboats. After a gallant struggle she was sunk, [but] not untill she had sunk two of her adverserys. The balance of our fleet then come on the scene and made short work of the Confederate gunboats, distroying all that came within reach of our guns.[20]

When the enemy fleet found themselfs worsted at all points, the few that remained tryed to escape back to the forts, or on up to the city. A few of them succeeded. The ram *Manassas* was making harmless attemts to strike our vessels as they came up. She struck at the *Brooklyn*, then crossed our bow. The *Mississippi* was in our rear [and] the Admiral signaled to her to engage the ram and run her down. The old *Mississippi* headed straight for her, intending to ram her. The *Manassas* escaped the butt, but received a full broadside at close range. The *Mississippi* began to turn to follow her, pouring in broadsides all the time when the *Manassas*, finding no other escape, ran along side of the bank when her crew set her on fire and left her. She soon after swung from the bank and drifted down the river in flames.[21]

When the last of [the] fleet past up out of sight of the vessels below the forts, Admiral Porter, who commanded the mortar fleet, and his people below knew little of their success or failure. Our fleet had disappeared from theirs in the thick smoke, and the heavy firing continued for two hours afterwards. When the smoke cleared away after daylight, the ram *Manassas* was discovered coming down the river, with great volumes of smoke coming out of her smoke stack, caused by the fire which was consuming her. The people below, thinking that our fleet had been distroyed and that the enemy's fleet, headed by the *Manassas*, was coming down to distroy them, emmediately cast loose and, amid the greatest excitement, started for the mouth of the river. Many of [the] steamers, in their haste, would not take the sailing vessels in tow, but left them to be distroyed or captured by the enemy.

The sailing vessels, however, soon had the joke on the steamers. As the *Manassas* approached near they discovered that smoke and flames was also coming out of her only hatch and that she was being consumed by fire. The dreaded monster drifted by them harmlessly and caught on the east bank of the river where she soon after sunk. Great quantities of cotton also come drifting down the river, which the sailing vessels gethered, many of them having a full freight of it to take north. The steamers returned the following day when they gradually learned of our success and Admiral Porter demanded the surrender of the forts, and, on their refusal, prepared to renew the bombardment.[22]

We now had an opportunity to look about us. The banks on either side of the river was lined with the burning and sinking vessels of the enemy. The engines of some were still going and the large side wheels revolving with lightning rapidity, as if the vessels were making a wild effort to follow their crews through the woods.

As the thick smoke cleared away, it revealed a beautiful morning, the bright sun just showing over the tops of the green trees that bordered the river. Our fleet, with few exceptions, still in line of battle, with flags flying from every mast head and peak, steaming towards New Orleans with no resistence and master of all the surroundings. We soon came upon our gunboat *Varuna* where she had been sunk in a death struggle with the enemy's fleet. Her top gallant forecastle was all that remained out of water where the most of her officers and crew were huddled waiting to be taken off which was being done. We soon after arrived at the Curintine [Quarantine] grounds where the fleet anchored to have breakfeast and repair damage and care for the killed and wounded.[23]

We found four of our fleet missing—the *Itasca, Winona, Kennebec* and the *Varuna*. The latter we knew had been sunk in the struggle with the enemy fleet, but the other three could not be accounted for and various were the speculations as to their fate, whether they had been driven back or sunk at the engagement at the forts.

(It was learned afterward that they had become entangled in the obstructions at the forts and disabled, drifted down the river among Admiral Porter's fleet where they anchored in safety.)[24]

Admiral Porter, with all the available vessels of his mortar fleet, brought up the rear and gallantly sustained the fleet while passing the forts, following with his flagship, the *Harriet Lane*, untill nearly abreast of the forts, thus drawing the fire from the vessels in line.[25]

Our fleet anchored at the Curintine [Quarantine] ground where we found encamped a Confederate regiment composed chiefly of Germans.

They displayed numerous white flags. After receiving their arms and equipments, they were paroled. They said they had been forced into the service and were as glad of our success as we were.[26]

The balance of the day was consumed caring for the wounded and burying the dead.

Two of our guns was disabled. An enemy shot entered the muzzle of one of them, breaking the muzzle off halfway to the breach.

At noon the fleet again started in the derection of New Orleans. The enemy in every way tried to check our progress, sending down upon us great numbers of fire rafts and burning ships, four and five full rigged ships lashed together. Some of them, loaded with cotton, would be swept down upon us by the rapid current in flames, at times blocking the river and making it difficult for our vessels to keep clear of them. At other times the whole surface of the river would be covered with bales of cotton, spars and debris from vessels which had burned and sunk. As darkness approached the sky in the derection of New Orleans was illuminated by the numerous fire ships sent down upon us which continued during the night.

It was reported there was heavy batterys at the English Turn. We anchored a few miles below it to await morning for the attack.[27]

About 8 oclock the following morning we up anchor and soon after cleared the ship for action. At 10 oclock we reached the Chalmette Batterys. They opened a heavy fire on the gunboat *Cayuga* and *Hartford*, they being a half mile ahead of the balance of the fleet. We fought both broadsides, continuing our course up the river. Their fire soon slackened.[28]

When we reached the upper end of the batterys, the ship was stopped and allowed to drift down again with the current, keeping up a continuous fire all the time. When we reached the lower end, the *Brooklyn* and the *Pensacola* had come up in range, closely followed by the rest of the fleet. The *Hartford* again started up almost side by [side] with the *Brooklyn*, she fighting the batterys on the west bank and the *Hartford* the east bank. We loaded mostly with grape and canister.

The *Mississippi* and the *Pensacola* were close in our rear [and] it soon became too hot for the enemy. Their fire rapidly slackened and through the intervals in the smoke we could see them deserting their guns and running across the fields in all derections. The engagement lasted nearly an hour when we stopped firing and the smoke cleared. The batterys were silent and deserted. The frigate *Mississippi* and a smaller gunboat was left to take charge of the batterys and spike the guns [and] the fleet continued up to the city.[29]

The enemy now redoubled their efforts to obstruct our way. The officers and men remained at their stations, ready for any emergency. As we neared the city, the destruction of property became greater. Everything ahead indicated excitement and confusion—large volumes of smoke, occasional explosions at different points in the derection of the city, [and] the face of the river seemed on fire.

There was a continual procession of burning vessels passing down with the current—the largest river steamers, then full-rigged ships, then three or four ships lashed together, some of them so weakened from fire, the cotton bursting from their sides; others sinking, leaving their cotton and other loose articles to float down the river. Our passage at times was very difficult and often looked impossible to keep clear of the burning vessels as they were floated down upon us.[30]

As fire seemed their only resort to check our advance on the city they used it for all they could. The vessels that had been blockaded in New Orleans from the commencement of the war, together with all other idle vessels, were fired and cut loose upon us.

About 12 April 26 we rounded the point that brought the city in sight. A large unfinished ironclad, pierced for 16 guns, passed us in flames. Here was a sight not soon to be forgotten—warfs, vessels, and buildings on both banks of the river along the whole front of the city was all in flames [and] the city was hidden behind the thick smoke. Another large Iron clad on the stocks on the Algiers side, together with the ship yard, was in flames. The fire fiend certainly had a feast.[31]

We continued our course up to the front of the city through almost a path of fire, the men standing at their places at fire quarters ready for any emergency. The heavens now added to the scene—a terrible storm of thunder and lightning and rain fell in torrents.

The *Hartford* anchored abreast of the center of the city, the *Pensacola* and the *Mississippi* ahead of us and the *Brooklyn* and the *Richmond* astern, the smaller gunboats filling the space between the larger ships, and all forming a line that brought the whole city completely under the guns of the fleet.

The men remained at their places at the guns for some time after we anchored, but it soon became evident they had no means of opposing us and the city was at the mercy of our guns.

The scene about us soon changed to a more agreeable form. The rapid current, assisted by our smaller gunboats, soon cleared the river of its floating conflagration and give us a chance to look about us. The houses set back some four hundred feet from the river. This space, the Levee, was soon crowded with the people of New Orleans, forming a sea of heads, swaying and crushing to get a look at the Yankee fleet, as they called us. In the rear, through the city streets, we could hear numerous forms of military music. It was the quick marches of Gen. [Mansfield] Lovell's troops leaving the city.[32]

At this time a few Union people displayed an American flag and attemted to show some wellcome to the fleet, but were fired upon by the retreating troops and the mob.

NEW ORLEANS FALLS

By the eighth census in 1860, New Orleans was the nation's sixth largest city and the South's largest, with a population of 169,675.

As a port city with much international trade, many foreign residents, and not long divorced from French rule, New Orleans had a cosmopolitan air about it. However, most inhabitants strongly supported the Confederacy.

After Federal warships passed the forts, with land forces not far behind, New Orleans's surrender was a foregone conclusion. Much of the defenseless city lay within reach of the Navy's cannon, and Butler's troops would soon arrive.

City leaders tried to stall for a bit, but they knew it was a futile exercise. Though still defiant, they had no choice but to yield.[1]

So the city fell, depressing its inhabitants, distressing Confederates elsewhere, and cheering people in the North.

In Washington, Elizabeth Blair Lee, wife of naval officer Samuel P. Lee and daughter of Postmaster General Montgomery Blair, reported a "frenzy of exultation" over New Orleans's capture. In contrast, Clara Solomon, a young woman living in New Orleans, described the fear, tumult, and uncertainty that wracked many. Writing in her diary, she lamented, "Such expressions of woe as were on the faces of everyone, & such sadness as reigned in every heart." In Mobile, Ala., another southern woman diarist wrote, "No more room for hope—New Orleans is gone to us."[2]

Yet that city's citizens remained defiant, resisting openly and covertly. "We are conquered but not subdued," Solomon insisted.[3]

As Diggins relates, initially mobs gathered to show their displeasure and rejection of the Yankee victors. Immediately Federals let the people know that they would rule with a firm hand. Farragut ordered Marine marksmen to fire at individuals in an angry mob on the levee; Butler, the army's commander, soon ordered the hanging of a man who had torn down the newly raised U.S. flag. And when the city's newspapers continued printed opposition, Butler shut them down, keeping one as a voice for his military administration.

But apparently many women felt they enjoyed immunity from retaliation because of their sex. One woman spat in Farragut's face as he sat in a horse-drawn street car. He calmly wiped his face and urged calm, lest the incident escalate into deadly violence. Butler, however, lost patience when women insulted his soldiers or dumped the contents of chamber pots on Yankee heads as they walked below apartments. That is when he issued his "women order," directing that any woman who so affronted order by insulting his soldiers should be treated as a woman of the streets plying her trade.[4]

While that order stirred outrage North, South, and abroad, eventually New Orleans's citizens learned to live under the occupation, as Diggins recounts.

In the afternoon, Capt. [Theodorus] Bailey landed under a flag of truce to demand the surrender of the city and that reb flag then displayed be hauled down and the United States flag be hoisted on all public buildings.[5]

As our boat neared the shore the crowd crushed and jammed in the direction of her landing so that it was with great difficulty that Captain Bailey could find landing room. It was with still more difficulty that he worked his [way] through the threatening crowd. Notwithstanding their jeers and insults, he reach[ed] the office of the mayor with his demands.[6]

The mob then turned their oaths and threats against the boat's crew. The men in the boat returned their threats in kind, untill to avoid a conflict the officer in charge of the boat ordered that she be shoved from the warf and lay on oars untill the return of Captain Bailey. All this could be seen by the fleet and caused some anxiety and excitement. Captain Bailey['s] return, however, with no greater damage than a ruffled uniform, quieted matters for the time.[7]

The mayor and city council answered the captain's demands with a show of much Rebel patriotism, [saying] that they being a civil body, they had no power to surender and that the man could not be found, so wretched and desperate a renegade, as would dare to profane with his hand the sacred emblem of their aspirations, and I [we] beg you understand that the people of New Orleans, while unable at this moment to prevent you from occupying this city, do not transfer their allegiance from the government of their choice to one which they have deliberately repudiated and that they yield simply that obedience which the conqueror is enabled to extort from the conquered. This and much more was signed by John T. Monroe, Mayor.[8]

This and other messages from the mayor, equel in spirit of resistance, made it plain that they would not haul down their flags nor hoist the U.S. flag.

On the morning of the 27th the United States flag was hoisted on the mint by men from the *Pensacola*. The men had hardly returned to the ships when a mob gethered and tore down the flag and, amidst the greatest uproar, trailed it through the streets, tearing it in small pieces for distribution to the crowd. This mob was headed by a man named Mumford, who was soon after hung for this offence by General Butler.[9]

On the morning of the 28th our crew landed with two boat howitzers, formed in line and marched through the surging crowds to the city hall where the state flag of [Louisiana] was hauled down and the U.S. flag was hoisted. The mob at times howled and jeered, often jamming our men as to compell them to draw cutlesses to keep them off. Notwithstanding the scornfull threats of the people, this flag remained until Gen. Butler's arrival.[10]

On this afternoon a portion of the mob on the levee waved a Confederate flag tauntingly at the fleet amidst great cheering from the crowd. When the Admiral's attention was called to it, he ordered the best marksmen of the Marine guard on [the] forecastle to open fire on the man waving the flag. The first fire caused a stampede in the neighborhood of the flag, leaving two still waving the flag. They soon fell and with them the last Rebel flag waved in New Orleans in our presence.[11]

On this afternoon also the Confederate steamer *McRae* came up from the forts, bringing the most distinguished of their dead, and a[s]ked the admiral's permission to land them at New Orleans for burial. The permission was granted, after which she returned to the forts and was destroyed with what remained of the Rebel fleet when the forts surrendered to Admiral Porter.[12]

This vessel was very much like one of our gunboats of the *Oneida* class and for which vessel she was mistaken during the battle at the forts by our vessels and to this she owed her existence.

On the 29th the fleet weighed anchor and steamed up to Carrollton six miles above the city to look after some batterys reported there. We found very strong earthworks running back on each side of the river as far as the eye could reach, well supplyed with heavy guns. They had what was called a boom across the river. This was composed of several heavy chains twisted and bolted through a raft of heavy logs, the whole completely closeing the river to passage of vessels. This place was considered impregnible to an attack from up the river, but coming in their rear made resistance useless. So they set everything on fire that would burn, spiked the guns and evacuated. An officer who landed from our ship reported everything distroyed when we once again returned to the front of the city.[13]

On our way down we took possession of the river steamers and other vessels lying at the warfs [and] men were put on board of them. They became useful bringing Gen. Butlers troops up to the city. We soon had a large fleet of captured tugs and river steamers, manned by Yankee sailors who seemed [to] enjoy steaming about in our prizes, racing and blowing whistles untill they were compelled to tie up in long strings behind the war vessels in front of the city.

The first fright of our arrival over, the people grew more insolent and abusive when ever we come in contack with them. They especially hated and dreaded Picayune Butler, or Butler, the Beast, as the[y] called him. Their great hope was that yellow jack [yellow fever] would relieve them of all of us. They would say, "wait till yellow jack comes, you will be dying in the street like dogs and no one to burry you."[14]

Our men would reply, "damned yellow jack, we can live where you can."

Day after day the levee continued crow[d]ed with people who stood staring at our ships and always ready to pick a quarrel with our men who had any business on shore. On one occasion a man from our third cutter jumped on the dock to chastise an insulting rowdy. He, being a powerful man, held his own against attacks from all sides untill the boats crew came to his assistance with cutlasses. These quarrels allmost stopped intercourse between the people and shipping untill the arrival of our troops.

The dinghy was exempt from these troubles, she being manned by five boys and the people did not think the boys worth growling with.[15]

I, being one of the dinghy's boys had a good chance to see and hear what was going on. We landed every morning with the stewards from the officers' messes for fresh provisions. The people were very anxious to trade with us, they taking our greenbacks greedily and giving their Shinplasters in change, their currency at this time being almost worthless. There was nothing in their currency less than one dollar, except street car tickets for five cents. They were called Picayunes [and] the city was flooded with this kind of money. They demanded enormous prices for everything. A poor breakfast would cost from four to five dollars, a cup of coffee and roll at the French market, 75 cents.[16]

While waiting the return of the stewards, the people would gather about us and question us about the battle—how many were killed on our vessels, how many of the enemy were killed, the names of the vessels that were sunk. Many had friends in the rebel navy and made special inquiry for them. Our general answer was that we had burnt or sunk the whole of them. They seem to have little or no information as to how the battle was fought.

Our boys soon became better acquainted. We used to resort to a coffee house kept by a man named Pete. I never heard the balance of his name. He was a Spaniard or Dago of some kind. His place was one of the most convenient to the warfs and was chiefly patronized by sailors, longshoremen and idlers about the levee. Pete had a kind word and a smile for every one that had money, Yankees included. The loafers about the place treated the boys of our boat kindly and never tired of questioning about the battle and our ships. One fellow named Snow used to lead in all the arguements. He could find numerous ways that our fleet might be got rid of, but their chief reliance was the yellow fever. They especially hated Gen. Butler and little storys to his discredit were always interesting. They did not dislike the sailors near so much as they did the soldiers and it was generally expected that there would be trouble when the soldiers arrived in the city.

After the passage of the forts by the fleet, Admiral Porter, who remained below, commenced negotiations for their surrender. The surrender was consummated at noon on the 28th of April [and] the news was received by our fleet with great rejoycing. Flags were hoisted at every masthead amidst great cheering. A salute of one discharge from each gun in the fleet was fired. Every available vessel was now hurried down the river to bring Gen. Butler with his troops up. The troops commenced to arrive on the following morning and, with a grand display of flags and music, they commenced landing in front of the custom house. The great mob looked on in sullen silence. There was a few cheers of wellcome as they marched up the levee from the boat. Gen. Butler came on the first boat and immediately took the St. Charles Hotel as his headquarters. United States flags were emediately hoisted on all possible buildings, with a company of soldiers at each to keep it flying.[17]

We found some important changes at Pete's Coffee House the following morning—the city Shinplasters and Confederate currency was worthless. Nothing but gold, silver or U S notes would be taken. Gold and silver money was very scarce, the working people having none of it.[18]

Another cause of trouble was communication was cut off with the surrounding country, stopping that source of supply of provisions.

31

Consequently, the price rapidly raised beyond reach of the great majority of the people. All business was suspended and matters seemed growing more desperate by the hour. The whole population seemed to be aimlessly roaming about the streets and staring in large crowds at the different places where our troops were quartered and along the levee facing the shipping.

That dispised Yankee, Picayune Butler (as they called him), was equal to [the] emergency. He established free store hours in all parts of the city and served out provisions to all who came without questions. Some were too proud at first to accept what they called Yankee charity, but hunger brought the fervendest to terms. The working classes, who suffered most, were very gratefull to General Butler.

The general soon after his arrival organized a city government. He organized a police force and a shrewd detective force. He levied taxes and made them heavyest on the more wealthy classes. The money collected this way was used in giving employment to the working people, repairing the damage to the warfs and government property destroyed by the retreating Confederates.

He also had large gang[s] cleaning the streets and alleys and he gave employment to all white men that applyed for it. It had been very dull at New Orleans for some time before its capture. The affairs of the city now seemed to take a new turn. Business was again in motion, every one seemed to have something to do.

The general opened recruiting offices for colored men who were quickly drilled and sent down to man the forts and batterys in the malarial swamps, reserving the more healthy stations for his unacclimated troops. He always had an eye to the health and comfort of his men. In return, they idolized him.[19]

After standing the abuse of the news papers for some time and as they would heed no warnings, he suspended all of them, took possession of their offices and published one paper himself. That adv[o]cated a Union sentiment and not the rebel.[20]

He organized a good detective corps, who turned up something surprising every day. They would stop a funeral on the street, take the coffin to headquarters and find it filled with gold and silver coin which had been taken from [the] mint by the retreating Confederates on the arrival of our fleet in front of the city and did not have time to get away with it. At another time they would dig up from the back yard of a good citizen several boxes of arms and ammunition.[21]

Nothing seemed to escape Gen. Butler. He seemed to know every thing. New Orleans was noted for its ruffianism before and after its capture. It was not unusual to find one or two people murdered on the street of a morning. If they had no friends, they would be burried by the city authoritys without further inquiry. The iron hand of Gen. Butler soon stopped these with many other evils. The inquest was instituted and the murderer hunted down and punished.

All open acts of sympathy with the rebellion was soon subdued, except from women who took advantage of the gallantry of our officers and men untill they became so insulting and aggressive they could bear it no longer. They would empty all kinds of filth upon our soldiers as they passed under their windows, they would use the most foulsome language to express their hatred of both living and dead as the funeral of a soldier passed through the street, and, when passing any of our soldiers on the street, they would gather their skirts and side off in the most insulting manner. They had many other way[s] of insulting and irritating our men. After repeated complaints from his men, together with his own personal experience, the general managed this as he did everything els. Effectually, he issued his famous order No. 28 that any woman who would wantonly insult soldiers or any other upon the public street would be considered a common woman and treated as such. This order had the desired effect but it raised a howl the lenth and breadth of the Confedercy. It was from this order that he was named the Beast Butler.[22]

Soon after this Mumford, the man who led the mob that tore down and dragged through the streets the first flag hoisted by us on the U S Mint was tryed and executed for that offence. This caused another howl through the Confedercy, and their sympathizers at the North. Regardless of the opinions of his enemy or the advice of his more timid friends, the general stuck firm to his policy untill New Orleans was the cleanest and the best governed city in the world.

During all this, the wealthy classes grew in hatred, as they did in acquaintance with the general, while the middle and working classes grew to like him. He opened the port to the world for trading purposes and did what he could to encourage all kinds of business. He personally seen to the needs of the poor and destitute, many familys of whom were left by their husbands and fathers to join the enemy. He seemed always doing something for the general good and made the wealthy pay for it.

Soon after the surrender of the forts, the English corvette *Rinaldo* came up to the city and anchored a short distance astern of our ship. She was soon made the headquarters of the Confederate sympathizers. Evenings, large numbers of men and ladies from the city would congregate on board of her and sing Confederate songs and airs. Her sailors would join in the chorous of the Bonnie Blue Flag when going on shore at midnight. They would take pains to pull their boat some distance out of the way to pass close to our ship, singing Confederate and Englesh songs. This, with other offences by them, caused the strongest feeling of hatred between the people of our fleet and those of the *Rinaldo*. Our men used to whip the Engleshmen when and where the[y] could find them untill they were afraid to go on shore.[23]

This, however, did not stop the singing. While passing under our bow one night, taking a large party of ladies on shore, when they all in loud chorous [were] singing the Bonnie Blue Flag, a large holystone was dropped on the boat by one of our men, causing her to sink and giving those in her a good ducking before they could be rescued by their other boat which luckily was only a little in the rear.

This brought matters to a climax. The English captain reported this with other troubles to Farragut, who replyed that if their taunting songs and other disagreeable habits were not stopped, he could not restrain his men and would not be responsible for any treatment they might bring upon themselfs from our men. This afterward became a subject of dispatches to Washington which ended in the *Rinaldo* leaving the port.[24]

After the arrival of troops at New Orleans, the smaller vessels were started up the river with the hope they would meet Admiral Foote's flotilla which was to come down and assist at the capture of New Orleans. Every thing working smoothly under General Butler at New Orleans, the U S *Pensacola* and *Mississippi* was left in front of the city while the balance of the fleet started up the river on the 10th of May 1862.[25]

BARTHOLOMEW DIGGINS,
Captain of the Watch, U. S. S. Hartford.

Bartholomew Diggins, ordinary seaman and Medal of Honor recipient. Naval History and Heritage Command.

General-in-Chief Winfield Scott's Anaconda Plan envisioned a blockade of Southern ports and splitting the Confederacy by securing control of the Mississippi River. Library of Congress.

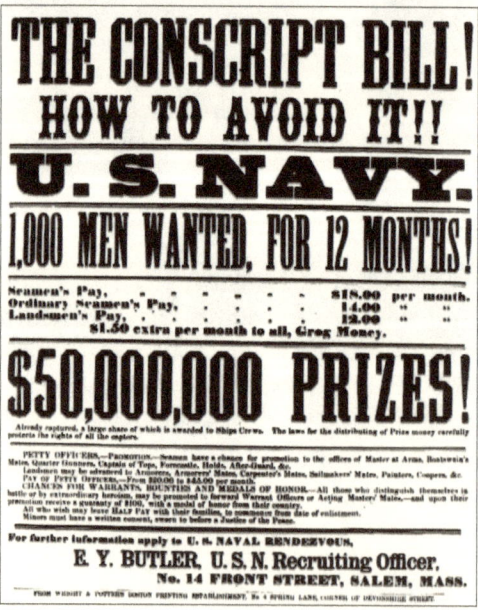

This recruiting poster promised millions in prize money for sailors. Naval History and Heritage Command.

USS *Hartford* at Mobile Bay in 1864. From *Miller's Photographic History.*

Rear Admiral David Glasgow Farragut. Library of Congress.

In the summer of 1864, *Hartford* sailors, many very young, wear their white hats while posing for a photograph. Courtesy Brian D. Caplan Collection, from the Metropolitan Museum of Art, NYC.

One of Diggins's favorite officers, Lewis A. Kimberly, here is a rear admiral in the 1880s. Naval History and Heritage Command.

Capt. James S. Palmer (*left*) and Adm. Farragut (*right*) were not popular with the men. Palmer was derisively called "Lady" Palmer, while Farragut was thought of as "a cold fish." US Army Heritage and Education Center.

Starboard side of the *Hartford's* gun deck of nine inch Dahlgren muzzle loaders. Library of Congress.

Rear Admiral David D. Porter energetically promoted himself and his mortar boats. Library of Congress.

Diggins and his shipmates watched in fascination as the 220-pound shells from the 13-inch mortars arched through night skies. From *Miller's Photographic History*.

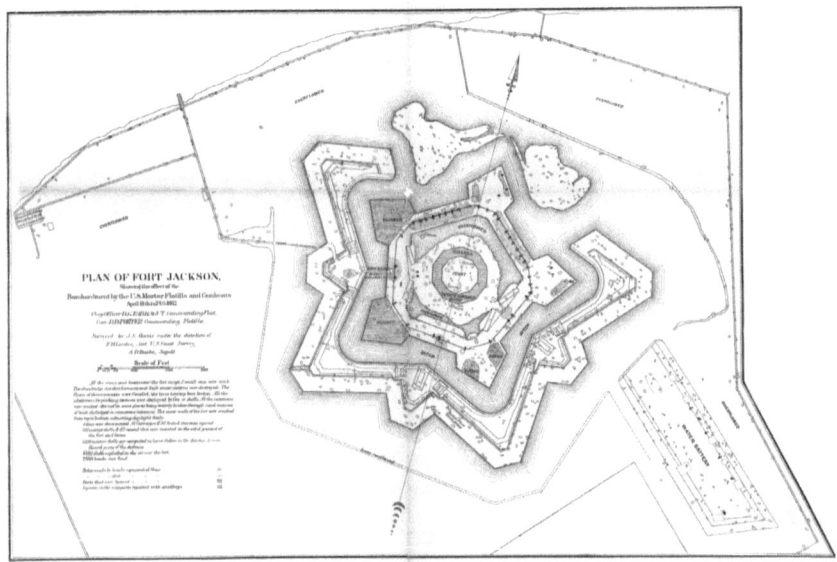

Fort Jackson (above) and St. Philip, New Orleans's guardian forts, failed to stop Farragut's advance to the city. *National Oceanic and Atmospheric Administration, coast survey of forts.*

JEFF'S NAVY.

This satiric and patriotic envelope cartoon might have buoyed Northern citizens' spirits, but Federal sailors knew the Confederate navy was no joke. *New-York Historical Society.*

CSS *Manassas*, the "dreaded monster" covered by 1½ inch thick iron plates, rammed three wooden Federal warships until she ran aground during the fight for New Orleans. National Archives.

Because she so closely resembled some Federal ships, the CSS *McRae* escaped early destruction when Farragut's fleet engaged Confederate vessels below New Orleans. Naval History and Heritage Command.

PART 2
VICKSBURG

Cheered by successfully passing New Orleans's guardian forts and capturing the city, Farragut may have thought he could repeat the process at Vicksburg, though he preferred first tackling the forts guarding the important port of Mobile, Alabama. But Gustavus V. Fox, assistant secretary of the navy, told Farragut that, "The opening of the Mississippi is of more importance than Mobile." He repeated that "it is of paramount importance for you to go up and clear the river with the utmost expedition."[1]

For Lincoln, opening the river was the supreme objective in the West. He saw Vicksburg as the key to unlocking the river, allowing the vital water artery to run unvexed to the Gulf.

Apparently neither Lincoln nor Navy Department leaders realized that, unlike New Orleans, Vicksburg was a fortress city. Ground troops, many thousands of them, would be needed to take that fortress.

So, obedient to the president's wishes and his orders, Farragut and his fleet steamed upriver toward Vicksburg.

SHIPS BATTLE "TO NO PURPOSE"

We arrived at Baton Rouge, the capitol of the state of La. It had surrendered to the USS *Iroquois*, which we found laying in front of the city. Our flag was flying from the Arsenal.[2]

On the following morning we continued up the river, passing Port Hudson, Natchez, Grand Gulf and up to Vicksburg, stopping long enough at each place to receive its surrender. At Vicksburg we found the balance of our fleet that had started up ahead of us at anchor. Vicksburg was well fortified and they could not proceed farther.[3]

Captain [Samuel Phillips] Lee of the *Oneida* had demanded the surrender of the city on his arrival and received for reply from the mayor that the Mississippians did not know how to surrender and refused to learn to surrender to an enemy and if Farragut or Butler thought they could teach them, let them come on. Brig-Gen M[artin] L. Smith, who commanded the defences, replyed with less bombast that having been ordered to defend Vicksburg he would do so as long as he could. This give us to understand that we had more fighting on hand.[4]

Vicksburg is located in a horse shoe like bend of the river. The bluffs on which the city is built commence about six miles below the city, fronting the river until about three miles above where the bank of the river is formed by low land. The city is built on a sharp slope which becomes sharper as we advance up the river untill at the upper end of the city, the high bluffs form the steep bank of the river and in the center of the bend on this bluff was located a battery of the heavyest guns commanding both approaches to the city. The other batterys were located in the city along the water front and terraced up the receeding hills, the whole forming a cresent of forts and batterys more than six miles long and so placed that the attacking vessels would be at all times under a raking fire. And when the center of the city is reached, a fleet would be surrounded on three sides by the batterys. There was a very heavy battery located in a large building in the center of the city, using the windows as port holes. From the building was kept flying a yellow hospital flag.[5]

After a thorough examination and getting all the information obtainable concerning the enemy's works and strenth, it was decided that our present force was not suficient to make a successfull attack.[6]

Leaving the balance of the fleet at anchor below the city, our ship started to New Orleans to order up all our forces and make preperations for the attack. On our return to Baton Rouge we found that while up the river, our flag, hoisted by the *Iroquois,* had been hauled down. Two boats were sent from our ship to replace the flag, the gig and dinghy. The dinghy being the soonest ready, reached the shore first and, while in the act of landing, a regiment of cavalry rushed down to the landing and discharged their carbines and revolvers at the dinghy crew and then disappeared through the streets of the town. The officer in command of the boat, Chief Engineer [James B.] Kimball was struck in the head and side [and] three of the boats crew were wounded, myself being one of them.

A ball past through my left arm and one through my right breast and through the upper lobe of my right lung. This wound paralyzed my whole right side.[7]

Owing to most of the crew being wounded, our boat became unmanageable and we were rapidly drifting down the river with the current when we were picked up by the gunboat *Kennebec* where our wounds were dressed. The *Kennebec* was the only vessel of our fleet present [and] was laying a short distance astern of us. [she] emediately opened fire on the town. Our ship was receiving coal from a schooner which was secured on the city side of our ship. It was necessary to drop her astern before the guns could be fired. This was quickly done, the guns firing as fast as the schooner cleared them, shooting away the schooner's headgear and a part of her cutwater in their anxiety.[8]

The order was soon given to cease firing as it was evident the cavalry had not delayed in the city after firing on the boat and we did not want to kill the innocent residents. During the short fire on the city much damage was done, but few of the buildings escap[ing] our shell.[9]

This style of fighting was now coming in practice by the enemy along the river from New Orleans to Vicksburg. They would plant light batterys on the river banks, the levee forming a breastwork, near some town or city, and open fire on our transports and supply boats. They would let the armed vessels pass without notice. They continually changed from one town to another so that our gunboats could not overtake or keep track of them. They would be heard from as firing upon our vessels from places 20 or 30 miles apart in a few hours. This had become such an anoyance, they at times firing into our hospital boats and killing many of the defenceless sick who were on their way to the hospital at New Orleans.[10]

The Admiral found it necessary to notify the authoritys and citizens of all towns along the river who permitted these attacks on our unarmed vessels that they would be held responsible and their towns distroyed if the offence was continued.[11]

Soon after this warning two transports from Gen. Williams camp, opposite Vicksburg, loaded with sick on their way to New Orleans, were fired upon at Donaldsonville and one of them sunk with all on board. This case was reported to the Admiral while laying at Baton Rouge.

We emmediately up anchor and steamed down and anchored in front of Donaldsonville and began to shell the town. After two hours shelling two boat crews were landed and set fire to what our shell did not distroy. We returned to Baton Rouge the same day.[12]

Soon after Grand Gulf was treated in the same manner by Comd [Lieut.] E. T. Nichols of the *Winona* and others of our fleet. Those prompt measures brought a howl from the people along the river and a complaint from Gen. Lovell, the commander of that Dept, charging Comd. Nichols and others of our fleet with introducing barbarous warfare. The Admiral replied that Comd. Nichols and others of our fleet had acted by his orders and that they [Confederates] choose the time and place for their attacks upon our vessels and should therefore see that the innocent and defenceless of their own people were out of the way before they made the attacks upon our vessels. For, said the Admiral, rest assured that your fire will be returned. The fate of the towns is at all times in the hands of your military who may at pleasure draw the fire of our vessels upon them and the community is made to suffer by the acts of its military.[13]

This had the desired effect. The firing was only done from the estableshed batterys at Grand Gulf, Port Hudson, etc., or if a planter was suspected of sympathy with our side, they would plant batterys so that the return fire would do the most damage to the persons thus suspected. In this way many Union men were ruined of which we found a considerable number along the river, who would openly declare their principles, if we had any way to protect them.[14]

After all necessary preparations were underway for an attack on Vicksburg, we again started up the river. When we arrived at Grand Gulf, it was a little after sunrise. In the morning the men were engaged washing decks when the enemy opened fire from the bluffs. This was not expected, but men hurriedly dropped the brooms and buckets and a spirited engagement of a half hour [occurred] untill we passed up the river out of range with the loss of 2 killed and 5 wounded.[15]

The enemy were industriously fortifying this place and it rapidly grew in strenth, giving our vessels more trouble each time they passed it, untill it grew to be one of the strongholds of the river and [was] afterwards captured by the combined forces of Gen. Grant and Admiral Porter.[16]

While moving up and down the river at this time, our vessel was always ready for action, nor was drum and fife necessary to call the men to quarters. As we neared the bluffs or suspicious places, the officers and men would naturally drift to their places at the guns. If not fired upon, [they would] resume their other duties again.

The people along the river gethered along the banks and at the landings and seemed to be much interested watching the long dark hulls and tall masted warships as they passed. The negroes looked upon us as friends and when we anchored at night, they would come off to the ship in large numbers and ask to be taken on board. We would receive all that we had room for and afterwards land them at New Orleans or turn them over to Gen. Butler where he had about two thousand of them at work digging a canal opposite the point at Vicksburg.[17]

The officers and men indured great hardships while passing up and down the river. The ship was continually getting aground and many times we were compelled to transfer all the stores and some of the heavy guns to smaller vessels to get her off. At other times, the men would run from side to side and fore and aft to loosen her from her muddy bed while two or three large river steamers would be trying to pull her off, breaking all the hawsers and ropes on the ship and, in the end, be compelled to take everything out of her to lighten her off. The men worked night and day in this manner.[18]

Being unacclimated, and compelled to drink the muddy water of the river, [it] alltogether commenced to tell on the health of the crew, so that when we returned to Vicksburg on the 23 of June 1862, more than one third of the men were on the sick list and more than half of the balance was complaining from the different forms of malaria, for which that river is noted.[19]

On our arrival, all preperations were hurried for the attack. The mortar vessels were placed in position above and below the city while Gen. Williams with a force of six thousand men was erecting batterys on the point opposite [the] city. On the 27th of June our mortars and shore batterys opened fire on the city. They kept up a rather sluggish fire during the day and received but few replys from the city. Toward evening the

48

signal was made from our ship [for] the fleet to clear for action. At the same [time], mortars, with the batterys under Gen. Williams, opened a vigorous fire on the city. About 2:30 oclock on the morning of the 28th, the fleet commenced to move up towards the city.[20]

The engagement become general soon after daylight. The mortars now redoubled their fire, keeping a stream of shell passing over our shipping and falling in all parts of the city, but with much less effect than at Forts Jackson and St. Philip, owing to the various elevations and the scattered positions of the batterys. However, they did much good, adding to the confusion of the troops and the people in the city.[21]

The smaller vessels were to take position between the three large vessels first mentioned [*Richmond*, *Hartford*, and *Brooklyn*], being equally divided along the line. The gunboats *Harriet Lane*, *Octorara*, *Clifton*, *Westfield*, *Jackson* and *Owasco* under Admiral Porter were to advance up in the rear of our fleet and engage the lower batterys untill our fleet either captured or passed the city.[22]

When the *Richmond* and other leading ships reach[ed] the bend in front of the city, they become so enveloped in smoke that we almost lost sight of them. All the surrounding hills seem alive with small batterys of three and four heavy guns each. Those with the water batterys along the river bank kept up a distructive fire upon us as we advanced up the river. Our ship moved up slowly close to the shore, silencing every battery as we come up with them.[23]

In a large building in the center of the city and about half way up the slopes was located the most formidable battery in Vicksburg. They seemed to fire the guns from windows. From the top of the building was flying a large yellow hospital flag.

This battery attracted the Admiral's especial attention. When we arrived abreast of it, as if angered at the flimsey disguise of a sick flag, he ordered the ship stopped and the whole fire concentrated on the hospital. We layed in front of it untill it was a silent mass of ruins. Many other batterys through the city was located like this in cellers or basements, using cellers for breastworks and windows for port holes, having the most innocent appearance when viewed from the river and showing no sign of their malignant character. Cellers and basements were also utilised by the troops as rifle pits from which they stormed upon us showers of bullets which buried themself in the ship's side and did little harm otherwise.[24]

After nearly two hours fighting we lay in front of the city in comparative peace. There was no reply to our last broadsides except from one heavy gun derecly ahead of us at the upper end of [the] city and

49

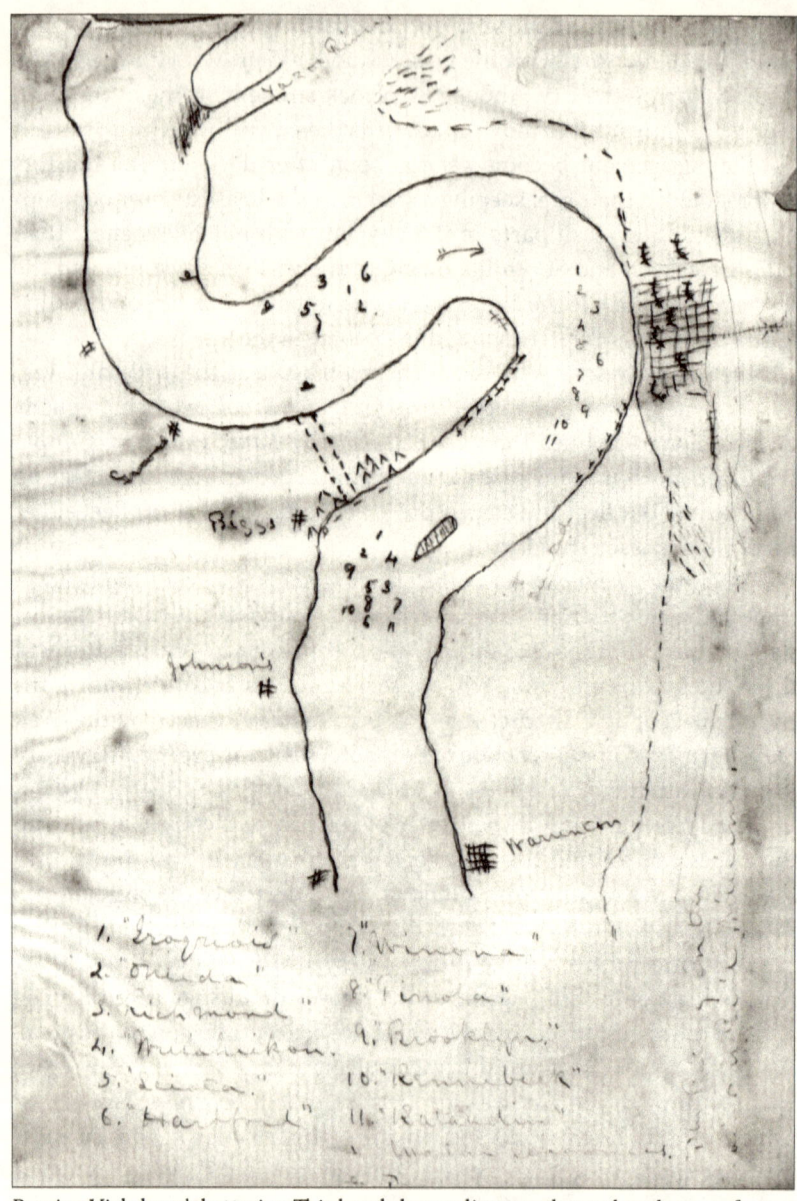

Braving Vicksburg's batteries. This hand-drawn diagram shows the advance of Farragut's fleet past Vicksburg's batteries on the river's right or eastern side. On the upper right the Yazoo flows into the Mississippi and upstream there was the CSS *Arkansas*. Here the *Hartford* is #6 as the ships steam against the current under fire much of the way. Courtesy American Antiquarian Society, diagram by Edward W. Bacon.

located so high on the bluffs that it was beyond the range of our guns. We ceased firing and as the smoke cleared from a beautiful clear morning, except for an occasional shot, the fierce batterys of Vicksburg lay silent before us. The Admiral ordered the signals made to seek close order. It was answered by the gunboats *Iroquois, Winona* and *Pinola.* They were all that remained of our fleet. The *Richmond,* whose captain so urgently sought the lead, had gone ahead as fast as she could until she had past the batterys. The gunboats in her emmediate neighborhood did as she did. The *Brooklyn* did not come up farther than the lower battery where she emmediately dropped back again and the gunboats in her neighborhood followed her example. It looked like it was intended to make this attack a failure.[25]

Farragut was at the beginning of his great career. He had received the thank[s] and congratulations of his government [and] the news papers from the North were loaded with his praise. The capture of New Orleans was considered the most important advantage gained from the Confedercy up to that time. There [was] little doubt that Farragut's growing popularity had excited some jelousey and envy among those who held equal rank with him at this time. Among them was Captain Thomas Craven of the *Brooklyn* and Captain James Alden of the *Richmond.*[26]

Be that as it may, the admiral found himself with less than one third of his fleet in front of the silent batterys of Vicksburg. It cost the government more than a year's efforts, millions of money and many lives to accomplish what we had that morning if our fleet had sustained the admiral. The capture of Vicksburg was certain. We could have anchored in front of the city and as far as our guns could reach, and they covered all important points we might defy the whole Confedercy. It was reported that there was 20,000 troops in the rear of the city. They could do nothing with us and would not dare [come] within range of our guns and might, with as much benefit to the Confedercy and danger to us, be encamped on any of the other bluffs along the river.[27]

Our signal to the rest of the fleet was kept flying, [but] it received no answer. The enemy gradually renewed the battle when the *Hartford* and the three small gunboats were not able to cope with the batterys longer, our hard earned victory fell back in the lap of the enemy as we slowly moved up the river out of range. This was our first failure and had a very depressing effect on the men and officers. All had a feeling that something was wrong. The big rifle on the bluff at the upper end of the city never ceased firing at us untill we got out of its reach.[28]

SHIPS . . . CAN NOT CRAWL UP HILLS

Diggins said that the fleet "suffered but little" in passing Vicksburg and that Confederate fire was wild. Relatively speaking, perhaps that was so—Fleet Surgeon J. M. Foltz reported just 7 killed and 30 wounded on the ships that completed the run. But the *Richmond's* log related that "their shots came crashing through our bulwarks, brains and blood flying all over the decks." More restrained, one of Diggins's shipmates simply called the fighting passage "very severe."[1]

Yet for all the thunder of ships' guns and the solid "one sheet of flame" from Confederate guns on the ridge above Vicksburg, the passage was pointless, proving only that the Federal fleet could do it, if willing to pay the price. In effect, that is what Farragut told Secretary of the Navy Gideon Welles when he wrote, "I passed up the river this morning, but to no purpose." Blunter still was Porter, who advised Assistant Secretary Gustavus Vasa Fox, "It was a useless sacrifice of life."[2]

Army and navy commanders on the scene knew full well that the fortress city would not fall like ripe fruit into their hands at the sight of Federal warships steaming past. Vicksburg was not New Orleans, a defenseless city. Here they needed ground forces and lots of them to overcome the city's defenders in their trenches and artillery emplacements. As Porter put it, "Ships . . . can not crawl up hills 300 feet high, and it is that part of Vicksburg which must be taken by the army."[3]

Farragut, a realist, said he knew that it was impossible for the Union "to take Vicksburg without an army force of twelve or fifteen thousand men." On the same day his fleet passed Vicksburg, Farragut sent a carefully worded appeal to Maj. Gen. Henry W. Halleck, the army's area commander, for help. He told Halleck, "My orders, general, are to clear the river. This I find impossible without your assistance." To strengthen the request, Farragut noted that he needed troops "to carry out the peremptory order of the President." Unmoved, Halleck refused. Obtuse about strategy, often marching to a drumbeat only he heard, Halleck said he could not oblige because his spare troops were needed elsewhere.[4]

Given all this, it is reasonable to ask why Farragut ran the Vicksburg batteries in the first place. There are several answers, some relying on informed speculation, some based on indisputable fact. Probably first and foremost, Farragut obeyed orders from officials in distant Washington who knew little or nothing about Vicksburg's defenses. Among the flurry of telegrams and dispatches directing Farragut to move up river was an imperative order, dated May 19, 1862, from Secretary Welles advising Farragut that "the President of the United States requires you . . . (without a moment's delay . . .) to open the river Mississippi and to effect a junction with Flag Officer Davis. . . ."[5]

Charles Davis's Western Flotilla, with his ironclad flagship USS *Benton*, would soon arrive just above Vicksburg. But a Farragut-Davis rendezvous in no way opened the river, something the naval commanders knew full well. They could clear the river of enemy warships, but they could not open it to undisturbed traffic until Vicksburg fell or they bypassed the fortress. In the end, Farragut simply obeyed misguided orders from Lincoln and Welles. Perhaps he also hoped that, by doing so, he could escape the river's confines, return to the open seas, and ultimately attack Mobile, a major Confederate port for blockade runners.[6]

The threat of a Confederate ironclad supposedly under construction above the city had little influence on the decision to steam past Vicksburg. Many in the Federal fleet viewed that ironclad as a chimera, a fanciful "myth," though persistent reports placed it up the Yazoo River, miles above where that river fed into the Mississippi. Even if *Arkansas* existed, Farragut did not think "she will ever come forth."[7]

But the *Arkansas* was real, and Diggins tells that story, after he backtracks a bit to describe experiences with fleeing slaves.

The antipathy and prejudice toward blacks that Diggins describes was not unique to sailors; they shared that animus with soldiers and most of the northern population of the time. However, greater and more frequent contact with newly freed slaves honed

54

sailors' animosity. Yet blacks had long served in the navy, unlike the army, and contradictions existed. On some ships, blacks messed and lived separately; on others, integration was the rule, though the navy limited African Americans to the lowest ranks.[8]

Like many southerners, one gunboat sailor questioned whether blacks were human. He asked, "Is he nearly a man or not? I am persuaded to believe he is not altogether." Such views often led to extreme positions. William W. Van Cleaf, serving on the USS *Benton*, swore that before he "helped to free them Niggers I would cut my throat from ear to ear." Less self-sacrificing but more blood-thirsty was a fireman on the little sidewheeler USS *Nansemond*. He wrote, "if I had my way I would cut every nigers throt in the united states they think more of a niger on this boat than they do of a white man."[9]

After an engagement of nearly three hours, we anchored in the midst of Admiral Davis's fleet where we found the *Richmond* and those of our fleet that ran by Vicksburg ahead of us.[10]

We suffered but little considering the lenth of time engaged. The enemy fire was wild, the most of their shot passing over us, damaging our rigging and spars. One shot cut away the after shrouds of the mizzen rigging just under where Admiral Farragut was standing, letting the upper portion with the Admiral swing in to [the] mast. The Admiral climbed lightly to the uninjured portion of the rigging where he continued to watch the battle till the close.[11]

While coming up the river, we picked [up] the many negroe slaves who would come out to the ships in small boats at every place we anchored. We had orders from Washington to take them as contraband of war. After we anchored above Vicksburg, they were still coming on board untill the ship was so crowded that they had become a nuisance. As they become used to the new state of things, they became quarrelsome, lazy and insolent. When they were brought up for any misconduct, the officers heard them with more favor than they did the crew. This was to discourage imposition upon them.[12]

The darkeys took advantage of this and grew in bad habits and at lenth became so unbearable that one night some of the men cut the fastening of a lot of rigging and spars under which they [the contrabands] slept on the spar deck, letting the whole come down with a rush upon them. Several of them was injured. One of the most insolent of them was caught by some of the men and thrown out of one of the forward ports overboard. The swift current carried him down to Vicksburg where he made a landing and told a terrible story of cruel treatment by the Yankees which was all published in the Vicksburg papers. This and other strong measures by the crew had a good effect on contrabands untill we reached New Orleans where they were all landed. [13]

A REBEL RAM MORTIFIES FEDERALS

Despite Farragut's doubts, early on the morning of July 15, 1862, the CSS *Arkansas* transformed from myth to dangerous adversary. Almost before Federal sailors knew it, the dull brown ironclad was upon the combined fleets, with all her guns firing at the surprised crews and motionless Federal vessels, most anchored with fires banked and unable to move.[1]

Yet such a surprise should never have occurred. Farragut's officers had received fair warning the day before of the ironclad ram's pending sortie. Deserters had revealed that information to *Hartford* officers on the evening of July 14, but the warning was ignored. A captain's clerk on the USS *Iroquois* lamented, "Consequently, the next morning saw us without steam and at the mercy of our bold and brilliant enemy."[2]

Still, as a precaution, Federal commanders had ordered three ships up the Yazoo River to learn the ram's condition and location. Under the command of naval officers, the three army ships were the ironclad *Carondelet* with fourteen guns, the wooden sidewheel river steamer *Tyler*, converted into a gunboat with seven guns, and the wooden sidewheel ram *Queen of the West*, with four guns. As they started up the Yazoo, they got their answers much sooner and at greater cost than they had expected. Round a bend ahead of them came the *Arkansas*, swiftly bearing down upon them, pushed along by her twin propellers and the river's current.[3]

Earlier, Confederate planners had shifted the unfinished *Arkansas* from Memphis to a secure place far up the Yazoo. There, navy lieutenant Isaac N. Brown took charge and, under very difficult conditions, did his best to prepare the ram for battle. But she was only partially girded with railroad iron, and her engines had proved unreliable. Nevertheless, Brown took her into action with a crew of two hundred, ten cannons, and with a listed top speed of eight knots.[4]

Quickly the *Arkansas* proved more than a match for the three Federal vessels. She pounded *Carondelet* mercilessly, forcing her to ground; then she hounded the other two, chasing them to the Mississippi. *Tyler* suffered heavy casualties, reporting thirteen killed, thirty-four wounded, and ten missing. A master's mate on the battered ship said that one enemy shell exploded on deck and "horribly mutilated and instantly killed" one officer and five enlisted men. Entering the Mississippi, *Tyler* and *Queen of the West* quickly took refuge in the assembled fleets. [5]

Without slowing, the *Arkansas* glided by thirty-three enemy warships. Brown, the *Arkansas*'s intrepid captain, said that all his guns fired rapidly while moving down the water corridor between the Federal vessels, and they did so "without the fear of hitting a friend or missing an enemy."[6]

Just the opposite bedeviled the Federals. Edward W. Bacon on the *Iroquois* explained that "we lay so badly that many vessels could not fire on account of the danger to others." Anchored in rows on both sides of the river and lacking motive power, many could not fire at the ram because other ships blocked their fire. In short, Farragut and Davis were not only surprised by the bold foray, but were unprepared in every way.[7]

Still, those ships with a clear field of fire or those that dropped down with the current for an open spot, rained shot and shell upon the ram. Edward M. Galligan, a sailor on the ironclad *Essex*, noted that many ships "had a crack at her as she passed." On the *Arkansas*, Brown reported, "The shock of missiles hitting our sides was literally continuous." One 11-inch solid shot penetrated above a gun port, killed three and wounded three, and then passed through smokestack, killing eight and wounding three men of a gun crew on the ram's other side.[8]

Meanwhile, *Arkansas* continued downstream until she tied up under Vicksburg's batteries, there to recover from her perilous passage. The romp through the Federal fleet killed ten and wounded fifteen of her crew; all told, Federals counted eighteen killed, fifty wounded, and ten missing.[10]

But casualty counts and damage reports paled in comparison to the brazen feat of the lone *Arkansas* sailing through two Federal fleets. Further, she remained afloat and still a potent threat to Lincoln's goal of clearing the river. Farragut admitted to "deep mortification" over the ram's jaunt past his ships, and Secretary of the Navy Welles also labeled it a "deep mortification." Both called for her destruction "at all hazards."[11]

Our fleet above Vicksburg formed a line on the north side of the river. The western flotelo, mostly ironclads, continued our line in our rear in the direction of Vicksburg. The numerous transports, hospital boats and non-combatants were tied up along the south bank, leaving a narrow passage between.[12]

The fleet lay in this position when about six o'clock on the morning [of] July 15th we heard rapid reports of heavy guns from up the river. As the reports grew nearer, the men, who were engaged in washing down decks, quickly took their places at the guns and before the cause of firing could be explained, it was in our midst.

The Confederate ram *Arkansas Traveler*, which was built up the Yazoo River, had been for some time awaiting an opportunity to run the blockade to Vicksburg. Few thought she would atemt it in [the] pressense of both fleets. The gunboats *Carondelet* and *Tyler* were blockading the mouth of the Yazoo river to prevent her escape when she made her appearance. Both vessels engaged her and continued a desperate struggle untill they reached the fleet. The *Tyler* especialy, though a wooden vessel, fought her side by side untill the fleet was reached where she pulled of[f] crippled and more than half her crew killed and wounded.[13]

The fleet, lying at anchor, now took up the fight, giving broadside after broadside as she passed down the narrow passage through the fleet with two confederate flags flying. She had closed her ports and our broadsides had little effect on her iron sides. As none of our vesels had steam up, there was nothing to obstruct her passage and she reached Vicksburg with little loss. Unfortunately, this was not our case. Every shot from our broadsides that missed the ram struck among our own transports and other vessels on the opposite side of the river, blowing up and sinking many of them, and causing great loss of life.[14]

The Admiral come out of his cabin in his nightgown while the ram was passing and seemed much surprised. He stood on deck in this attire untill after the engagement when he ordered a signal to be made to the fleet to prepare for action. There was none of our fleet had steam up. On our ship the machinery was apart being repaired and the men were scaling the boilers. Allthough the whole fleet were in hurried preperation, it was not till late in the evening that all was reported in readness.[15]

The Admiral in the meantime went on board of the *Benton*, an iron-clad, Admiral Davis' flag ship, and dropped down within range of the guns of Vicksburg. After exchanging shots and locating the ram *Arkansas*, they returned. Admiral Farragut returned to our ship about five o'clock when he ordered the fleet under weigh for another attack on Vicksburg. The chief object of the attack was to capture or distroy the ram *Arkansas Traveler*. The Admiral decided to do this with his own ship, so that we had prepared for that purpose. A kedg[e] anchor suspended at the end of our fore yardarm [was] ready to drop on the ram and our bow anchors were ready to let fall upon her that they might graple her while we hauled her out in the stream and, if possible, down the river with us.[16]

About 5:30 p.m. our fleet moved down the river. Admiral Davis' fleet accompanied us untill the first line of batterys was reached which he engaged while we passed down. They seemed to have added considerable strenth to the batterys from the reception they give us. When our ships reached the city the order was passed to watch closely for the ram. When we reached the center of the city where the ram was supposed to lay, our ship stopped for a few minutes, but oweing to the darkness of approaching night and the ram laying under the shadow of the bank, we could not discover her, being all the time under a terific fire from the hill and water batterys and musketry from the rifle pits, the latter peppering our sides with showers of bullets. Failing to discover the location of the ram and her distruction being the object of the attack, we followed the rest of our fleet down the river to our old anchorage below the city.[17]

On our ship we lost eight killed and several wounded. Among the killed was the Master's Mate George Loundsberry who I previously mentioned as having grabbed up a grating to jump overboard when the ship was on fire at Forts Jackson and St. Philip. He was standing behind the bitts near the fore hatch on the berth deck when a 10 inch shot struck the bitts, knocking them into splinters and scattering the upper portion of Lounsberry's body about the beams and side of the berth deck. A colored man who had the habit of standing behind Lounsberry at [the] bitts suffered the same fate, The legs and arms of both men [were] scraped together in a bag and burried together.[18]

The most reckless conduct during this action was remarkable of Lieut J. C. Watson, commanding the second division in which I served. [While] instructing his men to keep clear of the ports as much as possible to avoid the showers of bullets from the rifle pits, he took his own position where he was most exposed, on top of the main gangway, and from this dangerous position he coolly delivered his orders during the whole fight and luckily escaped without a scratch.[19]

Our fleet remained at anchor below Vicksburg untill the 22nd of July, 1862. On the morning of that day the ram *Essex* came down from Admiral Davis' fleet. This vessel was iron clad and supposed to be shotproof. She was just built and added to Admiral Davis' flotillo. It was intended that she would either sink or distroy the rebel ram *Arkansas* in front of Vicksburg. She was watched with great interest by the fleets above and below the city.[20]

As she advanced down the river the fire of all the batterys of Vicksburg was concentrated upon her. Our fleet moved up slowly towards the city, that we might assist her in case any thing happened. The officers and men crowded the rigging and rails to witness the fight between the two ironclads. Our mortars were placed in position the night before [and] they now opened fire on the city. The *Essex* kept her ports closed untill she got abreast of the *Arkansas* when she headed straight for her and opened fire with bow guns at the same time. The engagement was lively for a short time, untill in an attemt to ram her the *Essex* unfortunately grounded. When the *Essex* got off she was swept by the rapid current, passed the *Arkansas* when she again headed down the river and soon after arrived among our fleet. She escaped with one killed and three wounded. Her iron plating was some what battered without much injury to the vesel.[21]

After coming to anchor, Captain W. D. Porter of the *Essex* came on board our ship in a uniform composed [of] slouch hat, red flannell shirt, red top boots with his pants stuck in them. This rough and ready style was now becoming fashionable among the officers of the upper muddy water fleet.

It was now the begining of [the] unhealthy season, if it had any beginning. More than half the officers and men were sick with the many forms of malaria that affected the unacclimated. Gen. Williams troops seemed to suffer more than the men on the ships as every supply boat returning to New Orleans was loaded with his sick.[22]

All seemed heartily tired of the river and Farragut himself was opposed to river fighting and would much rather attack Mobile or some other of the coast defenses of the enemy. Previous to the appearance of the *Arkansas* it was intended to look after some of these places.

On the afternoon of the day the *Essex* came down all hands were called to muster on the quarter deck. The men soon gethered aft wondering what it meant. When Captain Wainwright, with the Admiral at his side, addressed us from the poop deck, he spoke feelingly of the great numbers sick among us [and] the hardships of the well trying to do the duties of all.

He said it was the intention, if we had succeeded in distroying the ram, to have left the river emmediately, that now it was not safe to leave the river with such a powerful enemy behind us. New Orleans itself would not be safe. He said he had considered the great dangers attendant to going up to the batterys and capturing her and had decided it a most desperate undertaking. In the present condition of the ship's company he thought it was better to consult them and let them decide whether we would go up to Vicksburg and capture or destroy the ram or wait a better opportunity by remaining in the river. He was quickly answered with loud cries of "We will follow you anywhere, we go to Vicksburg."

Those cries soon became a continual uproar and wound up with cheer after cheer for Captain Wainwright. The captain stood near the cabin hatch, his tall form reaching above all others, with a dignity of manner that never forsook him, his face aglow with paternal pride and affection. At the quick response from the crew, the captain then thanked them for their expressions of confidence and, with Farragut, went in the cabin while the men dispersed.

This was the first and only time the men were consulted as to any action the ship was to take part in. It was afterwards decided [it was] unwise to attack the ram under the Vicksburg batterys.[23]

Our fleet, with General Williams and what remained of his troops, started down to Baton Rouge where we landed Gen. Williams and left the ironclad *Essex* and some of the smaller gunboats with him while the *Hartford* continued to New Orleans.

BACK DOWN RIVER

Vicksburg, the key to free and safe passage up and down the river, remained securely in Confederate hands. No number of costly, risky ship parades back and forth in front of the fortress city would change that or the need for ground troops. Then there were other costs for Farragut's ships and men while they uselessly anchored above or below the city. In a letter to superiors, Farragut declared, "I fear we will have great difficulty in carrying out the views of the Department particularly as fever, dysentery and diarrhoea [*sic*] are beginning to affect our officers and men seriously."[1]

Loyall Farragut, the admiral's son and biographer, who was aboard the *Hartford* at that time, added that Farragut also thought it "imprudent" to keep his ocean-going, deep draft ships so high up the river when the river level was falling. But undoubtedly, Farragut sought any legitimate reason to escape idleness and the river's confines.[2]

On our arrival at New Orleans the men were given liberty on shore for twenty-four hours, the first we had since we left Philadelphia or nearly one year. We found New Orleans very much changed. The harbor was crowded with all kinds of shipping, many of them taking freight on board for New York and European ports, the streets and levee seemed alive with business. Gangs of workmen were handling freight on the levee while other gangs were cleaning and repairing the streets. There seemed to be plenty of employment for every body. The people who were loudest in their hatred of General Butler were now singing his praise. The business and working people seem as much devoted to him as those of his own district in Massachusetts.[3]

Soon after our arrival in New Orleans we suffered the greatest misfortune that could befall the ship's company in the death of Captain Wainwright. We knew that he was ill, but few were prepared to hear of his death. The men idolized him and spoke of him effectionately as the old man and he, by a thousand ways, showed his kindly feeling to the crew. There was not a man courtmarshaled during the time he commanded the ship.[4]

His remains were inclosed in a neat casket and lay in state on the quarterdeck for a few hours before being shipped on the mail boat for the North. As the men passed around the head of the casket in single file to take the last look at the remains, there was not a dry eye among them.

It was rumored among the men that his family were dependent upon his salery. Upon this report the crew decided to send a present to his family and a committee went to the mast for permission that each man be permitted [to] subscribe one month's pay and the paymaster charge it to their accounts and forward it to his family. For some reason the permission was refused by the officers.[5]

Captain Palmer succeeded Captain Wainwright in command of the *Hartford*. He was remarkable for his fine appearance. He was more than six feet in height and fully proportioned. He assumed a very proud and stately manner and was particularly neat about his dress.[6]

The morning that he came on board to take charge, before he reached his cabin, he stopped to issue his first order. Addressing the officer of the deck, with much dignity, he said, "Drive those men from the quarter deck and keep them forward of the mainmast."

The men thought this order a hard one as the ship had at least one third more men than her compliment in time of peace. We also carried a number of spare men to supply to the fleet as they were needed, making the ship very much crowded. Up to this time men were allowed to use the quarterdeck to the cabin door on the port side and the greater portion on the starboard side. The order was sullenly obeyed and, as the men moved forward, their expressions were anything but polite to Lady Palmer, as they called him.

On his arrival on deck the next morning, he ordered that the men be kept forward of the smoke stack. This the men thought needless cruelty, as now they had little more than standing room. To this was added stricter desipline in all other matters.[7]

The sudden change from the fatherly kindness of Captain Wainwright to the cold selfish dignity of Captain Palmer caused much discontent among the crew and, for want of a better remedy, they commenced deserting in large numbers at New Orleans, many of them joining the First and Second La. Cavalry, the first two Union Redgments raised in the South.[8]

Some excitement was caused by one of the city detectives bringing one of these men on board. After receiving his reward he thought to look over the ship and examine the shot holes. When he reached the berth deck, one of the firemen named Gallant struck the detective and knocked him down, then threw a division tub filled with water upon him. The cries of the detective soon brought the officers and Marines to his assistence.[9]

The first to reach the scene was [John] Duncan, the Gunner, who rushed at Gallant with a drawn cutlass. Some of the men grabbed Duncan from behind while Gallant wrenched the cutlass from his hand and, slashing right and left, soon cleared the deck. The detective made his escape during the scuffle. After a considerable trouble, Gallant and two others were overcome and confined in double Irons. They were afterwards tried by courtmartial and sentenced to ten years in the penitentiary. They, however, escaped from the mail boat while on their way north.[10]

While we lay at New Orleans Farragut received his appointment as rear admiral and the first Rear Admiral Flag in the U S Navy was emediatly hoisted to the masthead of the *Hartford*.[11]

The news was brought down that the enemy's ram *Arkansas* with other Confederate gunboats were coming down the river to support General [John C.] Breckinridge in an attack on General Williams at Baton Rouge. Our ship, with all other vessels lying at New Orleans, hurried up the river to meet this new force. Though we had lost no time, on our arrival we found the battle had been fought the day before. Gen. Breckinridge had been defeated and the ram *Arkansas* was distroyed. When she was about to enter the engagement her engines failed to work [and] her captain run her ashore where, after setting her on fire, she was deserted. After burning for a short time, her magazine exploded and she disappeared from sight in the river.[12]

On our return to New Orleans our executive officer, James Thornton, left the ship to take command of one of the small gunboats. (Capt. Thornton afterwards commanded the U S *Kearsarge* under Winslow, in her fight with the *Alabama*.)[13]

It was supposed it was through disagreement with Captain Palmer and, as he was a great favorate with the men, his departure added to the discontent and the number of desertions greatly increased, so much so that we sailed for Pensacola to stop it.

At Pensacola Lt Comd [Lieutenant Commander] Lewis A. Kimberly was ordered from the frigate *Potomac* to our ship as executive officer in place of Thornton. This officer had the most remarkable memory of names. From the moment he assumed his duties he addressed the men by their proper names and never seemed at a loss. He seemed to take more interest in the ship's company than other officers. He had all the ordanary seamen and boys examined and those that were qualified for better places were promoted. He was fair, inclined to leanancy in his dealings with men and rapidly won their good will and respect.[14]

An incident that would better show the man occurred at New Orleans a few months after this. A tough, one of the crew who had been on shore and come on board drunk, was brought to the mast for disorderly conduct. On Mr. Kimberly's appearance, Shaw, the prisoner, advanced upon him with his stomack distended and in this manner forced Kimberly some 10 feet back on the quarter deck.

Kimberly said, "What do [you] mean, Shaw?"

Shaw answered, "To run you down, you clipper built son of a bitch."[15]

As Shaw said this, Kimberly's face shaded red and white and his eyes flashed for a moment, then resumed its old calmness. All this caused great excitement among the officers and men, the officers calling for Kimberly to shoot him, cut him down, etc., some offering pistols. He quietly turned and said, "I will attend to this matter," and called the master-at-arms.

The man was confined in irons and soon after dishonorablely discharged from the navy.

While lying at Pensacola Captain Bell was ordered from our ship to take command of that portion of our fleet blockading the coast of Texas. He was relieved on our ship by Captain Thornton A. Jenkins. The Admiral's son, Loyall Farragut, also came on board as assistant secretary to the Admiral.[16]

While here there were several expeditious sent up the river for fresh provisions and beef for use in the hospitals. We also did a good deal of wrecking around the bay, raising sunken vessels and straitening up things generally about the Navy Yard which the enemy had wrecked and distroyed when they evacuated.[17]

PART 3
PORT HUDSON

HARD TIMES

Diggins prefaces his account of Farragut's own disaster at Port Hudson by recounting other reverses the navy suffered in the Gulf about the same time. However, then Diggins would not have had access to all the details, even if he had learned of the losses. So he wrote this portion later, when the facts became available through other sources, including newspaper accounts and official reports. Moreover, the reverses occurred in a different order than that narrated by Diggins.

We had been at Pensacola about three months when news began to arrive of disaster to our fleet at different points on the station. The *Hatteras* was sunk in an engagement with the noted priviteer *Alabama* off Galveston harbor. Two of our fleet were captured and burned at Sabine Pass. In an engagement in Galveston Bay the gunboat *Harriet Lane*, after a desperate fight, was captured by the enemy, another of our vessels was blown up and the balance of our vessels driven out of the harbor and our troops on shore were all captured.[1]

The *Harriet Lane* was commanded by Captain J. M. Wainwright, the brother of Richard Wainwright, the commander of the *Hartford*. It was said of them that they were the two most popular and bravest men in the navy. In the battle in Galveston Harbor Jan. 1st 1863 after two hours desperate fighting, when the U. S. Steamer *Westfield* was blown up and another of our vessels left the fight and the harbor. Wainwright still maintained the fight against odds of more than ten to one and, while defending his ship against boarders, fell to the deck of his ship riddled with bullets. His men emmediately wavered and the enemy took the ship.[2]

The Confederates emmediately began to fit her out for a privateer, but the arrival of Capt. Bell with gunboats from Pensacola spoiled their plans and the rebels distroyed her rather than she should fall into our hands again.[3]

The *Hatteras* was commanded by Lieut. Comd. Homer C. Blake. She was a new iron steamer, side wheels, built for the Merchant Service and bought by the government on account of her great speed for blockade duty. She was armed with one 100 pndr [pounder] rifle and 6 smaller guns. She was not equal [in] number of guns or men to the *Alabama*.

The *Alabama* appeared off the harbor of Galveston, Texas, about 3:30 oclock p.m. Jan. 11, 1863. She came in full sight of the blockading vessels. The *Hatteras* give her chase, at first thinking she was a blockade runner. The *Hatteras* gradually overhauled her untill 25 miles out when she came within speaking distance and hailed her. Receiving answer that she was her Britannic Majestys Steamer *Vixen*, the *Hatteras* was about to lower a boat to board her when she hailed again that she was the Confederate Steamer *Alabama* and emediately fired a broadside into the *Hatteras*. The crew of the *Hatteras* were not surprised and immediately answered the *Alabama* with a broadside and desperate battle continued for over three quarters of an hour when a shot from the *Alabama* struck the cylinder of the *Hatteras*, intirely disableing her engines.

Notwithstanding that she could no longer maneuver, she still kept up the fight. When the position of the *Alabama* made her heavy guns useless, they would use the small arms and shower the *Alabama* with musket balls. At lenth a shot from the *Alabama* tore a long hole in the iron side of the *Hatteras* under the water line. Her pumps could not be worked oweing to her damaged machinery and she began to rapidly sink. It was now some time after dark and the *Hatteras* ceased firing when [the] *Alabama*, seeing that she was sinking, hauled along side and took her crew and officers on board as prisoners and paroled and landed them days after on the Island of Jamaica.[4]

The *Hatteras* sunk a few minutes after the crew was taken off, her colors still flying as she disappeared. The great disadvantage of the *Hatteras* was that most of her machinery and boilers were above water and easily disabled and that she was an iron hull, a shot going through the iron alway[s] making a larger hole than the shot and tearing the iron, so that there is no way to stop the leak.

With a wooden vessel, after the ball passes through, the wood will emediately close together, making the hole much smaller than the shot was and then it is easily remedied by nailing a padded plank over the [hole] which [planks] are always prepared and ready for that purpose.[5]

We also learned that the enemy had fortified Port Hudson on the Mississippi River for the purpose of protecting their communication with Texas through the Red River, thus holding control of the river between Vicksburg and Port Hudson.

We learned also that the monitor *Indianola* was sunk and the *Queen of the West* captured by the enemy fleet which came out of the Red River. Those two vessels were sent down past Vicksburg by Admiral Porter to break up the Red River trade with points between Vicksburg and Port Hudson.[6]

This news started us in hurried preperation to leave Pensacola. We arrived at New Orleans on the first of March 1863.

DISASTER

On March 8, 1863, Andre H. Beauchamp, a private in the 1st Alabama Infantry at Port Hudson, complained to his wife that "it seems we are never to have any luck on the rivers."[1]

Yet luck and much pluck and daring had all helped Confederates along the Mississippi in early 1863. Vicksburg, the key to that river's traffic, still held, and they rapidly turned Port Hudson into another Gibraltar. While they had lost the *Arkansas* because of its faulty engines, they had captured the Union's *Queen of the West* and *Indianola*. Both Federal warships had run past the Vicksburg batteries to blockade the Red River.

Specifically, Beauchamp deplored the loss of the *Indianola* when her captors, busily repairing her, burned the ship when they fell for a Yankee hoax. Admiral Porter, above Vicksburg with his fleet, built a dummy monitor on a barge, complete with false turret, pork barrel smokestacks, and a smudge pot for smoke, and sent the "turreted monster" drifting downstream with the current. That threat prompted Confederate authorities to order the *Indianola* destroyed to prevent recapture by the fake monitor. Farragut's fleet surgeon called it "one of the most successful tricks in the grim game of war."[2]

But the loss of the *Queen of the West* and the *Indianola* had unintended consequences for both sides, though adverse mostly for the Union.

Porter, commanding the fleet above Vicksburg, needed his ships right where they were to support Grant's ground movements against Vicksburg, and that left the Red River unguarded, as well as that stretch of the Mississippi between Port Hudson and Vicksburg. Accordingly, Confederates sent supplies, livestock, and men to beleaguered Vicksburg. They also shipped some supplies across the river, although they attempted no more large scale troop movements from the Trans-Mississippi to the East.

Farragut lay below a strongly fortified Port Hudson that blocked water traffic at a commanding point on the Mississippi. Pressure from remote Washington and the imperatives of the strategic and tactical situation on the river pushed him to brave Port Hudson's guns and steam up river. There, he could intercept enemy shipping from the Red River and on the Mississippi itself.[3]

The preparations alone demonstrate that all knew they attempted a risky passage. Crews white washed the decks, sent down spars from the masts, arranged for river pilots to guide them through the dense black powder smoke of battle by arranging perches for pilots on the mizzen masts, erected splinter nettings, rigged chains over the side as armor to protect boilers, and lashed small gunboats to the port sides of the larger ships.[4]

Confederates also prepared. They collected and assembled combustible materials in huge stacks at intervals along the western bank of the river and on the eastern side bluffs, ready to ignite when needed. These giant bonfires would illuminate the river and silhouette Farragut's ships as they steamed slowly up against a strong current and the ever-present danger of new or shifting shoals. They readied signal rockets, dug new pits for sharpshooters, and even managed to ferry light artillery across the river to attack the mortar schooners.[5]

Confidence ran high on both sides, especially among Farragut's men, who knew they had successfully passed the formidable batteries at New Orleans and twice thumbed their noses at Vicksburg's heavy guns. Apparently few considered the possibility that most of them would never get past Port Hudson.

General Banks, who had relieved General Butler, was already preparing for an advance on Port Hudson. We remained but a short time at New Orleans when we started up the river for Baton Rouge which was to be the base of operations for all our forces. All preperations were hurried at this point. The vessels were taking in coal and ammunitions while Gen. Banks Army were arriving from New Orleans. On the 12th of March [1863] we moved up to Port Hudson, the Army at the same time marching up in the rear and surrounding Port Hudson.[6]

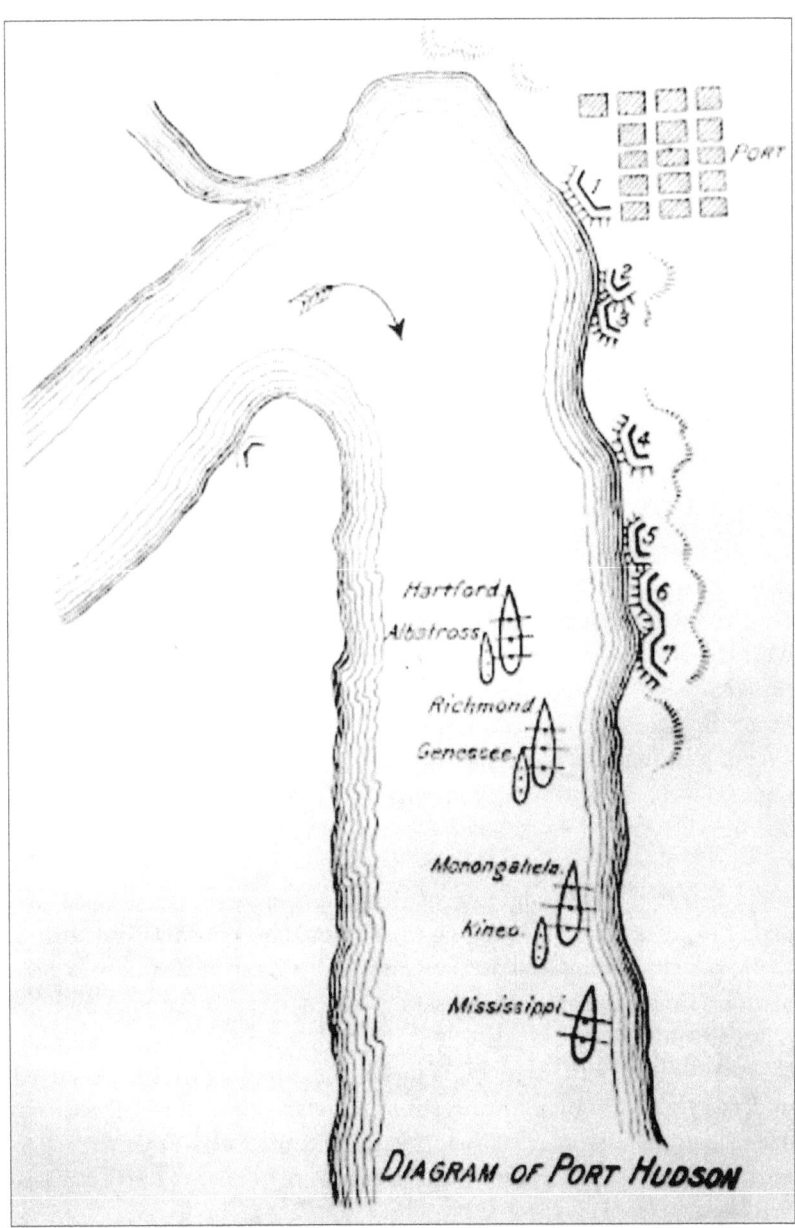

Passing Port Hudson. As Diggins relates, sailors lashed smaller gunboats to the bigger warships before steaming by Port Hudson's guns, thus offering some protection to the smaller ships and enabling one to help the other if disabled. Only the leading *Hartford* and *Albatross* made it through the gantlet of plunging Confederate cannon fire; last in line, the sidewheel Mississippi, disabled, abandoned and drifting, blew up downstream. From ORN 19.

We anchored below in full view of the place. This, like all other Confederate fortifycations along the river, was located on a sharp bend and on high bluffs, thus keeping our vessels under a raking fire during the greater portion of the engagement and giving our vessels little or no chance with their broadside guns oweing to the height of the bluffs. In this respect, this was the hardest place we had yet encountered. The river narrowed as it washed around the bend under the batterys, forming eddys and whirls that the most experienced river men found difficult to navigate through in safety. In addition, they had a fleet of armed river boats protected by iron and cotton. Among them [was] the lately captured *Queen of the West*, she now proudly flying the Confederate Flag, as she lately did ours.[7]

The mortar vessels were all placed in line on the north bank of the river [while] the ironclad *Essex* was moored ahead of them.

Gen. Banks forces having completely surrounded the place by land and the fleet being all ready, it was decided to make the attack on the night of the 14th of March 1863. The vessels were lashed together in pairs.

The vessels that took part were the *Hartford*, Capt. James S. Palmer, with the *Albatross*, Capt. John E. Hart, lashed together, were to lead; the *Richmond*, Capt. James Alden, with the *Genesee*, Capt. William H. Macomb; the *Monongahela*, Capt. J. P. McKinstry, and the *Kineo*, [Lt.] Comd. John Watters ; and the *Mississippi*, Capt. Melancthon Smith, being a side wheeler, it was not convenient to lash another vessel to her. The *Sachem*, Lt. Amos Johnson, and *Essex*, Comd. C. H. B. Caldwell were to engage the lower batterys while the fleet passed.

This was the first engagement that the ships were last [lashed] together in pairs. It was in case one vessel should become disabled or sink, the other could render assistance and that the larger would be a protection to the smaller, the successful passage of the fleet being the chief purpose of the attack.

At nine oclock the signal was made from our ship to the fleet to get underway and advance up the river. Through some cause, it was ten oclock before the whole fleet reported ready. The signal was then made to move up the river at full speed. The orders were to not fire untill we were fired upon.

Every thing along the river had the stillness of death. The night was very dark and heavy overhead. General Banks had opened fire in the rear to attract attention from the fleet. As we neared the batterys, the outlines of the high bluffs seemed to look down upon us. The usual lights were at the steamboat landing where at dock six of the enemy's steamers were laying.[9]

Oweing to the strong current (7 miles an hour), our progress up the river was very slow, so that [even] if not warned of our intentions, they had ample time to prepare a reception before we reached the batterys.[10]

They opened fire on our ships at 11 p.m. and, in a moment after, large fires were started along the whole lenth of the bluffs and at point[s] on the opposite side of the river, all of which in a few moments made the whole scene almost as light as day. We returned their fire with our two bow guns, all that would bear. Our mortars and the *Essex* opened fire at the same time with vigor. The battle soon became general. As we passed the first batterys, they opened a murderous fire upon us from the whole face of the bluffs which, oweing to the bend in the river, formed a half circle around us and thus raking us from all sides. We returned the fire with broadsides, but with little effect, our guns not having sufficient elevation to reach the high bluffs. The battle was now at its height with its deathly roar of cannon, screaming shell and crashing noises. The great volumes of smoke from the guns of both sides seemed to settle down over the river, shutting out from our view almost every thing about us.[11]

It was now evident the enemy had many advantages by a night attack while we were befogged and struggling in the smoke, fouling each other and running a ground, often requiring the compass to know which way we headed in the smoke and darkness. In fact, our chief and only guide was the flashes of the enemy's guns. On the other hand, the enemy by previous practice had good range of all parts of the river and, assisted by the fires on the opposite side of the river, they could locate the ships by their spars and rigging. They did not fail to make what they could from this opportunity. Their batterys kept up a continual roar.[12]

We lost sight of the balance of our fleet and continued to grope our way through the thick smoke and strong current of the most crooked river in the world. When at the upper batterys and where the river makes a sharp turn, the rapid current washing around under the bluffs caught the ship, swinging her half around head on to the bluffs and batterys and thus placing the ship in the greatest peril. The engines were stopped and for a moment we were at the mercy of the enemy.

To the pilot who had gone up in the mizzen top and Comd. [Commander] Kimberly, the executive officer, the *Hartford* owes much of her good fortune at this time.[13]

Comd. Kimberly seemed always where any thing was wrong. His exertions on this occasion saved the ship from grounding. After struggling for some time with the current, all the while under fire of the batterys, assisted by the *Albatross,* the ship was again headed up the river and soon after succeeded in passing the batterys. About 2 a.m. we anchored four mile[s] above Port Hudson, just out of range of their guns.

We now watched anxiously for the appearance of the balance of the fleet. The batterys continued, engaged with all their guns, untill 3 a.m. when the firing gradually ceased. We soon lost all hope of seeing any more of our vessels come up.[14]

After the firing ceased we could see a large fire start up apparently on the river in front of the center of the batterys. We correctly supposed it was some of our vessels [and] we afterwards learned it was the *Mississippi*. She, drawing the most water, had grounded and, after using every means to get her off while under the whole fire of the batterys [and] failing, Captain Melancthon Smith, her commander, decided to fire and abandon her, being in the last boat that left her.[15]

After burning for some time, she floated off and down the river with the current, discharging her loaded guns as she went along. When she reached our vesels which were now anchored three miles below the batterys, they give her all the room possible as it was expected every moment that her magazine would explode. She passed through them in flames from the water up, doing no injury, untill about eight miles below Port Hudson her magazine exploded, scattering her hull in all directions, not leaving a trace, thus ending her career beneath the waters of the grand old river from which she got her name.[16]

On board of the *Hartford* we now awaited anxiously for daylight, the men still standing at their places at the guns, awaiting any thing that might turn up. There was much uneasiness and surmising as to what happened to the balance of our fleet. It was thought that at least half of them were captured or distroyed as none of them had succeeded in following us through the batterys.

At daylight the men left the guns and commenced to repair the damage done during the fight. The ship was very much torn from the effects of the battle, the greater damage being to her spars and rigging, the most of the enemy's fire passing over the hull, causing us but a slight loss, one killed and three wounded.

The man reported killed was a Marine who had joined the ship but a short time before at New Orleans. He had been knocked or jumped out one of the port holes. He being a Virginian and supposed in sympathy with the enemy, many thought he jumped overboard intending to swim ashore.

Our little consort, the *Albatross*, which came through lashed to our side and shielded by us from the batterys, lost four killed and nine wounded.

After the ship was cleared of all the debris of the fight and the rigging temporarily repaired, the men had breakfast. In the forenoon we dropped down toward the batterys untill they opened fire on us. We returned it with our stern guns as we slowly steamed up the river again. This was done to let our fleet below know that we were safe and, if possible, to call their attention to our efforts to communicate with them by signals from our masthead over the tree tops. They failed to answer us, however. We anchored again on reaching our old berth of the morning. All seemed much depressed from the Admiral down. I never saw him show uneasiness before, [but] he had good reason at this time. His faithfull old *Hartford* and the little *Albatross* comprised his whole fleet, with Vicksburg, one of the enemy's strongest defences on the river above us and surrounded by an enemy's country, and thus cut off from all communication with his fleet and government. and where the enemy had a formislable [formidable] fleet to meet him.[17]

About four months previous, Admiral Porter sent two of his most powerfull vesels, the ram *Queen of the West* and monitor *Indianola*, down passed the Vicksburg batterys to blockade the mouth of Red River which was the greatest source from which the enemy received their war and other supplys through Texas, Mexico and thence from Europe. The Confederates had a large number of transports carrying this trade from the Red River to different points between Vicksburg and Port Hudson.

It was to protect it [supply route] that those two points were fortified and it had become of great importance to the Confederates at this time that these fortifications be maintained as their supplys at the coast ports were slowly but surely being cut off by the gradual capture of their ports and the great increase in the number of our blockading squadrons. So movements of the Union and Confederate forces on the Mississippi River at this time was watched with great interest by both sides.

The *Queen of the West* on her arrival at Red River attempted to go up the river. She was met by the Confederate fleet. After a gallant fight, she was captured. She was then manned by Confederate[s] and, with the Confederate fleet, attacked the *Indianola* which was found anchored halfway between Red River and Vicksburg. After a short fight, the *Indianola* was sunk by her own people to avoid capture. Her crew and officers were taken prisoner.

The Confederate fleet was composed of some ten river boats fortified with cotton [bales], some of them being provided with iron prows for ramming. The most of them were laying in front of Port Hudson, among them the *Queen of the West,* just previous to the battle. But [she] retreated as we advanced up the river.

We now expected an attack at any time after they learned that only two of our fleet succeeded in passing the batterys.

All efforts to communicate with our fleet below Port Hudson, by signals from our mastheads in daytime and rockets at night failed, [also] dropping several bottles into the river with reports of our safety with the hope that they might be picked up as they drifted by some of our vessels below.[18]

On the 16th of March we started up the river, our little consort, the *Albatross,* hugging effectionately to our side, never going beyond easy hail, we arrived at Bayou Sara about noon. We found a large barge being unloaded with provisions for the enemy. Two boat's crew were landed and the provision[s] distroyed except what was distributed among some half-starved looking country people who watched longingly the sacks of flour, meal, bacon, and hams as they disappeared in the muddy water of the river. The barge was sunk.

As our boat shoved off from the levee, some of the men on shore yelled to us to give them their gunboat.

Our men yelled back, "What gunboat?"

They answered, "The gunboat that surendered at [the] batterys."

We asked, "Why didn't you hold her?"

They said, "The current carried her down the river."

We said, "You can have that one," pointing to the *Hartford.*

They said, "We have got her any time we want her. Farragut is our prisoner."

By this time our boat had pulled out of hearing.

We then continued up the river, sinking and distroying everything we met afloat. When we reached the mouth of Red River, we anchored after gaining such a position that our whole battery would command the mouth. We then began to practice with heavy guns untill we got the exact range of the Red River channells. The guns were then left in position, [so] that night or day, all that was necessary was to pull the lock string when the enemy showed at the mouth of the river.[19]

We then made preperations to repel any attack from the enemy's fleet. The lower yardarms from the fore, main and mizzen masts were lowered across the rail and secured there. A heavy chain was then secured to the bowsprit and then continued to the ends of the fore, main and croquet yards, then to the spanker boom on both sides, thus forming a barrier to vessels coming along side.[20]

All the spare rope in the ship was brought up and used as a boarding netting. We commenced with the larger hawsers at the foot of the rigging at the fore stay, outside the fore, main and mizzen rigging, thus continually winding around the ship about 10 inches apart untill it reached half way to the tops. It was then interlaced with smaller ropes and lines at right angles, thus forming a network that a man could not get his head through.[21]

All the hammocks in the ship were then used as barricades around the men at the wheel, the officers on the poop deck and the men in the tops who manned the Hortzers [howitzers]. The men had little use for hammocks at this time and indeed but little rest as the men worked night and day to put the ship in condition against an attack from the enemy which was hourly expected. Every body worked during the day and early night when they would take their places at the guns, one watch lying at their places while the other watch stood at their places at the guns.

The largest trees along the river bank were cut down and towed off to the ship, some of them being three feet thick and 70 to 80 feet long. These were secured to the ship's side by being lashed to screw bolts made for that purpose. Two of these logs, one above the other, covered the space from the water line to the port sills and extended about fifteen feet beyond her bow and stern. These were intended to protect the ship from the rams of the enemy, of which they had several.

When all this was completed the ship seemed impregnable to any mode of attack and the Admiral remarked, "Well, they cant ram us, they cant board us, and I think they will have a hard task to take us any other way."

We layed here untill the 16th of March when we moved up the river toward Vicksburg with our little consort, the *Albatross*. We were naturally cautious and on the alert. The men and officers stood at their places at the guns night and day (leaving in watches for meals), which [guns] were always cast loose, ready for emediate action. On our approach to a suspicious point or bluff, the guns would be trained sharp forward upon it and kept upon it untill we passed out of range. All of this kept up a commotion among the ship's company, allmost as exciting as a regular engagement and no less labor.[22]

As we advanced up the river large numbers of negroe slaves or, as they were then called, contrabands, would come out to the ship and ask to be taken on board. Some times large familys with all their effects, children, ducks, chickens, pigs, etc. The most active portion of the males were taken, untill there was no longer room for more.[23]

We would occasionally capture boats crossing the river or along the banks. In one of them among some Confederate mails we found late Richmond and Vicksburg papers containing long accounts of the Battle of Port Hudson in which they claimed great credit, considering it one of the greatest victorys won by the Confedercy. They claimed the *Hartford* as captured and Admiral Farragut a prisoner of war and suggested the uses they could put the *Hartford* to. Through this source we also learned that the balance of our fleet was safely anchored below Port Hudson, except the *Mississippi* which grounded and burnt in front of the batterys.

If Farragut was a prisoner, he was mighty troublesome at this time. When we arrived a few miles below Natchez, two armed boats were sent on shore under command of Lt. J. C. Watson to cut all telegraph wires between Vicksburg and Port Hudson.

I was in one of the boats about dusk. In the evening we left the ship and pulled up a small creek untill the boat grounded. We then left the boats, one half of us armed with axes, picks, ladders, etc., the other [half] armed [with] revolvers, cutlasses, etc.[24]

After traveling inland about two miles we came upon the main road. All worked together cutting down poles and gethering the wire in large coils. We brought several miles of it back to the ship. When we had finished our work, we could distinctly hear the clatter of horses, we supposed cavalry sent out to intercept us. We took [to] the woods in the direction of the boat and soon after reached our ship about 11:30 p.m.[25]

On the following morning, 17th, we arrived at Natchez and anchored in front of the city. About a year previous the place [had] surendered to our ship. We now found them in a different state of mind. It was the first place we communicated [with] since the battle of Port Hudson and we found them very independent and boastfull and said their gunboats were coming out of Red River to capture us. They had a habit on previous occasions when a defenceless transport would pass to open fire with [a] battery of light artillery from the bluffs in front of the city. The Admiral administered the following caution to the Mayor:

March 17, 1863

Sir: I trust that it is unnecessary to remind you of my desire to avoid the necessity of punishing the innocent for the Guilty and to express to you the hope that the scene of firing on United States boats will not be repeated by either the lawless people of Natchez or by the guerilla forces.

Otherwise I shall be compelled to do the act most repugnant to my feelings by firing on your town in defence of my people and the honor of my flag

I shall be most happy to see his honor,

the Mayor, on board.

Very Respectfully,

D. G. Farragut, Rear Admiral[26]

On [the] following morning (18th), we continued up the river [and] on the morning of the 19th we arrived at Grand Gulf. As we drew near, the negroes from adjoining clifts [cliffs] warned us by waving and pointing ahead, but their kindly warnings were needless as we knew Grand Gulf of old and were then standing by our guns prepared for it.

When we came in range they opened a wicked fire on us from heavy rifles. We could not see their guns, they were so successfully hidden in the excavated bluffs. We aimed at their smoke and showered them with grape and canister untill we had passed out of range. We were struck several times, doing us little damage, however, except one shot that buried itself in the mizzen mast, weakening [it] considerably. Our losses were two killed and six wounded.

On the 22nd of March we arrived at Warrenton. This place was reported to be well fortified and we dropped anchor out of reach of its guns. Here commenced a range of bluffs that formed along the east bank of the river, six miles to Vicksburg and beyond. Fleet Captain T. A. Jenkins was sent by the Admiral on the opposite bank of the river to examine Warrenton and the bluffs toward Vicksburg for batterys and their strenth.

I was one of the boats crew and with other of the boats accompanied the Captain. After a long examination, going nearly opposite Vicksburg with powerfull glasses, Capt. Jenkins reported to the Admiral that he could see masked batterys on every bluff from Warrenton to Vicksburg and expressed the opinion that it would be certain distruction to ships to go up the river beyond Warrenton.[27]

After breakfast the next morning we were ordered to up anchor and prepare for action. This was a surprise to all. If Capt. Jenkins report amounted to anything, it was madness to attemt any farther up the river. While heaving up anchor, one of the quartermasters came forward and said that Captain Jenkins had been using every argument against going up, but the Admiral said he would feel them anyway.

The usual spirit of such occasions was not displayed among the men, all feeling how hopeless the chances were for our ship and the little *Albatross* against all the batterys reported.

After weighing anchor, we soon reached Warrenton. We were nearly abreast of it when they opened on us with a few field pieces and musketry from rifle pits. We drew close up to the battery and poured in broadsides untill it was silenced. We then continued up the river without further hindrance until we reached our old anchorage three miles below Vicksburg where we stopped.

While lying at anchor we opened fire on a warf boat lying at Vicksburg. Our shell completely distroyed her by fire. That night a heavy storm blew the steamer *Vicksburg* from her moorings in front of the city [and] she came down upon us about daylight . We boarded her from our ship and found, though nearly new and a magnificent vessel, her machinery had been removed for use in some gunboat and, there being nothing els on board, we set fire to her. She drifted down the river in flames.[28]

The first night of our arrival communication was opened with Admiral Porter, who, with his fleet, lay across the point above Vicksburg. The Admiral sent a request to Admiral Porter for a barge of coal, a barge of provisions and three or four ironclads as reinforcements. The Admiral was not present to receive the request, but the officer in command emmediately sent down one barge of provisions and a barge of coal. They come down with the current, passed the Vicksburg batterys about day light in the morning under a heavy fire. The provisions barge was uninjured, though struck several times, and the[y] were certainly welcomed as the ship's company were on reduced rassions [rations].

The coal barge did not fare so well. It reached us in a sinking condition. One third of our men were emmediatey ingaged in pumping and bailing her out while the balance of the crew and officers, including the executive officer, Mr. Kimberly, were throwing the coal on board through the ports as there was not shovels enough, many of them using their hands. After every place that coal could be stowed was filled, the barge was towed in shore where it emmediately sunk.[29]

While near Warrenton that morning the *Albatross* was fired [upon] from a new battery of heavy guns. On the following morning our ship dropped down and anchored in front of Warrenton. In about fifteen minutes we silenced their guns. We spent about an hour longer with our full broadside untill every thing like guns and batterys were leveled and distroyed. We then came back to our old anchorage.[30]

We dropped down again the following morning [and] there was no reply to our fire. We, however, shelled the place for an hour, distroying the greatest portion of the town. We were never fired upon again at Warrenton, allthough we visited the place every day or two to watch any attemt to rebuild batterys there.[31]

(Advice that made General Grant Famous:

About the middle of November, some four months before our arrival below Vicksburg, Gen. Grant, Gen. Sherman, Gen. McClernand, with Admiral Porter, made a combined attack on Vicksburg. Gen. Grant's forces were to attack by way of Jackson and Grenada and come down in the rear. Sherman and McClernand were to attack on the right by way of Haynes' [Haines's] Bluffs, with Yazoo and Mississippi as their base of supplys. Admiral Porter was to force his fleet up the Yazoo cover the attacking forces of Sherman and McClernand and protect their base of supplys.[32]

All this resulted in several grand assaults, each one a greater failure than the previous one, untill the whole movement was given up as a failure and the army retreated to the south bank of the Mississippi River opposite Vicksburg. Admiral Porter with his fleet also withdrew to the Mississippi, but he had accomplished his full share in the attack.)[33]

It was in this condition that we found matters when we arrived below Vicksburg with the *Hartford*.

While lying here General Grant came on board our ship [on March 26]. It happened that for a while my duty called me near where the Admiral and General were conversing. The Admiral sat with his thigh resting on the propeller block. Here I saw and distinctly heard Farragut advise the plan of attack on Vicksburg afterwards followed by General Grant. Drawing an imaginary line with his finger on the propeller block, he advised Gen. Grant to move his army below Vicksburg on the opposite bank, that Admiral Porter's whole fleet pass down by the batterys of Vicksburg and immediately transfer the army to the Vicksburg side of the river. This plan was soon after followed and the world knows how successfully. The world knows also how General Grant showed his ingratitude to Farragut when he became President of the United States.[34]

If any one doubts this story, they only need to carefully study the plan of attack on Port Hudson a month previous under Farragut to see that they were simaler in all the chief points to the attack on Vicksburg and originated in the same brain.)

Admiral Farragut sent a request to Admiral Porter to send him two or three ironclads down past the Vicksburg batterys as reinforcement and to assist in the blockade of Red River. Admiral Porter replyed that he could not spare the vessels at that time, but that he hoped to reach the Red River by another route in a short time.

Loyall Farragut, about 17 years old, the only son of the Admiral, who came on board as secretary to the Admiral at Pensacola and went through the battle of Port Hudson with us, left the ship at Vicksburg as the bearer of dispatches to Washington. The separation was very effectionate between him and the Admiral.[35]

Colonel Ellet commanded what was known as the Marine brigade. This consisted of four or five river steamers suplyed with iron prows for ramming and in other ways protected with iron. The brigade was under command of Charles Rivers Ellet, the most daring and recless officer in that section of the country. There was three or four of the Ellet brothers, all equally noted for their recless bravery. Each commanded one of the steamers of the Marine Brigade which were all manned by soldiers who were enlisted on the Western frontier, a lot equally as brave and recless as their commanders.[36]

Col. Ellet volunteered to send two of his vessels down to us. They started by Vicksburg about daylight in the morning. There was no one on board [as] their crews walked across the point to join them below. Vicksburg opened a heavy fire on them. One was intirely distroyed, floating passed us in pieces. The *Switzerland* was so much damaged it was doubtfull whether she could be made any use of, her machinery and boilers being much injured and the most difficult to repair. Those vessels were sent down on the 24th of March.[37]

The engineers and firemen from the *Albatross* and *Hartford* were put to work on the *Switzerland* [and] together with the carpenters going from our ship, patched [her] up so that by the last of March, she was ready to go down the river with us.

BLOCKING THE RIVERS

When the war began, Confederates had readily moved supplies, equipment, and troops across the river from the Trans-Mississippi. Regiments from Arkansas, Louisiana, and Texas joined the Army of Tennessee, the Confederacy's main field army, in what was then called the West, and Lee's Army of Northern Virginia in the East. But after New Orleans fell and Federal warships maintained a heavy presence on the Mississippi, such large troop movements became impossible. Individuals or small groups made the risky eastward crossing at times, and some took rowboat rides to the other side from the East. Troops from the Trans-Mississippi who served on the other side remained there for years with no home leaves.

Soon, the Confederate Trans-Mississippi became popularly known as Kirby Smithdom, after the area's commander, Lieutenant-General Kirby Smith. Though he had many thousands of troops, they might as well have paraded on the moon. However, Smith and his men did succeed in repulsing Federal forces during the Red River campaign mentioned by Diggins.

Although isolated in the Trans-Mississippi, Confederates still strove to move food and supplies to their garrisons at Vicksburg and Port Hudson. It was this traffic that Farragut hindered by his presence on the Mississippi and at the mouth of the Red River.

On the 31st of March the *Hartford, Albatross* and *Switzerland* started down to continue the blockade at the mouth of Red River. At Warrenton, they opened on us from some new batterys. The *Hartford* stopped to shell them untill the two weaker vessels had passed down when the *Hartford* continued on down the river.[1]

There was scarcely a mile of our way that we did not distroy some of the enemys property. Flat boats, warf boats were hauled out from their hiding places up the creeks and given to the flames. Tons of provisions which had been landed from Red River at different points, sheep, hogs, beef, pork, bacon, hams, corn meal, sugar, molasses and numerous other kinds of provisions was either burnt or thrown in the river.

The *Switzerland* was especially useful in this work. Being a river steamer and easily handled, she could go up the small creek or alongside the levee at any suspicious point while the *Hartford* was confined to the deepest water channell. The Admiral, however, would not let our two little consorts go beyond the reach of *Hartford*s guns and at night, while at anchor, they would tie up effectionately under our quarter.

This kind of work was continued, clearing the river of all kinds of boats, large and small. On our passage down, on the afternoon of the 31st, we anchored near the spot where we saw the wreck of the *Indianola* while going up the river. It was the intention of the Admiral to distroy all traces of the *Indianola* as it was reported that some one had entered into a contract with the Confederate Government [to] raise and repair her.

The heavy storms of the last few days had saved us all trouble in this respect as it was found that she had slipped and turned keel up in deep water.[2]

We then up anchor and come in sight of Grand Gulf about sunset. The Admiral ordered the *Albatross* and *Switzerland* to come up on [our] starboard side and shelter as much as possible from the fire of the batterys. The battery had been strenthened with a number of heavy guns while we were up the river.

[For several reasons, this page in Diggins's manuscript defies full and accurate transcribing. From what is readable, Diggins relates the concerns about Confederate plans to board and capture the *Hartford* and the effort to prevent or repel such an attack. Deciphered passages follow, even if incomplete.—Ed.]

On the following day we continued our work of destruction down the river, capturing and destroying everything we found afloat. We captured several small boats crossing the river with mail. We learned from newspapers and letters thus captured that the enemy were determined to attack us with a fleet of river boats . . . which they were preparing up the Red River.

We were always on the alert for this attack. One half the men never left their places at the guns while the balance of the men were engaged in adding to the boarding netting and strengthening the weak points about the ship. All our defences were prepared against boarders. If we could keep them off the ships, our broadsides would make short work of the river steamers. The crew were drilled in [what to do] in case boarders got possession of [certain portions] of the ship.

[Here resumes Diggins's usually legible narrative.—Ed.]

The men in the tops were also well supplied with hand grenades which were to be thrown among the enemy. Those and many other propositions, original the most of them, and suited to the occasion, were adopted to meet the threatened attack.[3]

On the first of April we again reached the mouth of Red River. The two rivers run nearly in the same direction where they join, thus forming a long narrow point between them. We took our position on the Mississippi side of this point, making it necessary for vessels coming out of Red River to pass our broadside at close range, then pass nearly a half mile down the Red River before they could turn to come up the Mississippi where we lay. The *Albatross* anchored ahead of us and the *Switzerland* was secured to a line from our stern.[4]

Our first day was spent practicing to get the range of the Red River channell. When this was done, the elevating screws were secured so that it was only necessary to pull the lock strings when the enemy cleared the mouth of the river. Several refugee[s] come on board of us here, some of them no doubt spies. They all reported that they [Confederates] were making hurried preperations fitting out a fleet to come down Red River to capture us.[5]

Soon after dark each night two men in a skift [skiff] were sent some five miles up the Red River who were instructed, on the approach of an enemy boat, to send up rockets. During the day the *Albatross* and *Switzerland* would move up and down the river. They were instructed to distroy or capture all public or Confederate property where soever found, but not interfere with private property, except for food, and to buy that, and if they would not sell, take what was necessary of it. This order was carried out to the [letter] by Captain [John E.] Hart of the *Albatross.*

During some portion of each day the *Switzerland* leaves her anchorage with instructions to distroy whatever she could of the enemys property as far down as Port Hudson and the same distance up the river. She could afford to do more steaming than the *Hartford* or *Albatross* as she could use wood for her boilers of which she could get an abundant supply along the river. She often captured the mail boats while [they were] crossing the river. The *Switzerland* did a good deal of foraging and would often return to our ship with a welcome supply of beef, mutton and poultry. She was well suited for that purpose. Her crew was composed of the hardest frontiers men [who] had little respect for God or man. Where they once landed, they were always feared afterwards. At Pointe Coupee, after taking everything of value from the inhabitants, they horrified them by robbing the church and the priest's house and chasing [the] priest across the fields, compelling him to take to the woods.[6]

They were not sectarian in this respect. The Admiral received complaints from every place they landed from priest and preacher and all others that come in their way. Their robberys included money, if it could [be] found, silver plate, bedding, clothing, pianos and, in fact, anything of value that could be taken away. On hearing these complaints, the Admiral ordered the *Switzerland* to be fastened to the stern of the *Hartford* for the purpose of stopping their freebooting propensities. The northern papers gave the *Hartfords* crew credit for doing these robberys.[7]

The robberys by the *Switzerland* done us incalculable injury for which there was no remedy left.

The people along the river, thinking that Admiral Farragut approved those robbery and that they would be a part of his method of warfare, removed with their stock and valuebles from the vicinity of the river, thus exiting our only source of supplies, especially as our own supplys of food was growing rapidly less with each day.

After a week blockading Red River, we started down to Port Hudson and anchored out of reach of their guns above it. Mr. [Edward C.] Gabaudan, the Admiral's secretary, volunteered to attemt the passage of Port Hudson in a skiff to open communication with the fleet below. On the night of April 6th he left the ship in a skiff, surrounded by green limbs and branches of trees. He had mail and dispatches from our ship and carried a negroe contraband to scull the boat when out of danger.

He had the good wishes of all as he left the ship about 10 p.m. He soon drifted out of our sight. We listened anxiously to hear him fired upon from the batterys but all remained quiet, and we concluded they had passed in safety.

In accordance with an agreement with Mr. Gabaudan, we made an attemt to communicate with the lower fleet from our masthead by army wig-wag signals. To our delight we were answered from the masthead of the *Richmond*. We found that Mr. Gabaudan, after considerable trouble, had [reached] the lower fleet about 10 oclock that morning with the dispatches and mail. This was the first communication we had with our fleet or friends for nearly a month.[8]

On the 9th of April we started again for the mouth of Red River. [At] Bayou Sara we came upon a lot of provisions which had been land[ed] by steamers from Red River to be sent thence by rail to Port Hudson.

The ship was hauled close to the landing and, after bring[ing] all we had room for of bacon, meal, sweet potatoes, etc., on board, the balance was distroyed and thrown in the river.

Soon after leaving Bayou Sara we discovered two columns of black smoke ahead. We knew they were rebel steamers, [so] the ship was started ahead at full speed. The steamers were on their way with freight for the place we had just left. As they rounded a bend in the river, they discovered us coming up when they immediately turned up the river again. Then commenced an exciting chase. Our engines were doing their best. The *Albatross* being the fastest, she gradually worked ahead of us. The rebels were also doing their best [as] we could tell from the great volumes of smoke coming from their smoke stacks. When we would come to a strait portion of the river, which would bring them full in sight, we opened fire on them with our bow guns when they would again disappear around another bend.

After two hours of great excitement, it was evident that one of the steamers was getting away from us and we were gaining on the other. We at lenth overhauled the *J. D. Clarke* [while] the other made her escape up the Red River. The *Clarke* had a rebel colonel and a small quantity of flour on her, all of which we took on board and sunk the steamer.[9]

We soon after arrived at our old position at the mouth of Red River. We now give ourselfs to feasting on the food captured at Bayou Sara, which was a great relief as our own rasions [rations] was stale and short. The meal was cooked in a variety of styles while it lasted. It was greatly enjoyed as mush, flap Jacks and other styles. Necessity forced more invention to making fish hooks and what little leasure time the men could find was spent trying to catch catfish, the only fish that could exist in the thick muddy water of the Mississippi. On lucky days we would catch single catfish weighing over one hundred pounds, one such making a meal for half the ship's company.[10]

An attack from the enemy was still looked for at any moment and there was no relaxation from the strick vigilance and watch kept over the mouth of Red River. For over two months there was not a man had his clothes off, including the Admiral, the officers setting around or pacing the deck, while the men stood at their places at the guns. At night one watch was allowed to lie down alongside their guns. The heavy April rains of that climate added much to their discomfort, being at all times exposed to it, drenching them to the skin, then being compelled or having no remedy but letting the cloths dry on their bodies. In addition to this the men were on short rations and what provisions remained was unfit for human food. What remained of the bread had been consumed by wevils and worms. The only way it could be eaten was by boiling the whole mass like mush. It was at first thought repulsive, but at last they would be glad to get it.

It was remarkable that notwithstanding the hardships, exposure and starvation, at this time the health of the men was excellent while six months previous, while lying at Vicksburg, two thirds of the crew were on the sick list and the bad health of the crew drove us from the river. Whether this was due to want of supplies to feed [the men], decease [disease], the continual excitement and exertion the men were subject to or being better acclimated, I do not know, but I know it was the case.[11]

About the middle of April we again run down to Port Hudson and communicated with the *Richmond* below the batterys. Mr. Gabaudan, with Ensign [Robert P.] Swann and some of the men from the *Richmond*, came up bringing us the first mails since the battle of Port Hudson. They also brought the cheering news that General Banks had invested Port Hudson while another portion of his forces were then but a few miles from us, marching up the west bank of the river in the direction of Alexandria on the Red River to cut off General Taylor and Kirby Smith who were trying to reach Port Hudson with reinforcements which had been gethered in Texas and Arkansas.

Gen. Taylor had several engagements with Gen. Banks who was driving him before him. The Admiral sent the steamers *Albatross* and *Switzerland* up Red River to help Gen. Banks at the capture of Alexandria, after which the Rebel forces in that section were scattered.[12]

When Gen. Banks returned to Port Hudson with his whole forces and attacked the place with renewed vigor, there was also a battery of four nine inch guns and 70 men landed from the fleet under command of Lieut. Comd. Edward Terry, Ensigns R. P. Swann and E. M. Shepard. This battery did excellent work and were highly complimented [by] the artillery officers of the Army.[13]

On the 22nd of April we again arrived at the mouth of Red River. During our passage from Port Hudson, we seldom failed to capture some of the enemy property, such as boats, barges, cors [?], etc., which were alway[s] distroyed, not having any way to care for them.

On the 25th of April the steamer *General Tyler* of Admiral Porter's fleet came down to tell us that the Admiral with his whole fleet had passed down by the Vicksburg batterys, captured Grand Gulf, and that Grant's army was advancing on Vicksburg and, what we liked best of all, give us a supply of provisions.[14]

On the night of the first of May a rocket was sent up by our picketts up the Red River. Several other rockets soon followed. We were ready for action in a moment and the men watched anxiously for the coming attack when the order was passed to not fire untill ordered to. Soon bright red lights were displayed by a vessel coming out of Red River [and] the order was again passed not to fire.

Every thing was still as death on the ship. As she cleared the trees, we could see she had masts and was not a river steamer. It proved to be the U. S. Steamer *Arizona.* She had come up by way of the Atchafalaya River with dispatches for the Admiral and mails and provisions for the ship.[15]

This placed us again in full communication with the balance of our fleet and government, though in a roundabout way.

Our little fleet now gradually increased in numbers. The U. S. Steamer *Estrella* arrived soon after the *Arizona,* our fleet now being sufficient to resist any attemt from the enemy's steamers. While the ships were kept ready for action at a moment's notice, the strained watchfullness was relaxed and the men were allowed to sleep in their hammocks.[16]

Our fleet now [lay] between Port Hudson and Vicksburg, being of sufficient strenth to meet any force the enemy could command. All their Red River fleet having been distroyed in different engagements on Grand Lake and the Atchafalaya River, including the *Queen of the West,* with our gunboats, there was little left for our fleet to do but blockade the Red River. [This] the *Hartford* did while the smaller vessels patrolled the river from Port Hudson to Vicksburg, capturing all that came in their way that belonged to or would be of service to the enemy.[17]

On the 7th of May the Admiral left the ship on the USS *Sachem* for New Orleans via Red River, Atchafalaya River, Grand Lake, etc. His personal attention [was] required by the attacks made by the enemy at different points below Port Hudson from the west bank of the river upon the supply vessels of Gen. Banks while passing from New Orleans to Port Hudson.[18]

The Confederates were commanded by Gen. Green and were mostly from Texas. They would lay quietly behind the levee while an armed gunboat passed, but open a murderous fire on the transports. They made Donaldsonville their headquarters and, from this point and from twenty miles above and below it, our transports would be certain to be fired at. Donaldsonville, White Hall and other places were thoroughly shelled by our vessels with little effect.[19]

In fight[s] with those Texans we lost many of our men killed and wounded, among them Comd. Read of the USS *Monongahela.* When a battery was distroyed at one point by our gunboats they would [set up] at another point and thus continually keep up the annoyance. It was the only means of warfare left to the rebels on the west bank of the river. It was at last found necessary to send a strong convoy of gunboats with the transports as they passed up and down the river.[20]

On the 23rd of May the *Hartford* arrived above Port Hudson. On that day Gen. Banks was to make a concentrated attack on Port Hudson. It began soon after our arrival. The vessels took part, especially the *Essex* and mortar boats. From this date followed a constant bombardment, with occasional charges on the works by our troops. It was a continual battle every day for more than a month.[21]

On the 6th day of July 1863 the U S Steamer *General Price* arrived with dispatches for the Admiral and Gen. Banks announcing the surrender of Vicksburg to Gen. Grant on the 4th of July.[22]

This news was received with great cheering and a grand salute from the guns of the fleet. The people in Port Hudson refused to believe that Vicksburg surrendered and the attacks continued with all the possible strenth of the Army and fleet combined.

On the 9th of July at daylight they hoisted a white flag, instead of the rebel. On the appearance of the white flag the *Hartford* up anchor and dropped down and anchored in front of Port Hudson. Many of us landed. We found a deplorable condition of thing[s] within the fortifycations. For more than two weeks they had lived intirely on corn shelled and on the cob. Twice a week [they] received a small portion of mule flesh. There was nothing living within the fort that had not been eaten, except human beings, and all the corn had been consumed. The people were lank and hungry looking, some of them scarcely able to stand.[23]

Their bravery and indurance won the admiration and respect of our side. We emmediately give them all our provisions, except enough to take us to New Orleans. Other ships and the Army did the same untill they had a full supply of clothing and food.

Port Hudson being the last Rebel stronghold on the Mississippi River, its capture put the union forces in possession from its source to its mouth.

There being no further need of our fleet on the river, [we] left Port Hudson for New Orleans. At New Orleans a board of survey decided that the *Hartford* was so torn and weakened that she could not stand another battle and she was ordered home for repairs. We arrived in New York early in August and was hauled up on the dry dock at the Brooklyn Navy Yard.[24]

As soon as the ship got in the dock, the officers all left her, making no provision for the men. There was now nearly 400 men with out an officer except Lewis A. Kimberly, the executive officer. No Paymaster to give us money to reach home, no one to sign our furlows.

Breaking up the wardroom mess made it necessary for Mr. Kimberly to live on shore. He, however, visited the ship every day [and] he always brought some cheering news. He had written to the Admiral of the conduct of the officers and the condition of the men and he told us he would stay by us untill we were paid and received our furlows.

After two weeks delay, through the efforts of Mr. Kimberly the paymaster at the Navy Yard paid each man half what was due him and Mr. Kimberly himself made out the furlow passes. As the men followed him in an irregular drove, as children would an effectionate father, the men made several attemps to express their gratitude by cheering him, but he plainly showed it would be disagreeable to him. But as he turned to leave us, the men could hold no longer [and] they burst into cheer after cheer untill he turned into an office at the Navy Yard [to] avoid it.

Before Vicksburg fell in 1863, this is how Diggins saw the steeply sloping city from the Mississippi River. Library of Congress.

Down from the Yazoo River came the CSS *Arkansas*, shooting her way through two immobile Federal fleets tied up along the banks above Vicksburg. Naval History and Heritage Command, from a sepia wash drawing by R. G. Skerritt.

USS *Essex,* a river ironclad, failed in an attempt to ram the CSS *Arkansas.* Naval History and Heritage Command.

Farragut's effort to pass Port Hudson's batteries in March 1863 is a disaster. Side-wheel ship is presumably the doomed USS *Mississippi.* Courtesy Boston Public Library, lithochrome by Louis Prang.

The sidewheeler USS *Mississippi* was abandoned by her crew before drifting down from Port Hudson until her magazine exploded with a roar heard for miles. Naval History and Heritage Command.

U.S. Gunboat "Albatross"

After the Port Hudson disaster, Rear Admiral Farragut commanded a two-ship fleet, the *Hartford* and the little three-gun *Albatross* (above), both locked in the river between Vicksburg and Port Hudson. Naval History and Heritage Command, sketch by W. M. C. Philbrick.

Manned by freebooting soldiers, with her guns on the second deck, the *Switzerland* joined Farragut's river-locked fleet. Sepia wash drawing by F. Muller, circa 1900, depicting the ship on the Western Rivers during the Civil War. Naval History and Heritage Command.

At Mobile, Ala., and other Southern ports, Federal blockaders tried to intercept fast, sleek blockade runners such as this one, the ex-*Robert E. Lee*, captured by two Federal ships in 1863. Library of Congress.

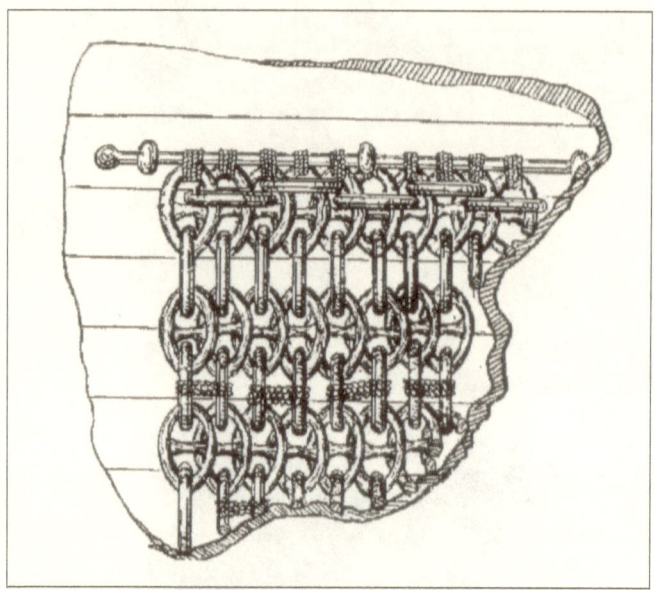

Ships' crews draped chains around boilers and machinery before battles as impromptu armor, as illustrated above. From *Battles and Leaders*.

Fort Morgan, the masonry bastion guarding Mobile Bay's entrance, could not stop Farragut's fleet and finally fell to a combined sea and land siege. National Archives.

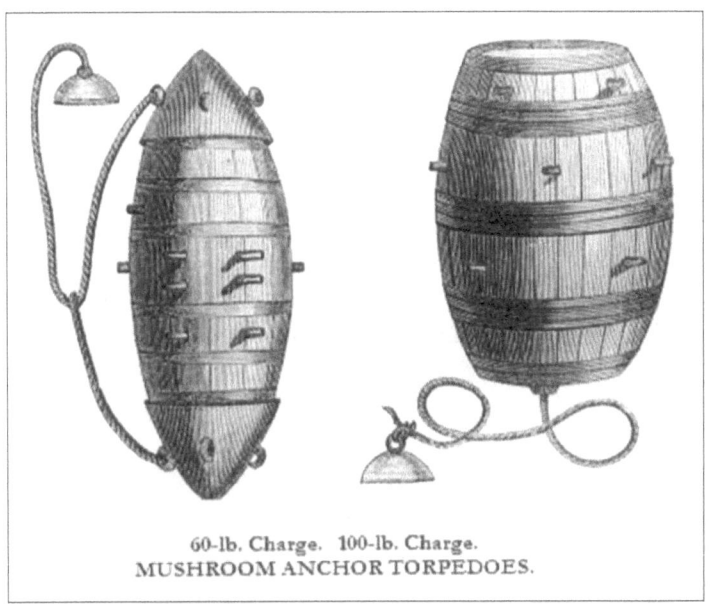

60-lb. Charge. 100-lb. Charge.
MUSHROOM ANCHOR TORPEDOES.

These Confederate "torpedoes" or mines, though primitive in construction, posed a serious threat to Farragut's ships in Mobile Bay. From *Harper's Weekly*, April 29, 1865.

Tunis A. M. Craven, the *Tecumseh's* captain, warned about Mobile Bay's mines, said he did not care "the snap of my fingers for them." Library of Congress.

USS *Tecumseh*, a *Canonicus* class monitor like the one above, speedily plunged 30 feet to the bottom where she remains, an iron shroud for most of her crew. Library of Congress.

Quartermaster John H. Knowles, an old salt, waves his cutlass long after the battle of Mobile Bay when he lashed Farragut to the rigging to prevent the admiral from falling. Courtesy Nimitz Library, US Naval Academy.

Rear Admiral Franklin Buchanan, CSN, did not hesitate to fight the entire Federal fleet in his clumsy, slow-moving ironclad, the CSS *Tennessee.* Naval History and Heritage Command.

CSS *Tennessee,* crippled and overwhelmed, surrendered during the Mobile Bay clash whereupon Federals provided her with a new smokestack, flag, and crew to bombard Fort Morgan. Naval History and Heritage Command.

PART 4
MOBILE

WAITING GAME

After five months of repairs and refitting in New York, Diggins and the *Hartford* sailed in January 1864 for the Gulf and renewed war operations. Now the goal was the port of Mobile, Farragut's long-favored target.

By this time the Union's blockade of southern ports, declared by Lincoln in early 1861, had become increasingly effective, sharply reducing the flow of war materials from abroad and the export of cotton, the South's main source of cash to finance the war.

Another consequence of the blockade, intended or not, caused many hardships for the civilian population. An acute shortage of many ordinary household goods ensued, some of which became luxuries in the agrarian South. Few or no factories existed to manufacture such simple things as pins and needles, toothbrushes, wool cards, and shoes, while imports such as coffee, tea, salt, and bolts of fabric became very dear or unobtainable. To satisfy the demand, some southerners became rowboat blockade runners, crossing the Potomac River from Virginia to Maryland to buy pins, needles, combs, and other small items to sell on their return. In doing so, they risked capture and imprisonment or, in the case of one Confederate soldier, execution as a spy.[1]

By the war's second year, shortages had reduced many southern troops to stripping fallen Federals of shoes and clothing. When they came upon a well-equipped but dying Federal, some showed a certain sensitivity: they waited until the soldier expired before pulling off his shoes or knapsack. One soldier reported others sometimes dug up those already buried for their footgear and coats. When scouring a recent battlefield, scavengers also looked for Yankee haversacks with coffee and perhaps clean socks. Then, towards the end, they began to steal basic necessities from each other. Orderly Sgt.

Robert A. Jarman, 27th Mississippi Infantry, reported that fellow foot soldiers stole shoes and boots from cavalrymen on the theory that they did not need footgear, having horses to ride.[2]

Both the civilian and military population suffered from the severe inflation, stress, loss of morale, and acute shortages of simple necessities caused in part or entirely by the blockade. Imports such as salt, those "precious crystals" as one southern gentlewoman called the common condiment, and coffee rapidly became scarce, and prices rose accordingly. Personal hygiene suffered in 1863 when households lost toothbrushes "because we can't buy any more," as another southerner complained.[3]

Blockade runners crossed the Atlantic with salt from Europe while Federals destroyed southern coastal sea water processing sites or inland salt mines or springs. Eventually salt cost $100 a barrel, $25 to $80 a sack, or $1 for a pint at a salt mine. Soon coffee cost $25 a pound and $5 a cup in a restaurant.[4]

Still, there would never be enough ships to detect and stop every blockade runner. Designed and built for the task in England, low-slung, speedy blockade runners continued to evade northern blockaders. In late 1862, Farragut conceded, "It is impossible to prevent these fast steamers from running the blockade in very dark nights." In April 1863, while watching the port of Wilmington, N.C., an officer aboard the USS *Florida* wrote that the blockade runners "come upon us & flit by like a phantom." But by 1864, many thought they were catching more and more of those swift phantoms, though junior officers on the USS *Gettysburg* still thought the blockading effort was poor, while others on the North Atlantic reported great progress in catching blockade runners.

All involved, including Lincoln, admirals, Federal sailors, and their Confederate counterparts, knew the only way to seal off the South was to capture either the ports or the guardian forts so that blockade runners had nowhere to go, no safe harbor to unload their cargoes of war supplies, staples, and luxury items. Modern historians, aided by postwar statistics, also argue that the blockade was porous and that seizing southern ports was the answer.[5]

Opening the Mississippi significantly improved the blockade's effectiveness. Ports west of that river immediately lost much of their importance. Blockade runners could and did slip into ports along the Texas coast or sail into Mexico's port of Matamoros, but their cargos nourished only the trans-Mississippi Confederacy, as any large-scale movement across the Mississippi became almost impossible. That left the guarded ports to the east of the river on the gulf and then up along the Atlantic seaboard. Major southern ports such as Mobile, Ala., Savannah, Ga., Charleston, S.C., and Wilmington, N.C., continued as inviting destinations for blockade runners. Some smaller harbors existed, but they often lacked the ability to handle freight efficiently and, even more important, had no rail line connections.

So Confederate leaders, knowing that Union forces would try to capture or close major ports, prepared a vigorous defense. Usually, they strengthened former Union forts guarding the entrances and embraced innovative weaponry. Unable to float a navy remotely approaching the Union's naval strength, they necessarily relied mostly on defensive technology, though they also deployed some new offensive weapons.

Their submarines and semi-submersibles enjoyed only limited success. The CSS *Hunley*, a primitive hand-powered submarine, sank the blockader USS *Housatonic* off Charleston's harbor on February 17, 1864—and also went to the bottom; CSS *David*, a steam-powered semi-submersible, detonated a 100-pound charge against a Charleston blockader, the USS *New Ironsides*, an iron-plated 3,500-ton steamer, causing "very serious" damage, according to her captain. These novel threats compelled Union naval authorities to expend much time, energy and money in developing counter-measures.[6]

Far more effective were the "infernal machines" or "torpedoes" so profusely and widely employed by Confederate forces in the water and on land. Both terms referred to what are now called mines, but the first conveys the then prevalent notion that such "devilish engines" were underhanded, unfair, disreputable, "cowardly," or "treacherous" weapons for use in honorable warfare. Farragut himself thought the use of mines "unworthy of a chivalrous nation." By their very nature, mines must lie concealed from sight to be effective. That meant sailors and soldiers might be killed by soulless machines they could not see or confront face to face. In an understatement, an officer on the USS *Gettysburg* wrote that "it is very annoying to have to contend with an enemy . . . that lies hid."[7]

Confederate's enthusiastic embrace of mine warfare forced the North to adopt new defenses against the devices. They tried many mine sweeping methods to protect individual vessels, including pushing a big raft ahead to trigger mines, slinging hooks from a spar attached to a ship's bowsprit, torpedo rakes, and grapples. Mine sweeping by pairs of small boats dragging chains between them pulled up the devices, but they could not do that while under fire at a place like Mobile Bay. One mine clearing method not endorsed by the Navy Department was that allegedly employed by Thomas O. Selfridge, Jr., commanding the USS *Cairo*. George W. Brown, the USS *Forest Rose*'s skipper, with tongue in cheek, said his fellow captain removed torpedoes "by placing his vessel over them," eliminating the devices but sinking the *Cairo*.[8]

Soon Federals began to design, construct, and place their own torpedoes in eastern rivers. In short order, the James and other navigable waterways were clogged with Confederate mines upstream and the Federals' downstream. While Union ships continued to sink after striking torpedoes, the mostly immobile Confederate warships there escaped a similar fate.[9]

Besides a respectable war toll of twenty-nine Federal ships sunk and fourteen others damaged, Confederate torpedoes or mines proved very effective as psychological warfare weapons. Their ghostly, invisible presence caused fear and alarm in many Federals. A paymaster declared, "I am decidedly opposed to this cowardly method of warfare; I had much rather be blown up by my wife than by one of these things." But gallows humor failed to help some and in one instance, a naval officer reported that a crewman was "loosing courage" and so was sent home before he demoralized others. And a naval surgeon confessed in a letter home that they lived in "constant dread of torpedoes." That widespread concern influenced plans for several naval operations, particularly at Mobile Bay.[10]

After a thorough overhauling of her hull and rigging, the *Hartford* sailed from New York on the 22nd of December 1863 and arrived at New Orleans early in Jan. 1864. Preparations were now hurried for the attack on Mobile.

Our stay at New Orleans was a short one. We arrived at Mobile blockade Jan. 20th. After two days here we sailed for Pensacola. At Pensacola we stripped ship to her fighting trim, sending down every thing above her topmast, which together with all spare boats and other articles were landed at the Navy Yard.[11]

The other ships of the fleet which were to take part in the battle come into Pensacola on turns [and] were stripped, some of them taking aboard more heavy guns when they could find room to work them.

While we were at Pensacola the Admiral received information that the ram *Tennessee* had arrived at Fort Morgan from Mobile and, with the Confederate fleet, were about to attack our vessels on the blockade. The *Hartford*, with the other vessels of the fleet, then at Pensacola, set sail at once for the Mobile blockade.[12]

We anchored in the center of a half circle formed by our fleet around the entrance to Mobile Bay. We had a good view of our enemy. On the east side of the entrance and occupying the whole point of land lay Fort Morgan with its nine acres of walls and guns. Commanding the main ship channel on Dauphin Island, about three miles across the entrance to the bay, is Fort Gaines. From Fort Gaines in the direction of Fort Morgan are several rows of piles with other obstructions extending to the bank of the main ship channel, thus compelling vessels going in the bay to pass close under the guns of Fort Morgan where the narrow channel thus left was filled with torpedoes. About four miles within the bay on the west side, Fort Powell commanded Grant pass, an entrance to the bay from Mississippi Sound behind Dauphin Island.[13]

A little west of the mouth of the bay and about three miles nearer to our fleet lay Sand Island, a barren pile of sand on which nothing could be seen but the remains of a horse which was said to have fallen overboard from a shipload that was being landed at Fort Morgan early in the war.

From where we lay we could watch the movements of the ram *Tennessee* and the enemy fleet behind Fort Morgan.

This place was now the greatest and only stronghold remaining to the enemy in the West Gulf. Its importance, as a means of communication with the outer world and to receive supplys through blockade runners grew greater as their other ports were captured or more closely invested by our now rapidly increasing navy. The Confedercy was unsparing in their efforts to make Mobile impregnable to any attack by water.[14]

The ram *Tennessee* was built at an expence of over two millions of Dollars and with many diffucultys brought her down the river untill at lenth she was floated in Mobile Bay. She was admitted at this time to be the most powerfull warship in the world. She was over two hundred feet long, fifty feet beam and plated with six inches of Iron, backed with two feet of solid wood. She had an iron prow extending twenty feet from her bow under water for ramming. She carried six guns of the best European make (Brook[e']s Rifles) which, together with her engines, were brought from England through the blockade.[15]

It was her arrival at Fort Morgan that called the Admiral to the blockade. An occasional deserter would tell us of the wonders expected of the *Tennessee* by the people of the city and at the forts and that they were only waiting for favorable weather to come out and sink or drive the Yankee fleet from the blockade. This was no doubt the intention of [Confederate] Admiral [Franklin] Buchanan and the continued increase in our fleet from all quarters at this time rather put him on the defensive.[16]

Blockading was not the most agreeable duty. [With] an unfriendly shore on one side of us and the great waste of water on the other, there was no communication with the outer world, except through the irregular mail boats from the north. We were continually on the alert for blockade runners. Our ships lay thick around the mouth of the bay and some were in motion at all times, yet some tried to run through us, few succeeding, however.[17]

We also experienced some terrific storms. On some of the ships, their guns broke loose from their mooring, causing great trouble, for if not captured and secured at once or let overboard, [they] would cause certain destruction to the ship.[18]

The *Hartford* was singularly fortunate in this respect, being one of the best sea boats in the fleet, if not in the Navy. Often she lay comparatively comfortable while others wallowed their lower yards under while the heavy seas run.[19]

On the 23rd of July two double turreted monitors, the *Winnebago* and *Chickasaw* arrived from the Mississippi River. They anchored inside of Sand Island just out of reach of the guns of Fort Morgan. On the first [of] August the monitor *Manhattan* arrived from the North and took position. with the others behind Sand Island. All the vessels that were to take part in the battle were now present, except the monitor *Tecumseh* which was hourly expected from Pensacola. Sixteen wooden vessels and four ironclads, besides a large number of mail and freight boats altogether [made] a formidable appearance.[20]

THE *IVANHOE* SAGA

One hapless blockade runner became an obsession for both sides during early July 1864.

She was the *Ivanhoe*, a fast English iron-hulled paddle-wheel steamer that grounded near Fort Morgan in the dark night of June 30, 1864, after Federal blockaders spotted her on her inward run and the USS *Glasgow* fired at her. *Ivanhoe* was moving "at fourteen knots per hour when she went ashore," a Confederate observer noted, stranding her firmly on the beach. Carrying medicines, shoes, blankets, and provisions, both the *Ivanhoe* and her cargo were sorely needed by the Confederacy.[1]

Immediately, Federals tried their best to destroy her and Confederates did their best to save the steamer, salvage the cargo, and repel attacks. In a weeklong series of actions, both sides had some successes. However, Farragut too quickly reported the *Ivanhoe's* destruction, though he knew that she "still lies on the beach," with little visible damage.[2]

For the first five days of July, Union warships constantly shelled the beached blockade runner. The trouble was that they could not approach within sure range lest Fort Morgan's guns hit and cripple their ships. Ensign Purnell F. Harrington, aboard the USS *Monongahela*, admitted, "Those [Morgan's] shells make a horrible noise when they come at us." He also admitted he was "a little nervous" when one of those shells burst right over his head, but did not flinch "to set a good example for the enlisted men." From the beginning, Federal sailors thought all the cannonading mostly missed the stationary target. Capt. Percival Drayton, the *Hartford's* commander, on July 1 wrote, "I must confess that I could see no signs of the least damage to the blockader, although wonderful stories are told." On the same day, the captain's clerk of the USS *Galena* confided that his ship had fired forty-eight times and hit her just once. On July 2, a *Hartford* Marine reported that gunboats fired at her all day but "we could not see that they had done any damage." To see for himself, Farragut boarded the small sidewheeler USS *Glasgow* and steamed so close to the *Ivanhoe* in shoaling water that the admiral risked grounding, inviting heavy shelling from Fort Morgan when he went back. Three ships bombarded the *Ivanhoe* the night of July 3, and one sailor wrote that the three ships "humbugged around all night." On July 4 the *Lackawanna's* captain wrote in his journal that he did not think any of his shots had struck the *Ivanhoe*.[3]

Yet a Confederate midshipman, whose cutter reached the *Ivanhoe* shortly after she beached, reported that "solid shot was tearing great holes through the upper works and shells were bursting every minute above and around" and that the Federal fire killed one seaman and badly wounded another. Further, one shot knocked in an iron plate, "causing her to take water fast." By July 5, a USS *Galena* sailor said that a small boat raiding party found the beached steamer "riddled with holes" and 2½ feet of water in her hold. Apparently the ships' gunners aimed better than thought by many, probably including Farragut, who had a close-up view.[4]

Concurrently with the daytime barrages, Farragut launched nighttime small boat expeditions against the *Ivanhoe*. He ordered his sailors to either blow up or fire the iron-hulled steamer. In a private letter, Drayton, the *Hartford's* captain, wrote that "We . . . have been trying to destroy her without receiving too much injury ourselves, which is presently scarcely worth risking at present unless for cause."[5]

For Farragut, sufficient cause was the *Ivanhoe's* continued existence. He presumed correctly that Confederates had promptly removed the blockade runner's valuable cargo, so that was not a consideration. But he did not want Confederates to salvage and use the damaged sidewheeler in Mobile Bay, so he ordered night raids, one after the other.[6]

Diggins took part in two of those expeditions and reported dramatic events not narrated in the official reports. Confederates described equally hair-raising incidents on the *Ivanhoe*, as when five men found themselves trapped in an oven-like empty coal bunker during a fire, also missing from official correspondence. Both sides suffered casualties, and most did their duty, though Diggins describes some as paralyzed by fear.[7]

In the end, Confederates could not salvage the ship, though they saved much of the cargo and removed her machinery. Federals got much target practice, and the affair busied many ships and sailors, honing their fighting skills for the work ahead.

On the night of the 30th of June an English blockade runner succeeded in getting through the fleet. She was so pressed by our gunboats, however, that she ran too close to shore and grounded under the guns of Fort Morgan. The Admiral was much annoyed that such a large amount of stores should be landed at Fort Morgan at this time, for want of which he hoped to conquer it.

He immediately ordered an expedition of two boats from each of the larger ships to go in that night and cut her out or distroy her.

The expedition was composed of about one hundred men in ten boats. They left the *Hartford* about 10 P.M. and returned at 3 a.m. and reported they could not find her. Another [expedition] went in on the following night with as little success.[8]

When these failures were reported to the Admiral, he was still more annoyed and calling Lieut. J. C Watson of his staff, he said, "Mr. Watson, I want you to take the barge, gigs, crews, and go in tonight and distroy that vessel." [9]

There could not have been a more agreeable selection to the men who were to form the expedition. Lieut. Watson was one of the few officers remaining on the ship who sailed from Philadelphia with us and his cool, determined bravery under many trying circumstances in the previous fights of the ship had established a confidence that no other officer could inspire. I was one of the barge's crew and we were soon making preparations. The men were mustered and asked if there was any among them that did not want to go. There was no answer.

We were ordered to wear white caps that we might better distinguish our men from the enemy in the darkness and each man was provided with a revolver, cutlass and carbine. The boat was also provided with combustible matter with which to fire the blockade runner.

Soon after dark we pulled alongside the gunboat *Metacomet* which towed us within three miles of Fort Morgan where we cast off and rowed in the direction of the fort which soon loomed up in the darkness ahead. We soon discovered the blockade runner lying in the shadow of the fort and headed direct for her and boarded her on the after part of her port wheelhouse.[10]

115

After a short struggle her crew was driven before us, escaped to the fort where they gave the alarm. The fort immediately opened fire on the vessel. Though under a heavy fire, we distributed the combustibles and, placing a large tank of powder in the center of her machinery, we set her on fire. After seeing the flames well started, we retreated to our boat, still under a heavy fire from Fort Morgan which was kept up untill we had pulled out of range. Their shot made the water foam about us, but fortunately none struck the boat.

When about two miles from her the tank of powder placed in her machinery exploded with a loud report. We reached the ship about daylight without loss or accident.[11]

On the following morning the iron hull of the blockade runner could be seen as plain as before in her old place and the Admiral, thinking it might be of use to the enemy if taken in the bay, decided to send us in again. Accordingly, preparation[s] were now made by the barge and gig crews, each boat carrying two hundred pounds of powder which we hoped to blow her to pieces. The two officers added were Lieut. [Herbert B.] Tyson and [acting master's] Mate [William H.] Hathorne who were to command the barge. Lieut. Watson commanded the gig.[12]

We were again towed in and come in sight of the blockade runner about one a.m. after pulling over three hours. Pickets along the shore, as they discovered us, galloped off in the direction of the fort, thus giving information of our approach. When within fifty yards of the blockade runner we stopped to let the gig come up, she being about a half mile astern so that the two boats might go alongside together. As soon as we stopped, they opened fire on us from the blockade runner with musketry. There could not be less than a thousand men on her, judging by the rapidity of their fire. The water around us bubbled like rain.[13]

Mate Hathorne, in a paroxysm of cowardice, threw himself his full lenth up[on] the thwart board between the men, making it impossible for the men to pull the boat and causing much confusion. We at lenth, by much kicking and threatening to throw him overboard, we removed Hathorne to the stem of the boat. He was asked to look after the killed and wounded [and] he whined that he did not know what to do for them. Nor was Lieut. Tyson much better, he having coiled himself up behind a tank of powder in the stern sheets of the boat. James Gallagher, the Coxswain, now assumed command and, coming from the coxswain box, assisted in removing the wounded to the stern. Then, standing in the stern, tiller in hand, amidst the showers of bullets, with great coolness [he] headed the boat for sea. We soon pulled beyond reach of their fire.

We reached our ship at [blank] a.m. [and] we made no farther attempts to distroy the blockade runner.[14]

On the 4th of August the monitor *Tecumseh* arrived from Pensacola and took her place with the other monitors. On that evening we made what little preparations necessary to attack the Forts on the following morning.

"DAMN THE TORPEDOES"

With a mixture of piety, diffidence, and resolve, Farragut wrote his wife a few days before the battle of Mobile Bay, "My monitors are all here now, so that I begin to feel that I am the one to attack." He also noted, "When I shall attack I know not, as I am waiting on the army. . . ." In addition to the monitors and the army, he also sought God's favor, saying, "I hope for the best results as I am always hopeful . . . trust to God for the Rest. He has thus far been gracious beyond my desserts but should he think proper to withdraw that position, I am ready to submit to his will."[1]

While he and other senior officers might disparage or scorn ironclads and prefer a navy of wooden sailing ships manned by iron-hearted sailors, Farragut was pragmatic enough to know that he needed iron warships to counter the enemy's. Percival Drayton, his fleet captain and also an officer in the prewar navy, embraced the new realities. A few weeks earlier, he wrote, "I have . . . some doubts about wood against iron." In another private letter, he thought that the odds favored iron ships in a contest with those of wood. He also wanted monitors to reinforce the fleet before the attack.[2]

As Farragut also knew, the attack required a combined operation, a cooperative effort of land and naval forces. The army needed the navy to transport troops on the waterways and the fleet's guns to help subdue the forts. Without troops to seize the entrance forts, just passing those guns and fighting Confederate ships in Mobile Bay would serve only as a costly exercise. Farragut's fleet could not sustain itself for long inside the bay and could not pass out again without risking more losses from Fort Morgan or torpedoes.[3]

But neither troops nor monitors came easily to Farragut. While he waited impatiently, uncertainties and needs elsewhere delayed the movement of soldiers to Mobile and equally frustrating difficulties, real and imagined, delayed the monitors.

Serious planning for the land operation began in June under Maj. Gen. E. R. S. Canby, who had replaced the bumbling Banks in a newly created area of command. Canby named a commander for the attack force and figured the expedition would start off for Mobile about July 6.[4]

Then events in the distant Virginia battlegrounds forced a change in plans. Grant had lost heavily in the spring campaign and needed reinforcements. So he ordered Canby to limit his operations to defensive actions and to send immediately "all available white troops" to Virginia. Grant figured that Canby could spare the 20,000 strong 19th Army Corps or its equivalent. Obeying the order meant suspending army operations against Mobile, and Canby promptly so wrote Farragut on July 1, 1864.[5]

Then, ignoring Grant's injunction to engage solely in defensive operations, a little more than two weeks later Canby announced that he had found about 4,000 soldiers to throw against Forts Morgan and Gaines, Mobile's outer defenses. About a week after that announcement, Canby said soon he would send a 2,000-man contingent, then another 3,000 troops when they arrived from Texas.[6]

For his coordinated land and sea attack, Farragut needed the monitors on hand as well as troops. Two monitors would come from the eastern seaboard while two river monitors would steam down the Mississippi. Never was it smooth sailing—shipboard fires, mechanical difficulties, a near grounding, and petty obstructionism delayed and hampered the monitor mobilization.

On June 9, well in advance of an attack at Mobile, Secretary of the Navy Gideon Welles ordered Rear Admiral David D. Porter to detach two monitors from his Mississippi River squadron and send them to Farragut. Four days later Porter, then at Mound City, Ill., began stalling. He argued that the river monitors were not seagoing vessels, that "[t]hey would break to pieces in the least swell, and they are not fitted to go anywhere but in the smoothest water. . . ." He added that the monitors were "very vulnerable" and "unfit" to cope with fortifications or ships with heavy guns. He doubted that they would ever reach Mobile and declined to send them without direct orders, orders which he already had.[7]

Whether Porter acted from envy, spite, or jealousy, as one of Farragut's biographers speculated, is uncertain. But perhaps it was just another of Porter's self-serving exercises in gross exaggeration. In any event, his objections cost precious time, even though Welles would have none of it. He repeated his direct orders, telling Porter to dispatch the twin-turret monitors *Winnebago* and *Chickasaw* to Mobile.[8]

The two single-turret *Canonicus*-class monitors assigned to the Mobile operation departed from their Atlantic coast stations several weeks apart. *Manhattan*, launched in June 1864 at Jersey City, N.J., "left the Capes of Delaware on June 20," while the *Tecumseh* began her southbound voyage July 5 from Hampton Roads, Virginia.[9]

Though steamers towed them during the ocean voyages, all the monitors experienced difficulties of one kind or another. The *Chickasaw* almost ran aground, and her steering gear gave trouble; one of the *Winnebago*'s turrets jammed; fires broke out on the *Manhattan*; and the *Tecumseh* had engine trouble, and three of her chief engineer officers were hospitalized. Officers and men alike labored in miserable conditions of poor ventilation, enervating heat below decks, excessive moisture, poor food, and a lack of restful sleep. Lt. Robert B. Ely, serving aboard the *Manhattan*, called it a "filthy iron-pot" and thought "three month's service in an ironclad ought to insure a man's promotion to brigadier general." The day after arriving at Mobile, Ely in vain requested a transfer to a regular ship.[10]

Though the blockading Federals had feared the Confederate's ironclad ram, the CSS *Tennessee*, might sally forth some dark night and sink their ships, they worried needlessly. When the *Tennessee* did try such an attack, it ended in ignominious failure shortly after getting underway and long before she was anywhere near the Federal blockaders. Barely making headway at about two or three miles per hour, her surgeon said she was unseaworthy. He recalled that "every sea tumbling over her came inboard in such masses that fires in engine room nearly put out." In that brief venture, the crew learned that the engines, lifted from an old river boat, were old and weak and could not be strengthened. Like the Federal monitors, crewmen found that it was very hot and humid within the casemated ironclad, making sleep almost impossible. Furthermore, John C. O'Connell, the *Tennessee*'s 2nd assistant engineer, said that the abortive attack experienced another setback when she ran aground.[11]

After watching the *Tennessee* in action, John C. Watson, Farragut's favorite lieutenant, agreed that Federal concerns were all for naught. He described her as "unseaworthy and so slow and sluggish ... even in smooth water, as to be a failure as a ram." But, as noted, that realization came after the battle.[12]

Small semi-submersible Confederate torpedo boats should have worried Federal sailors much more than the big and clumsy *Tennessee*. Drayton, the *Hartford*'s captain, was concerned when he saw a torpedo boat near Fort Morgan, writing "so I suppose an attempt will be made to treat us like the *Housatonic*." He referred to the Confederate submarine *H. L. Hunley*'s sinking of the USS *Housatonic* off Charleston on February 17, 1864. Probably more than one low-slung torpedo boat operated in Mobile Bay, and there the CSS *St. Patrick*, a fifty-foot-long semi-submersible, attacked the sidewheel USS *Octorara* on January 28, 1865. But the Confederate's explosive charge failed to detonate, and both vessels survived the encounter.[13]

Most Federal sailors had a healthy respect for Confederate torpedo boats and an even healthier regard for the hidden torpedoes or mines. Whether from bravado or ignorance, some scorned the new weapons. James M. Jouett, the *Metacomet*'s captain, cautioned Tunis A. M. Craven, commanding the monitor *Tecumseh*. Jouett recalled, "I particularly warned him against the torpedoes. I had been in the harbor at night. I warned him to be careful. He looked at me in his bright confident way and said, "Jouett, I don't care the snap of my fingers for them.""[14]

At 2 a.m. on the 5th August 1864 all hands were called. At daylight the men were served with coffee. At 5:40 a.m., the *Hartford* signaled the fleet to get under way and form in line of battle. The ships were soon all in motion and were lashed together in pairs, a large one and a small one, so that in case one should become disabled or sunk by torpedoes, the other could afford relief. The smaller one [was] on the sheltered side from Fort Morgan.[15]

As we moved ahead, the ships formed in the following order:

the *Brooklyn*, Commander James Alden, with the *Octorara*, Lieut. [Lt.-Comdr] C. H. Green, lashed to her side

the flagship *Hartford*, Captain P. Drayton, with the *Metacomet*, Lieut. [Lt.-Comdr] James E. Jouett

the *Richmond*, [Captain] T. A. Jenkins, with the *Port Royal*, Lieut. [Lt.-Comdr] B. Gherardi

the *Lackawanna*, Capt. J. B. Marchand, with the *Seminole*, Commander Edw. Donaldson, the *Monongahela*, Commander J. H. Strong, with the *Kennebec*, Lieut. [Lt.-Comdr] W. P. McCann, [with] the *Ossipee*,

122

Commander W. E. LeRoy, with the *Itasca*, Lieut. [Lt.-Comdr] Geo. Brown, [with]the *Oneida*, Commander J. R. M. Mullany, with the *Galena*, Lieut. [Lt.-Comdr] Clark H. Wells.

The four monitors, *Tecumseh*, Commander T. A. M. Craven; *Manhattan*, Commander J. W. A. Nicholson; *Winnebago*, Commander T. A. Stevens; and *Chickasaw*, Lieut. [Lt.-Comdr] G. H. Perkins, formed a line abreast of the four leading ships and between them and Fort Morgan.

The *Brooklyn*, which was in the lead, had a boom rigged across and braced under the head of her bowsprit. From this was suspended numerous graplines dragging the water and reaching below her bottom and wide enough to clear a passage by exploding or displacing the torpedoes which filled the channel through which the fleet were to pass. The balance of the fleet were to follow in the clearing made by the *Brooklyn*, each vessel keeping in the wake of the one directly ahead.[16]

The troops, under General [Gordon] Granger that were to aid the navy in the attack, had been landed the day before in the rear of Fort Gaines [by a] fleet of small vessels commanded by J. C. P. De Krafft of the *Conemaugh*.

At 6 a.m. the ships were all formed in line moving up the main ship channel towards the forts. Each ship had her largest flags, the Stars and Stripes, flying from her mast head and peak. It was a beautifull sight just before the battle commenced. [When] we reached a gentle curve in the channel, we could look back and see this mass of colors grandly unfurled by the strong westerly breeze.[17]

We had two important points in our favor for which the Admiral [had] waited[:] a full flood tide going in the bay with us and a westerly wind to carry our smoke towards the enemy, thus at times the forts were enveloped in the smoke from our guns and much of their firing was guesswork.

At seven oclock the monitor *Tecumseh*, which was a little in the lead, opened the battle. The forts was a little slow in responding and did not fire untill the *Brooklyn* opened with her bow guns. The forecastle guns of the *Hartford* commenced firing at the same time. The forts and Confederate fleet now opened on us vigoriously.[18]

The *Hartford* was almost abreast of the fort when it seen that [the] monitor *Tecumseh* struck a torpedo. After one or two lurches, she disappeared in front of Fort Morgan.[19]

A moment later the *Brooklyn* stopped. The *Hartford*, to avoid fouling her, stopped also and ceased firing, thinking to give assistance, thinking that she too was going to sink.

The Admiral, who up to this time had remained on the poop deck or lower mizen rigging, now hailed the *Brooklyn* and asked, "What's the matter[?] Why dont you go ahead[?]"

George S. Waterman, a Confederate navy midshipman, drew this diagram of successive stages of the Mobile Bay battle. At top, the Federal fleet advances while Confederate warships wait in foreground. He shows the USS *Tecumseh* hitting a mine and, at bottom right, the CSS *Tennessee* surrounded by Federal ships. Naval History and Heritage Command.

There was no answer.

The Admiral waved his hand several times, crying, "Go ahead, go ahead."

At lenth, Captain Alden answered, "I am right in a nest of torpedoes." The Admiral replied, "Go ahead, damn the torpedoes, go ahead."[20]

There was no answer from the *Brooklyn*, but a moment later she commenced backing. Our helm was put hard astarboard to avoid collision and we commenced to lap her port quarter. In the mean time we were receiving the full fire of the forts.[21]

The Admiral seemed much distressed upon perceiving that the *Brooklyn* continued to back, he hastily jumped to the deck and cried, "Give her four bells, go ahead full speed."

Admiral Farragut did nothing in all his previous battles that so completely won the admiration of his officers and men as his quick decision on this occasion. The *Brooklyn*, being between us and the forts, for the moment the men had nothing to do but wait the outcome of the *Brooklyn*'s movements. At the order to take the lead, the *Hartford*'s crew burst into cheer after cheer which was in turn taken up by the other vessels of the fleet untill they reached the whole length of the line.

Though we had stopped but a few moments, we did not start ahead any too soon. The *Richmond* had to sheer to clear our stern and was lapping our port quarter. A few moments indecision and we would have been huddled in a helpless mass, struggling among thousands of torpedoes and at the mercy of the enemy's guns. Short as the delay was, it caused considerable confusion. The vessels were all compelled to stop in turn and the line of battle was partly broken.[22]

Our guns were idle while passing the *Brooklyn*. During that time our men were engaged [in] hooting, groaning and howling, "Coward, take him out; he ran away at Vicksburg; etc."[23]

As we cleared the *Brooklyn*, taking the lead, we entered a storm of shot and shell. Our broadside guns were soon again in full action while we dashed on through the main ship channel, over and through the buoy that located the beds of torpedoes.

About this time the Admiral observed what remained of the *Tecumseh* & crew were still struggling in the water between us and the fort. He hailed the *Metacomet* to send a boat to their rescue.

This was what Captain Jouett was preparing to do and, in a few moments later, a boat commanded by Henry C. Nields cleared our stern with the American flag flying full to the breeze and pulled fearlessly through a storm of missiles from both friend and foe toward Fort Morgan where the men were still struggling in the water.

No one could witness this act of heroism with out emotion. The ships' crews for a moment ceased their murderous work to jump to the rail to cheer the little boat on her mission of mercy. She was anxiously watched, but as if under divine protection on she went. A part of the time she was completely hidden by the dense smoke, but at intervals she could be seen pulling here and there to rescue the drowning men. She was all the time the center of the fiercest part of the battle. Shells were bursting and striking on all sides and the air above her was almost darkened by the flying missiles from fleet and fort. As we entered the bay we saw her almost under the walls of Fort Morgan where she had gone to recover some men who attemted to swim to shore.

Few thought it possible for her to return. But after rescuing ten men, all that were left of the *Tecumseh's* crew, the balance having gone down with her, among them Captain Craven, she was headed for our fleet again and made the trip in safety. She was thrown a line from the *Oneida* and towed safely into the bay.[24]

After the *Hartford* took the lead and increased the distance between her and the balance of the fleet, Fort Morgan on our right, Fort Gaines on our left, Fort Powell and the enemy fleet ahead seemed to concentrate their whole fire upon her and made it warm work [for] two minutes. The hurried steps of powder boys and shellmen from the stearage and fore hatches with supplys for their guns added to the apparent confusion. The nois from the cannon was so great and so continuous that it was impossible to distinguish a single report. We could hear, however, the peculiar scream of shot passing over us, the bursting shell, and the quick snapping crash of those that struck us. The cut rigging swung aloft while some of it came on deck by the [rail? illegible word]. The men were smeared and begrimed with burnt powder and the smell of it was almost suffocating.

The dead and wounded were hurried from all parts of the ship to the main hatchway where they were placed in a swinging cat and lowered to the temporary hospital in the main hold. One poor fellow, when placed in the cat, in his agony attempted to turn and fell nearly thirty feet and ended his suffering. The explosion of one shell killed or wounded eleven men at no. 7 gun. Guns one and two were disabled for a few moments by the loss of fifteen men untill re-enforced from other guns. Our men were dropping all over the ship. A man working at one's side would the next moment be hurried to the main hatch in his last agonies. The decks and sides were smeared and tracked with blood which ran in crooked streams to the scuppers. Mangled portions of the human body were shoved in out-of-the-way places or stuck to the sides, ropes and masts.[25]

Those were a few of the sights on the *Hartford* during her passage through the deadly storm of shot, shell and torpedoes between Fort Morgan and Fort Gaines.[26]

During this time Captain Drayton remained about the poop deck with his glasses in hand, closely watching all that was going on. He was nearly always accompanied by Lieut J. C. Watson, the signal officer, who invariably wore the same agreeable smile whether fighting or at morning drill.

Commander Kimberly, speaking trumpet in hand, slowly walked fore and aft [on] the main deck, always the first to be present at any mishap and superintending the case of the killed and wounded.

ONE AGAINST MANY

After the Federal fleet passed Fort Morgan and entered the bay, Farragut had fourteen wooden warships and three monitors still afloat with crews in fighting trim. Confederate Admiral Franklin Buchanan opposed him with the ironclad *Tennessee* and three small ships, the *Selma*, *Morgan*, and *Gaines*.

Besides the obvious 4–1 numerical advantage, the Federals had a central command in Farragut who directed the attack in the fluid battle. Farragut used signal flags and shouted orders to deploy his ships in a coordinated, cohesive effort. Buchanan had no signal flag mast, and his small ships soon fought independently of each other until eliminated one by one.

Buchanan, on the *Tennessee*, then attacked Farragut's fleet by himself in his slow-moving ram, in a fight that quickly exposed some of the ironclad's design defects.

Perhaps the stout-hearted Buchanan thought he could duplicate his feat on March 8, 1862, at Hampton Roads, Va. Then, he had rammed and sunk one Federal warship and forced the surrender of another with his ironclad *Merrimac* (CSS *Virginia*). Perhaps he thought he could so damage the Federals in Mobile Bay that they would break off the fight and that somehow he could outfight or outfox the three monitors.

Most likely, however, he did not ponder possibilities and alternatives but took the only immediate course of action open to him: attack.

After one hour of this murderous work, we cleared the iron hail of the forts and entered the bay where the enemy fleet awaited us. They were formed in a line on the east or right side of the channel. The ram *Tennessee*, the nearest, advanced to meet us.

We now loaded with solid shot and the guns were trained sharp forward. Neglecting all els for the moment, we gave her the benefit of our whole broadsides untill we had passed her. Much to our surprise, she gave us no more attention than to return our fire and then continued in the direction of the engagement at the forts. We were now more than a half mile in the bay. The other vessels seemed not to have recovered from the confusion caused by the *Brooklyn*, as none of them had yet appeared inside the forts.

The *Hartford* was now beset by the whole of the enemy's fleet: The confederate Steamer *Selma* ahead and raking us fore and aft, the *Gaines* on our starboard bow, the *Morgan* on our starboard beam, and the *Tennessee* across our stern, all keeping up a distructive fire. The *Selma* was doing us the greatest damage. Her position ahead was such that we could only bring one forecastle gun to bear on her and a shot from her disabled that and killed half its crew. One of them was literally blown to atoms, nothing remaining together but his boots which were found in different parts of the ship.[1]

The Admiral ordered Commander Jouett of the *Metacomet* to go forward and engage the *Selma*.

The *Hartford* and the *Metacomet*, which up to this time had been lashed together, were now hurriedly cut apart, Commander Jouett himself cutting many of the fastenings with a hatchet. The *Metacomet* was the fastest vessel in the fleet and in a few moments was spinning ahead, receiving a hearty cheer as she left the *Hartford*. We now gave our full attention to the *Morgan* and *Gaines*. The *Tennessee* either thought us too insignificant or that the other three gunboats would take care of us as she continued in the direction of the forts. Our broadsides soon proved too much for the *Morgan* and *Gaines*. The former hauled off in the direction of Fort Morgan and the latter ran for the beach in a sinking condition and grounded to avoid sinking about a half mile east of Fort Morgan where she was fired and abandoned by her crew.[2]

After the *Metacomet* cast off from the *Hartford*, she gradually gained on the *Selma*. They were equal in number of guns and men and a desperate running fight followed for nearly an hour when the *Metacomet* boarded and captured the *Selma*, bringing her back in tow, with those of her officers not killed or wounded [as] prisoners of war.[3]

The *Hartford* anchored about six miles inside the forts and the balance of our fleet soon after appeared coming up the bay and anchored about us. All hands were at once engaged clearing the wreck of battle, washing the blood from the decks and making the wounded comfortable. The ship's boilers were relieved of the high pressure of steam and the fires were banked.[4]

We had started to get ready for breakfast when it was reported that the ram *Tennessee* was coming up from the forts to attack the fleet. This was an agreeable surprise to us, for we were well aware that we would have no rest while the *Tennessee* floated in the bay, our enemy.

Admiral Farragut and Admiral Buchanan were of equal rank in the navy from boys up. Both were captains at the beginning of the war when Farragut was on duty at the Norfolk Navy Yard and, though a Southern man by birth, joined the Union Cause and came north. Buchanan commanded the Washington Navy Yard at that time when he made a speech to the employees in which he extolled the Confederate Cause and invited his hearers to follow him. He joined the Secessionist[s] and went South. Both were the most active and had attained the highest rank in their respective navies and now met for the first time in the war.[5]

Admiral Buchanan[']s previous experience [was] with wooden vessels. When he commanded the rebel ironclad *Merrimac* in Hampton Roads [that] encouraged him, for the *Tennessee* was a much superior vessel. But he did not have a Farragut to deal with at Hampton Roads.[6]

The signal was made from our ship to ram the enemy. All our vessels now slipped their cables. The *Monongahela*, which had her bow strengthened and an iron prow fitted, struck her at full speed without the slightest effect on the monster, but had her iron prow carried away and her stem crushed and splintered. The *Lackawanna* next struck her with no better results. Each vessel after striking poured a broadside against her iron sides with no more effect than to dent them. The *Tennessee* kept up a murderous fire on the vessels that struck her but continued her course towards the *Hartford.* Soon all was clear between the two flag ships. They headed for each other at full speed. Admiral Buchanan showed the first weakness as a direct blow was avoided by the *Tennessee*, probably fortunate for both vessels. They would [have] hurled] against each other's bows on and crushed and telescoped, both go[ing] down together.[7]

It was believed that Admiral Farragut had this in view as he was heard to say he would willingly lose any of his ships to sink or distroy the *Tennessee.* However, fate did better by both. The *Hartford* struck her on the port bow as she came under our port cathead. She so jammed the anchor stock as to cause the flukes to fly up in the air and, as if in great anger, fall on the roof of her casemate. Captain Drayton, who was standing on the forecastle, seeing Buchanans head above the hatch on top of the casemate, cried "Infernal traitor" and threw his field glasses at him. Lieut. Watson, who was standing near at the same time, fired his revolver at him and Buchanan quickly disappeared.[8]

Both vessels then came side by side. We fought the port battery with solid shot, which bounded in the air from her iron sides, clearing, however, all loose articles, such [as] railing, boats, davits, flags, etc., and jamming her port shutters so as to make many of her guns useless during the rest of the fight.[9]

It was supposed that at this time, while superintending the work clearing one of his jammed ports, Admiral Buchanan was severely wounded in the leg by either the hammer or chisel used by the mechanic, a shot striking outside the spot where the chisell [was] being used, causing both hammer and chisell to fly. The mechanic who was using them was instantly killed.[10]

The *Tennessee* now passed astern of the *Hartford* and the other ships took up the fight in turns.

The Ram's guns did terrible execution on our berth deck, killing and wounding most of the powder division. The percussion shell[s] fired by the *Tennessee* never failed to explode just as they entered the side, pieces of them going up through the spar deck, kill[ing] and wounding men. The men killed and wounded between decks were replaced from the gun crews while the *Hartford* made a half circuit and headed again for the *Tennessee*. The position of the ram prevented a fair blow [but] as the two ships come together we poured in broadside after broadside while a very dense smoke enveloped both vessels.

We discovered the *Lackawanna* bearing down on us at full speed, intending to strike the *Tennessee*. Upon discovering her mistake, her engines were immediately reversed and her helm put hard astarboard. Her force was broken and a square blow avoided, but she struck us two guns forward of the mizzen rigging, throwing two guns in on deck, carrying away the rail to the mizzen rigging and cutting our side down to the water. She then glanced off and passed around our stern. While this was going on at starboard side, we continued fighting the ram with our port battery.

The *Hartford* again separated from the ram and, after a hurried examination, it was found that a large opening had been made in the side from the water up, but there was no serious leak.[11]

Our three monitors had now arrived in action. Their want of speed being their greatest failing, [they] were seeking close quarters with the ram, one on each side and the third across her stern. An ordinary water bucket could have been placed in every dent made by the fifteen inch solid shot from the monitors, but none of them went through.

The vessels not engaged in ramming now formed a rough line outside the monitors and poured in broadsides of solid shot.

After clearing the wreck made by the *Lackawanna* and nailing a tarpaulin over her injured side, the *Hartford* again headed for the ram. The *Tennessee* now began to show signs of weakness. She had not fired a shot for some time and seemed trying to make her way back to the fort. Every thing that shot could affect had been swept away. Her flat hull and battered casemate were the only targets for our fleet.

The Admiral had never shown such anxiety in any of his previous battles. He wanted to be continually with the ram and only left her to secure a better position or when crowded by other vessels. Lieut. Watson, signal officer, was kept busy signaling the other vessels how to conduct the fight.[12]

The *Hartford* was again bearing down on her on one side and the *Ossipee* on the other when a white flag was waved from the hatch on top of her casemate. The *Ossipee* was so close that she with difficulty avoided a collistion [collision]. She rounded to, alongside the ram, and lowered a boat which went alongside and received the surrender of the *Tennessee* after a desperate fight of one hour. The swords of the officers and a portion of the men were brought on board of our ship. The officers were sent to New Orleans as prisoners of war, except Admiral Buchanan who being severely wounded was sent to the hospital at Pensacola. Admiral Farragut did not see him.

Captain Johnston, who surrendered the *Tennessee*, explained that her stearing apperatus was defective and disabled, her smoke stack was shot off close to the deck, letting the smoke and heat between decks which almost suffocated the men.

Her port shutters, which worked on pivots, were nearly all jammed and disabled by our shot, so that her guns were useless during the later part of the fight. She was very much dented and some of the plating was loosened, but none of the shot went through her sides.[13]

The fleet dropped anchor where we lay, the *Tennessee* among us. A prize crew was put on board of her [and] they soon rigged a mast to which they hoisted a new American Union flag.

The *Hartford* was terribly torn and riddled in the engagement. On the berth deck, the mess things, hastily laid aside mess chests, clothing, partitions, splinters, etc., were all jumbled together, almost covering the whole deck, while mingling with the debris were the killed and wounded of the morning fight at the forts, together with those killed of the powder division by the *Tennessee*. This part of the ship was well christened the Slaughter House. At one time during the fight with the *Tennessee* it was found necessary to send down a gun's crew to take the place of the killed and wounded. This part of the ship, together with fire rooms and engine rooms, was under command of Chief Engineer Thom Williamson. Notwithstanding the many variations demanded of the engines and, at times, the disorganization caused by the killed and wounded, they acted as promptly as if we were working our way in[to] one of the docks in New York harbor.

The sight forward of the fore hatch was a ghastly one. After the fight at the forts, the wounded and dying were placed in this part of the ship and made as comfortable as possible. Those were now massed together with those killed later by the *Tennessee*. Some that had been but slightly wounded at the ports had been cut to pieces by the *Tennessee*. Those in whom life still remained were recognized by their groans and soon cared for while some of the men were engaged in clearing the debris. Others were gathering legs, arms and other parts of the human body and sewing them up in bags, with two shot to each bag. The bodies were sewed up in their hammocks with their allotted shot at their feet, preparatory to being sent to sea the next morning with [the] killed of the balance of our fleet.[14]

In a few hours, the wreck of battle was all cleared away and the decks and sides were scrubbed and relieved of all stains of the conflict.

Our losses were,

Hartford, killed 25, wounded 38; *Brooklyn*, killed 11, wounded 30; *Oneida*, killed 8, wounded 20; *Lackawanna*, killed 4, wounded 25.

The other seven wooden vessels had killed 4 and wounded 34. Our monitors had no one injured except the *Tecumseh*, sunk with over one hundred and twenty men.[15]

The *Richmond* passed the forts in the smoke of the vessels ahead and scarcely took part in the fight with the *Tennessee*. When the doctors report [of] two slightly wounded was laid before her captain, he became enraged, saying, "What! Only two wounded! Is that all? What, none killed? Why, how is that? They will think at home that this ship was not in the battle."

An old sailor who overheard the captain suggested to the doctor to kill a couple of afterguard sweepers to fill out his report.[16]

The Steamer *Philippi*, a frail dispatch boat, attempted to come in the bay in the smoke at the rear of the fleet. She grounded in front of Fort Morgan and was blown to pieces after the fleet passed in.[17]

Captain Jouett of the *Metacomet* sustained the flag ship throughout the fight. After he captured the *Selma*, although his [ship] was too frail to ram the *Tennessee*, he hovered near and when an opportunity offered, he poured in a broadside of his hundred and twenty pounders.[18]

Commander George H. Perkins, who was on his way home, hearing of the impending battle, ask[ed] the Admiral to be assigned to duty. He was given command of the Monitor *Chickasaw*. He fought her well. From the [moment] his guns came in range of the *Tennessee*, he did not leave her till she surrendered. He located across her stern [and] when she moved, he moved, and when she stopped, he stopped, all the time hamering her with 11 inch solid shot as if determined to make an opening in that end of her. He jammed her stern port shutters and is supposed to have disabled her steering gear. When she surrendered, he hauled alongside and towed her abreast of the flag ship.[19]

On the same afternoon, he went down to Fort Powell and, after engaging it alone for half an hour, he brought out the barge *Ingomar* from under its walls. He then went over to Fort Gaines and gave them a half hour's turn with his broadsides when he returned to Fort Powell and brought out another barge.[20]

The *Oneida* suffered most at the passage of the forts. She brought up the rear of the line and received the full fire of the forts after the other vessels had passed. Her captain, J. R. M. Mullany, had his arm shot off and was wounded in the leg. A shell set her on fire and a ball entered her boilers, completely disabling her. The *Galena*, Commander C. H. Wells, which was lashed alongside, pulled her through to an anchorage in the bay with the other vessels.[21]

Commander J. H. Strong of the *Monongahela*, with our own Lieut. Watson, were the two most noted for their fine Christian principles and piety and were the two hardest fighters in the fleet. Strong, who was chaplain as well as captain of his ship, was the first to run his vessel against the *Tennessee* and continued to ram and fight her untill his own ship was in a sinking condition. Indeed, it was the younger blood, forming the middle and rear of the line, that forged ahead, compelling the vessels that faltered in front of the forts to enter the bay or be run down and afterwards gallantly sustained the Admiral all through the desperate struggle with the *Tennessee*.

Comd. De Krafft came in the bay by Fort Powell soon after dark, his gig bringing the mails to our ship. While the fleet were engaged at the forts entering the bay, Commander De Krafft with his fleet in Mississippi Sound advanced on Fort Powell and give them a teast [taste] of what Fort

Morgan had a feast. When the *Chickasaw* shelled and took out the barges from Fort Powell, De Krafft's vessels again shelled it from the outside. The Confederates could not stand so much of that kind of treatment and as soon as there was sufficient darkness, they evacuated, leaving a [powder] train to the magazine which exploded about 10:30 p.m., the explosion giving us the first warning that the fort was abandoned.[22]

As one of the Admiral's boat crew, I landed with him the next morning. The little island was covered with debris. Where Fort Powell once stood was a great hollow. Around the edges was guns, gun carriages [and] broken timbers burried through the loose earth.[23]

This was an important gain for us, opening us to full communication with the outside.[24]

The following day some of De Krafft's vessels come in from Mississippi Sound while De Krafft himself was a frequent visitor to the *Hartford*, going in and out as he pleased in his gig.

FORT MORGAN RESISTS

Even before Federal land and sea forces could concentrate on Fort Morgan, many in the garrison saw their prospects as dim and believed they fought and lived on borrowed time. On Aug. 4, 1864, one of Fort Morgan's artillery officers wrote his betrothed, "We are in a position from which there will be no retreat.... I sincerely hope they will try to take us by an attack and not by cutting us off and starving us out."[1]

That was a vain wish, as Federal leaders had no intention of launching costly frontal assaults. Instead, they immediately began regular siege operations by emplacing artillery and mortars and constructing parallel approaches, thus moving ever closer to the isolated fort from their protected positions. Joseph B. Wilkinson, a 1st Tennessee Artillery lieutenant and the post adjutant, confided to his diary, "The siege has commenced & God only knows how long it will last though in the end there can be no favorable result."[2]

Like Wilkinson, Brig. Gen. Richard L. Page, Fort Morgan's commander, did not know how long it would last, but he also saw no happy ending. He declared, "The only question was: Hold it . . . or save life and capitulate?"[3]

No such uncertainties plagued Farragut and Maj. Gen. Gordon Granger, a regular Army Mexican War veteran and a leader who helped save the day at Chickamauga. Clearly and simply, they intended to force the surrender of Forts Gaines and Morgan, and to open Mobile Bay to their traffic while closing it to blockade runners. To that end, they planned a combined navy-army operation to capture Gaines and to lay siege to Morgan, denying the latter reinforcements, supplies, and hope.[4]

Yet, despite its reach, it was a limited operation, confined to eliminating Mobile as a blockade runners' port. Farragut and

Granger entertained no plans to capture Mobile itself or the city's strong inner defenses. Mobile was not New Orleans, captured by the navy, nor did it pose a threat to shipping, communications, and troop movement as had Vicksburg.

In firepower, numbers, and morale, the odds favored the Federals and aligned against Fort Morgan's defenders. Fleet gunners and army artillerymen could bring an overwhelming weight of cannon and mortar fire to bear upon the fort, while Page would see his guns dismounted one after the other. Further, Page said that Yankee sharpshooters "could pick off my men as fast as they appeared at the guns." His post adjutant added that those sharpshooters were "very daring."[5]

Federals had about 2,000 troops to use in Morgan's investment, a mix of artillerymen, infantry, and engineers, as well as some sailors shifted ashore with naval guns; Confederates had about a quarter of that number in Fort Morgan. But both sides had learned the hard way that such a numerical advantage evaporated should the superior force try frontal assaults against an entrenched or fortified enemy. Heeding that lesson, Federals accordingly besieged Morgan as a less costly, though more time-consuming, solution.[6]

Whether sailor or soldier, Federal or Confederate, most knew that Fort Morgan must fall. So while morale remained high among Federal forces, Confederate spirits steadily deteriorated. As the days went by, more and more of Morgan's defenders questioned why they should die in a losing fight and, as the besiegers moved closer to the fort's walls, many feared being blown skyward by a big explosive charge placed under the fort. Second Lieutenant Hurieosco Austill, 1st Alabama Battery, chronicled the declining morale among fellow garrison soldiers. Austill denounced as a "silly rumor" the whispers that Federals undermined the fort, but noted the men "exceedingly" disliked the idea of being blown up. And, as rumors go, that one may have had some basis in fact. Second Lieutenant Rufus Kinsley, leading a black infantry company in the siege lines, said army engineers would soon have "five or six tons of powder under the walls of the fort," although he may have heard exaggerated reports.[7]

But mine or no mine, the constant bombardment alone steadily reduced Fort Morgan's defenses until soon the garrison would have only rifles, pistols, and swords to counter Federal artillery.

On the day after the battle (Aug. 6), the whole fleet were engaged in repairing damages to their hulls and rigging. The *Tennessee* was not neglected. A few men from the larger [ships] made up a full crew for her [and] they emmediately went to work clearing her port shutters, repairing her steering gear and putting [her] back in her old fighting condition. The Admiral sent to New Orleans for a new smoke stack.

While the men was engaged in this manner, the officers were demanding the surrender of the forts. Gen. Page at Fort Morgan was still defiant and said that he would never surrender. He seem[ed] to have not got over the slathering he got the day before. The boat that went to Fort Gaines under a flag of truce to demand its surrender returned in the afternoon bringing Col. [Charles D.] Anderson, the commandant, and his staff. They were received on our ship with every show of respect (the spider and the fly). They were taken to the Admiral's cabin where the surrender was soon agreed upon. The next morning our troops occupied Fort Gaines.[8]

Preperations were now began to reduce Fort Morgan. Troops were landed by Gen. Granger at Navy Cove four miles in the rear of Fort Morgan, thus cutting it off from all communication. This force now fortified across the peninsula and began a regular siege and as fast as guns and mortars could be got in position, they opened fire on the doomed Fort.[9]

In about a week a new smoke stack arrived from New Orleans for the ram *Tennessee.* When this was put in place and flying a large new United States flag, she went down to Fort Morgan, accompanied by the *Chickasaw, Manhattan* and *Winnebago*, three monitors, and shelled the fort for three hours. The fort seemed in an angry mood and returned the fire with its whole strenth. This was kept up a portion of each day.

Nine inch guns were [sent] from the fleet which formed a naval battery under command of Lieut. Herbert Tyson of our ship to assist the bombardment. They were highly complimented afterwards by Gen. Granger for their effective work.[10]

On the 20th of August there was sufficient guns (40) in position to keep a continual fire on Fort Morgan night and day. About this time several fires occurred in the fort. Our batterys grew nearer to the fort. On the 21st a battery of 4 heavy guns opened on them within five hundred yards of the fort.

On the 22nd the whole fleet was ordered to take part and took position in front of the fort and, together with the shore batterys, made one of the most furious bombardments ever witnessed. This was kept up during most of the day. Fires again started within the fort [and] we could plainly

139

see the flames. The enemy fire now grew weaker and it was evident they were having a troubled time within the fort. We learned after that the citidel had been fired several times by our shell and the last fire had consumed it altogether.[11]

The fire from our side was kept up with intermission untill daylight while the return from the fort grew weaker and weaker. Soon after midnight they ceased firing and at daylight a white flag was displayed from the ramparts. It was received with great cheers from the fleet and the batterys on shore. The fleet anchored close under the walls of the fort and soon after fired a salute of one charge from each gun in the fleet in honor of the capture.[12]

We found the fort battered to a shapeless mass, nearly all the guns dismounted or disabled, the Citidel and all the wood work consumed by fire. There was wreck and confusion every where, arms, provisions and stores of all kinds forming a jumbled obstruction to the passage ways. The garrison were worn and jaded. They held out till they could hold no longer. By their bravery and indurance they won the respect and friendship of the victors.[13]

A few of them were brought as prisoners on the *Hartford*, among them a little Irishman who had been opposed to us in nearly all the previous fights of the *Hartford* along the Mississippi River. We knew he was telling the truth from incidents he related and that none could know except he was there. He told us he was shifted with the reinforcements to the points we were to attack and what a dread they had of the *Hartford*, they knowing her by the Admiral's pennant. She was alway[s] the center of their fire. Many thought she had a charmed existence, notwithstanding their heaviest fire directed against her, she always came out of battle as trim as she went in.

This old enemy was treated as an old friend. He was naked and hungry when he came on board. The men supplyed him abundantly with every thing he needed, treating him with the greatest kindness untill he was paroled and sent to New Orleans.

After we found ourselfs in possession of Mobile Bay and its emmediate surroundings and as the enemy had sunk a number of vessels in Dog River, obstructing the channel which at the best only carried nine feet of water. It was impossible for our fleet, drawing from ten to twenty feet to reach the city of Mobile.[14]

So the *Hartford* sailed for Pensacola. Here we refitted with our masts and spars and did some temporary repairs, getting the ship back to her usual appearance.

PART 5
HOME

WAR SERVICE ENDS

Diggins compresses the time frame and the *Hartford's* itinerary in his closing section. Ship and crew remained in Gulf waters, mostly at Mobile, until November 28, 1864. Then the flagship sailed for Pensacola, leaving there on November 30 for New York, where she arrived on December 13.[1]

Omitted from his account were a princely gift to Farragut and his promotion. First came the promotion, when Congress created the grade of vice admiral on December 22, and, on the next day, Lincoln signed the bill and named Farragut as the first to hold the rank in the United States Navy. Pay for the new vice admiral was $7,000 a year while at sea, $6,000 for shore duty, and $5,000 when awaiting orders. Next came a munificent present of $50,000 from the city's merchants and citizens, with which they hoped Farragut would buy a home to live among them. Farragut did just that, with some cash left over, when he and his wife bought a handsome brownstone on East 36th Street in Manhattan for $33,000.[2]

In conclusion, Diggins offers an assessment of Farragut as leader, officer, and man. With many others, he praised Farragut's courage and leadership. Quartermaster John H. Knowles declared that "When ever there was any fighting going on he was always in the lead." Knowles recalled that when steaming down the Mississippi, Farragut summoned all hands to muster and "thanked us for our good behavior during the Mississippi campaign. . . ." Still, Diggins found the admiral wanting as a human being, saying that he and other crewmen thought Farragut was a "cold fish."[3]

Then or now, however, warship captains and fleet commanders do not engage in popularity contests, nor do they fraternize with underlings. In the kingdom of a naval vessel, large or small, success and survival require strict discipline, quick decisions, and immediate obedience. For many free-born Americans or Americanized immigrants, many aspects of that authoritarian regime were hard to swallow. As a consequence, the navy found it difficult to attract Americans, and the result was that a large proportion of enlisted men were foreigners. In early 1863, *Hartford*'s crew of 324 had 216 who were foreign-born, more than two-thirds of her complement.[4]

In any event, the "cold fish" label was probably as much a matter of perception as of fact. Very junior officers often described him as affable, and he concerned himself about crew morale and well-being. A young captain's clerk who had chatted with Farragut irreverently said he "is a very clever old salt," while a midshipman said he was "jovial and talkative" and had "a winning smile and a most charming manner." With that same charm, Farragut answered a mother's plea for her son's promotion and, while steaming down the Mississippi, mustered all hands to thank them for their "good behavior" during the long upriver campaign.[5]

Further, Farragut expressed his worries about the welfare of his men and told his civilian superiors that it was vital to care for his Jack Tars, the then prevailing term for sailors, the ordinary enlisted men. Concerned about a shortage of navy doctors and medical supplies, he wrote, "My greatest anxiety now is to proper comforts for the sick and wounded . . . It is a great gratification to *Jack* to see that his comforts are looked to, when he is sick."[6]

We sailed for New Orleans and, after a short stay, for New York where the fighting cruise of the *Hartford* ended December 1864.

On our arrival in [New York] harbor, the forts fired a salute. As we advanced up the bay the foreign man of war lying in harbor saluted in honor of the Admiral, all of which we returned. As we neared the city, a steamer came along side with a committee of citizens on board to take the Admiral to the city where a grand reception by the citizens awaited him.[7]

We had a very rough passage from Key West to New York. Off Hatteras we experienced one of the heavyest gails ever known of that stormy cape. We were hove to for three days untill much of our headrails were stove in and all but two of our boats carried away, among them the dinghy and the Admiral's barge. Those two boats were all that remained of the boats that we began the cruise with. The others were all shot away. The Admiral's barge had been often riddled and patched untill not half of the old boat remained. The Admiral seemed attached to her and every effort was made to save her. She shipped a sea and a moment later was dangling in two pieces from the davits and all the fittings went with her.[8]

The *Hartford*'s crew was discharged at the Brooklyn Yard Dec. 24th 1864. Of about 380 men that made up her crew when she sailed from Philadelphia three years [earlier] only forty remained of them and only a few of them escaped being more or less injured. We had three captains during the cruise, two executive officers and continual changes among the lesser officers. The Admiral and Lieut. J. Crittenden Watson and Lieut. Herbert Tyson were all that remained of the original officers of the ship.

[Appraisal of Farragut]

Admiral David G. Farragut was a man slightly below the medium height with a body well rounded and filled out, not at all reaching corpulency. He had a full head and face in full proportion with his body. He had rather a serrious cast of countenence which seemed always ready to change to a smile. He could be most agreeable or stern, his face always expressed his feeling as plain as words. He was plain and unassuming in his dress and manner, very sociable among the officers and would heartily enjoy a good joke. He was approachable to any one at any time and had a pleasant business like way of bringing matters to a point.

He was as light and active in his movements as any boy on the ship, climbing any where through the rigging with natural ease, never using more than one hand at one time while standing in the rigging. While on the blockade, when bringing him along side the ship in a heavy seaway, he would grab the swinging manropes and go up the side hand over hand. At one of the battles of Vicksburg, while standing in the mizzen rigging, the two after shrouds on which he was standing were shot a way, letting him swing suddenly towards the mast. Before any one could help him, he quickly grabbed some of running rigging at mast and slid to the deck and in a moment later was at his old place on the poop deck.

He was as cool and calm in the height of battle as at morning drill and always seeking with the *Hartford* the position where he could do the most damage to the enemy, regardless of danger.

He was inclined to be religious, but made no display of it. I never saw him angry or excited but twice, when the Rebel ram *Arkansas Traveler* escaped from Yazoo River to Vicksburg, passing through Admiral Davis' and Farragut's fleets. Farragut come on deck (it was about 6 a.m.) just as she was passing our ship. He was in his night cloths and a white night cap on. He remained on deck in this attire untill she passed out of sight. As he turned to go below, he remarked, "There is damnable neglect or worse some where."[9]

He then ordered signals to the fleet to get under way and prepare for action. That evening we made the second attack on Vicksburg.

He was both excited and angry when the *Brooklyn* stopped in front of Fort Morgan when he hailed Captain Alden several times to go ahead and hailed to Alden, "Damn the torpedoes, go ahead."

While he had the full respect and confidence of the crew as a fighter, he was not popular with the men. As one of the men expressed it, he was as cold blooded as a fish. He was the naval laws and regulations personified. The interest of the government was his first thought, in all matters great and small, [rather] than his own.

Beyond these he showed no interest. He certainly showed no partiality to the crew of the *Hartford*. If one of the men who had been through all the battles with him fell in error, he received no mercy at the hand of the Admiral. After the Battle of Mobile Bay, though the *Hartford* crew stood the brunt of the battle and lost more men than the rest of the fleet together, there was thirty-seven of his crew recommended by their emmediate commanding officers for Medals of Honor for distinguished bravery during the action. He ordered the number reduced to ten, while the *Richmond*, which was scarcely in the fight, received 35, the *Brooklyn* 30, and all other vessels proportionately larger than the *Hartford*.[10]

After a battle he would go through and carefully examine the shot holes and the damage done to the ship. He would pass and step over the wounded and dying without remark or notice, but examine critically all injury to the ship.

He had none of those qualities that would warm men's heart to him. The old ship had a warmer place in the men's heart than their Admiral. But he knew how to command respect and obedience.

EPILOGUE

Bartholomew Diggins, though honorably discharged after three years of service, did not stay out of a uniform for long, nor did he ever stray too far from the navy and Civil War days.

He joined the Washington, D.C., police force, advancing to sergeant's rank. Then he became captain of the watch for the Navy, State, and War Building in the nation's capital.[1]

He married Mary H. Wallace, another native of Ireland and four years younger than Diggins, on May 12, 1869. They produced eight children, the last three dying in their first years of life. Their second-born was a boy, promptly named David Farragut Diggins.[2]

During those peaceful postwar years, Diggins became an officer of the Medal of Honor Legion, a Mason, and regularly attended various official ceremonies, including the 1881 unveiling of a statue of Farragut in Washington, D.C. Probably the ceremony most filled with memories and nostalgia occurred when Diggins gave Farragut's old pennant to Admiral George Dewey on the latter's triumphal return from the Spanish-American War in September 1899. According to a *New York Times* reporter, tears glistened in Dewey's eyes as he accepted Farragut's flag, as both he and Diggins perhaps remembered the star-crossed passage of the Port Hudson batteries. It was then that Confederate fire disabled Dewey's ship, the USS *Mississippi*, forcing surviving crew to abandon her to drift down stream and blow up. And it was then that Diggins and shipmates found themselves isolated on the Mississippi River for months as Farragut commanded a two-ship fleet.[3]

While that was long ago, Dewey wrote Diggins that of all the gifts he had received, "[n]one . . . has given me more pleasure than this, the flag of my great predecessor." Dewey added that he would treasure it as "one of my most valued possessions."[4]

Even as Diggins relived those exciting days, he also attended to practical matters. In 1872, he applied for a Civil War pension. An examining navy surgeon ruled that Diggins suffered "Five eighths" disability as a consequence of gunshot wounds to his left arm and right chest inflicted by the enemy on May 28, 1862. By 1916, this earned him a pension of $24 a month, a fair sum in those days.[5]

However, a later effort to have himself placed on the retired list as a chief boatswain met resistance from the Navy, though he submitted a raft of supportive letters from Civil War officers who had become admirals. Navy Department officials told members of the House Committee on Naval Affairs that such a private bill "would establish a harmful precedent." Furthermore, they said, Diggins last served in the navy more than thirty-seven years before and, besides that, there were more suitable lesser grades than that of chief boatswain.[6]

Diggins succeeded in two other endeavors during those years, both legacies: most important and lasting, he wrote his recollections, and he also invented and patented a combined "hammock-support and shelter-tent." Apparently his patent, issued in November 1899, did not enrich him, as he pushed for a promotion on the navy's retired list and an increased pension after that.[7]

While it is unknown exactly when he penned his recollections, he probably wrote them at intervals and after some official records became available. He may have relied upon a diary, journal, or letters home to aid his memory. However, he never speaks of keeping a written record or sending or receiving letters during those war years, so it is merely speculation to suggest he may have had recourse to contemporary notes. Yet some of his narrative's anecdotes are so fresh and detailed that a reader can justifiably suspect a real time source.

Again, it is also unknown how and when his manuscript ended up in the New York Public Library's archives, though there is no doubt as to its authenticity. Over the years, many historians have learned of his recollections, abstracted information, and cited Diggins in their own works.[8]

He left behind a solid, noteworthy legacy when he died on February 24, 1917. His wife had died just about a year earlier, on January 29, 1916. Both are buried together at Arlington National Cemetery in Virginia.[9]

Diggins's hero, David Glasgow Farragut, named the navy's first vice admiral in December 1864, also became the nation's first full admiral on July 25, 1866. On that same day, the Senate confirmed Lieutenant General Grant as the first four-star full general.[10]

Soon the navy appointed Farragut commander of the European squadron and sent him off on a goodwill tour. Leaving behind light official duties and many social engagements, Farragut sailed with Mrs. Farragut in 1867, both aboard the USS *Franklin*, a big and new screw frigate. During this grand tour, Farragut chatted with European heads of state, his naval counterparts, reviewed fleets, and toured shore installations.[11]

Returning to New York, he and his wife then traveled to the West Coast, visiting the Mare Island Navy Shipyard. Going back East, he suffered a heart attack in Chicago. In failing health, Farragut repaired to Portsmouth, N.H., where he died on August 14, 1870.[12]

David D. Porter, who visited the *Hartford* during the Mississippi River phase and was often mentioned by Diggins, followed in Farragut's footsteps in the postwar navy. He became a vice admiral in 1866 and in 1870, the year of Farragut's death, won the full admiral slot. As the navy's senior officer, Porter became very influential in naval affairs, too much so for some in the government. So they furled his sails for him, launching an effort to reduce his salary from $13,000 to $8,000 yearly. His influence upon the naval establishment soon waned. Porter died early in 1891 and is buried in Arlington National Cemetery. In his honor, the navy has named five warships after him.[13]

Lewis A. Kimberly, Diggins's favorite officer and a man he admired, also sailed to Europe in early 1865 aboard the USS *Colorado*, the deep-draft frigate that could not pass over the bar on the approaches to New Orleans in 1862. After varied duties, he took command of the Pacific Station and was promoted to rear admiral, both in 1887. Retiring in 1892, he died ten years later in Massachusetts.[14]

John Crittenden Watson, Farragut's flag lieutenant, was another officer Diggins respected. After a variety of ship and shore duties, Watson rose to commodore's rank on the battleship *Oregon*. He and his ship helped win the battle of Santiago, Cuba, on July 3, 1898. Advanced to rear admiral in 1899, he commanded the Asiatic fleet until 1900. He retired in 1904 and died in Washington, D.C., on December 14, 1923.[15]

Captain Percival Drayton, who commanded the *Hartford* during the Mobile Bay fight, never achieved flag rank. Death cut his navy career short when he fell ill and died in Washington, D.C., on August 4, 1865. However, in the next century, the navy named two destroyers after him.[16]

Quartermaster John H. Knowles, the seasoned old mariner who lashed Farragut to the rigging during the Mobile Bay fight, wound up at the naval academy, assigned to the USS *Philox*, a sidewheel steamer used as a practice ship for the midshipmen. In 1878, he complained that he had got little prize money but plenty of fighting during the war. In a letter to Loyall Farragut, the admiral's son, Knowles confided that he had married, remained sober for twelve months, and that he hoped to buy a shanty for himself and his wife of four years. Born in 1830, he died in 1895, always an old salt.[17]

Confederate leaders who fought Farragut often experienced several reverses. First, was the defeat; then blame or distrust from their own side; next came loss of freedom as prisoners of war. Finally, those who had served for years in the prewar army or navy forfeited their pensions when the North won the war.

Major General Mansfield Lovell, ordered to defend New Orleans, was an 1842 graduate of West Point who was severely wounded during the Mexican-American War. Later he worked as a civilian in New York City, but threw his lot in with the Confederacy in 1861. Even though General Robert E. Lee praised his line of defense at New Orleans, and though a court of inquiry cleared him of responsibility for the city's loss, he was largely sidelined for the rest of the war. Afterwards he returned to New York City, where he worked as an engineer until his death in 1884.[17]

Lieutenant General John C. Pemberton, Vicksburg's defender, was born in Philadelphia, Pa. A member of West Point's class of 1837, he served with distinction in the Mexican-American War. In 1848, he married a Virginia woman, and that likely influenced his decision to resign his commission and join the Confederate Army. But his northern birth prompted many to doubt his loyalty to the southern cause, particularly since he surrendered Vicksburg on July 4, 1863. As a consequence, he never again held a post of command commensurate with his rank. So, in 1864, he resigned as a lieutenant general and accepted an appointment as a lieutenant colonel of artillery. He served in that capacity until the war's end. Then he returned to Pennsylvania, dying there in 1881.[18]

Franklin Buchanan first spent two months in the naval hospital at Pensacola for treatment of the compound fracture of his left leg. On the mend, Federals then transferred him to a prison cell at Fort Lafayette in New York's harbor. He won exchange as a prisoner and returned to Mobile, just in time to see Union troops occupy the city in April 1865. Soon he was a prisoner again, and Federals carried him north once more, to Hampton Roads.

Released, Buchanan returned to the charred ruins of his home, burned during the war, on Maryland's Eastern Shore. Neighbors and friends aided the crippled Buchanan and his family while they rebuilt their home. But with his navy pension forfeited, he suffered financially until he was appointed president of the Maryland Agricultural College. An academic dispute ended that arrangement, whereupon he returned to Mobile to work for an insurance company there for more than a year. Back in Maryland, he died in 1874 at seventy-four years of age.[19]

Less than half a century after his death, when the Civil War's fiercest passions had subsided, the navy named three destroyers after Buchanan, launching the first one on January 2, 1919.[20]

Brigadier General Richard L. Page, CSA, was formerly a commander in both the United States and Confederate States navies. After his capture, Federal authorities tried him on charges of destroying surrendered property, such as spiking cannon and ruining gunpowder, a violation of the rules. However, he was acquitted and subsequently imprisoned at Fort Lafayette in New York until released in September 1865. Ten years later, he became superintendent of public schools in Norfolk, Va. He held that post until 1883. Finally, Page moved north to Blue Ridge Summit, Pa., where he died at the age of ninety-four in August 1901.

A little more than one hundred years after the Mobile Bay battle, the navy named a guided missile escort after him, the 3,400-ton *Richard L. Page.*[21]

Colonel Charles DeWitt Anderson endured vilification by some Confederates for his "inexplicable" surrender of Fort Gaines. Farragut, however, praised Anderson for doing the sensible thing and said Page and others were in no position to criticize him.[22]

Neither denunciations nor plaudits affected his immediate status. He was a prisoner of war until January 1865, when he was exchanged. Anderson returned to his native Texas, where he worked as a civil engineer, including two years as Austin's engineer. Somehow he wound up as a lighthouse keeper at Galveston, where he and his wife barely survived the great 1899 hurricane. He died there in 1901 at seventy-four.[23]

Most places where Diggins fought are now historic landmarks or parks. Forts Jackson and St. Philip on the river approach to New Orleans are now overgrown National Historic Landmarks. Both have suffered much damage from hurricanes and flooding and are now in poor condition.[24]

About seventy miles upriver, New Orleans is as lively today as it was in Diggins's time. Though the horse-drawn street cars and many Civil War–era buildings are gone, the city itself stands as a large Civil War landmark. Also, museums, plaques, and tours enlighten visitors about the city's role in the war.[25]

More than two hundred miles above New Orleans is Vicksburg, the focus of the Mississippi River campaign. There now is a National Military Park and a National Cemetery, together embracing more than 1,800 acres. The park includes more than 1,300 monuments, plaques, markers, and tablets, as well as miles of trenches, earthworks, and 144 emplaced cannon; the national cemetery holds about 17,000 Union soldiers, many unidentified. There also is the USS *Cairo,* a gunboat sunk by a mine in the nearby Yazoo River and raised in 1964.[26]

Down river, between Vicksburg and New Orleans, lies Port Hudson, the scene of Farragut's disastrous effort to pass its batteries. While thousands on both sides became casualties and the Confederate defenders were reduced to eating mule and rat meat during the forty-eight day siege, the battle there has not attracted as much interest as the campaign and siege of Vicksburg. Now it is belatedly a National Historic Landmark, a Louisiana State Historic Site, and also holds a National Cemetery.[27]

Though the fighting in lower Mobile Bay had ended, its many torpedoes continued to take a toll of men and ships. Just a few days after Fort Morgan surrendered, sailors clearing the waters of mines wrestled one ashore with careless vigor. That caused an explosion, killing five and wounding nine.[28]

When Federal forces advanced on Mobile's inner defenses in March 1865, mines caused casualties and more sinkings. By one careful tabulation, eight ships and a ship's launch went down after contacting the "infernal machines." Those losses included three gunboats and two monitors.[29]

As early as May 1862, Confederates had thickly seeded Yorktown, Va., with land mines and booby traps. Omitting the booby traps, they followed the Yorktown example at Mobile. To defend Fort Blakely and Spanish Fort, works guarding the city, they planted many land mines, or "subterra torpedoes," as they were then called. Usually these were improvised devices, using converted mortar rounds or simply burying artillery shells with percussion fuse nose up. Confederates buried mines before the forts or on approach roads, gently covered them with a board and sprinkled dirt on top. When a man or horse stepped on these devices, the blast killed or maimed nearby troops and animals. During the final assault on Spanish Fort, attacking black troops tripped a mine, killing and wounding thirteen.[30]

After the forts fell and Federals occupied Mobile on April 12, 1865, Grant declared the costly attacks should never have happened. He said, "The war was practically over . . . if left alone, it would within a few days have fallen into our hands without any bloodshed whatever."[31]

Mobile Bay ended battle operations for the USS *Hartford*, so no more blood was shed on her decks. After repairs in New York, she became the Asiatic squadron's flagship and, in 1882, she served as flagship of the North Atlantic Station. After more reconditioning and rebuilding, *Hartford* served as a training and cruise ship for Naval Academy midshipmen. Sea-going days ended in 1912, when the navy moved her to Charleston, S.C., as a station ship. Finally, in 1945, the navy classified her as a relic and towed her to the Norfolk Navy Yard.

Neglected for years, the *Hartford* sank at her Norfolk berth in November 1956, almost one hundred years after her launching.[32]

However, she still survives in parts and pieces. Some of her anchors and cannon greet visitors here and there. There is a lively trade in pieces of wood reportedly pried from her husk, and a fragment of the flag that she supposedly flew during the Mobile Bay battle sold at auction for $3,459 in 2011.[33]

When the real thing is not available, reproductions and replicas are. The Maine Historical Society offers for sale a reproduction of a gangway board in its possession, "believed to be from the USS *Hartford*." Finally, the National Civil War Naval Museum in Columbus, Ga., has recreated and housed the *Hartford's* berth deck, wardroom, and captain's cabin.[34]

NOTES

INTRODUCTION

1. Joseph P. Reidy, "Black Men in Navy Blue during the Civil War," *Prologue* 33, 3 (Fall 2001):1, www.archives.gov/publications/prologue/2001/fall/black-sailor-1.html.
2. Ibid, 5; Michael J. Bennett, *Union Jacks: Yankee Sailors in the Civil War* (Chapel Hill: Univ. of North Carolina Press, 2004), 9, for a "whopping" 45 percent after he scoured enlistment records; Ella Lonn, *Foreigners in the Union Army and Navy* (1951; reprint, New York: Greenwood Press, 1969), 637.
3. Bennett, *Union Jacks*, 5; Robert Means Thompson and Richard Wainwright, eds., *Confidential Correspondence of Gustavus Vasa Fox, Assistant Secretary of the Navy, 1861–1865* (New York: De Vinne Press, 1918), 2:34, for captain's complaint.
4. For ships, see Lonn, *Foreigners*, 618; for chart on numbers, also see John A. Grier, "A Sketch of Naval Life," in *Military Essays and Recollections* (Chicago: Dial Press, 1899), 3:303, where he reports that fifty-two of the eighty-nine ships were sailing vessels; for manpower, see Spencer C. Tucker, *Blue and Gray Navies: The Civil War Afloat* (Annapolis: Naval Institute Press, 2006), 1, 5.
5. George W. Dalzell, *Flight from the Flag: The Continuing Effect of the Civil War on the American Carrying Trade* (Chapel Hill: Univ. of North Carolina Press, 1940), 237–62; Bern Anderson, *By Sea and By River: The Naval History of the Civil War* (1962; reprint, New York: Da Capo, 1989), 9, 12; John A. Butler, *Sailing on Friday: The Perilous Voyage of America's Merchant Marine* (Washington, D.C.: Brassey's, 1997), 100–1.
6. See *Red Rover* entry in *Dictionary of American Naval Fighting Ships*, Naval History and Heritage Command, access at NHHC website, http://www.history.navy.mil/ (hereafter cited as *DANFS*, NHHC). The ship marked another first when female nurses helped staff that hospital ship.
7. Porter to Fox, Dec. 5, 1862, and Fox to Porter, Dec. 11, 1862, in Thompson and Wainwright, *Confidential Correspondence*, 2:151, 152–53; Saunders to Mother, Jan. 28, 1864, in Ronald K. Huch, ed., "The Civil War Letters of Herbert Saunders," *Register of the Kentucky Historical Society* 69 (January 1971): 20.
8. Dennis J. Ringle, *Life in Mr. Lincoln's Navy* (Annapolis: Naval Institute Press, 1999), 21–22, for sailor enlistment bonus.

9. Vail to Sister Carrie, Oct. 13, 1864, in I. E. Vail, *Three Years on the Block-ade: A Naval Experience* (New York: Abbey Press, 1902), 5, 12; Joseph T. Collins to father, March 11, 1863, in James J. Heslin, ed., "Two New Yorkers in the Union Navy," *New York Historical Society Quarterly* 43, 2 (April 1959), 191.

10. Journal of Carston DeWitt, p. 1, G. W. Blunt White Library, Mystic Seaport Museum, Mystic, Conn. (hereafter cited as DeWitt Journal); William N. Bock to brother George, Feb. 17, 1864, Abraham Lincoln Presidential Library, Springfield, Ill. (hereafter cited as William N. Bock Papers); W. H. Price to Sir, May 2, 1864, Lincoln Presidential Library (hereafter cited as W. H. Price Papers).

11. Muster roll, USS *Hartford*, Dec. 20, 1864, National Archives and Records Administration, Washington, D.C.; letter from Kim Y. McKeithan, National Archives, to editor, Dec. 3, 2012, in editor's possession.

12. Jan. 10, 1863, entry in Gideon Welles, *Diary of Gideon Welles* (Boston: Houghton Mifflin, 1911) 1:218; Ann Preston to Fowler (son), April 30, 1862, Preston Family Papers, Bentley Historical Library, University of Michigan, Ann Arbor, Mich. (hereafter cited as Preston Papers); William W. Van Cleaf to mother, March 14, 1862, William W. Van Cleaf Papers, 1861–1897, Archibald L. Alexander Library, Rutgers, The State University of New Jersey, New Brunswick, N.J. (hereafter cited as Van Cleaf Papers); William N. Bock to Mother, May 5, 1864 (William N. Bock Papers). Bennett, *Union Jacks*, 182, citing *Report of the Secretary of the Navy . . . December 1866*, 41; William F. Fox, *Regimental Losses in the American Civil War* (Albany, N.Y.: Albany Publishing Company, 1889), 537–39. Fox also lists casualties by ship. Some other historians report slightly higher figures, but Fox and the Secretary of the Navy are reliable.

13. James E. Campbell, "The Mississippi Squadron," *Ohio Archaeological and Historical Quarterly* 34, 1 (January 1925): 62.

14. For the *Tecumseh,* see Jack Friend, *West Wind, Flood Tide: The Battle of Mobile Bay* (Annapolis, Md.: Naval Institute Press, 2004), 181–82. For the *Mound City,* see C. H. Davis, "Memoir of Charles Henry Davis, 1807–1877," 39, accessed November 23, 2013, http://books.nap.edu/html/biomems/cdavis04.pdf; Van Cleaf to Mother, June 22, 1862, Van Cleaf Papers; W. H. C. Michael, "The Mississippi Flotilla," in *War Sketches and Incidents*, vol. 1: Military Order of the Loyal Legion of the United States, Nebraska Commandery (all similar citations will be hereafter cited as MOLLUS with the state commandery specified, as in MOLLUS-Neb.) (Omaha: Burkley Print, 1902), accessed at MOLLUS War Papers, http://suvcw.org/mollus/warpapers/NEv1p21.htm/; "Ben" to Roxbury City *Gazette,* dated June 21, 1862, published July 17, 1862. For the *Tyler,* see *Official Records of the Union and Confederate Navies in the War of the Rebellion* (hereafter cited as *ORN*), 30 vols. (Washington, D.C.: GPO, 1894–1922), 19:37–41, 68–69; S. B. Coleman, "A July Morning with the Rebel Ram 'Arkansas,'" *War Papers,*

vol. 1, MOLLUS-Mich. (Detroit: Winn & Hammond, 1890), 9–10, accessed at http://suvcw.org/mollus/warpapers/warpapers.htm/. Lastly, for the *Cricket* and the *Underwriter*, see Fox, *Regimental Losses*, 539, and *DANFS*, NHHC. Confederate Navy surgeon Daniel B. Conrad, who treated the *Underwriter*'s wounded, found one sailor whose "head had been cleft in two" by a cutlass. Neil Kagan and Steven G. Hyslop, eds., *Smithsonian Civil War: Inside the National Collection* (Washington, D.C.: Smithsonian Books, 2013), 266.

15. Fox, *Regimental Losses*, 537, lists 373 navy deaths by accident, drowning, and scalding, but that is a minimal count. For fatal falls, see John R. Bartlett, "The 'Brooklyn' at the Passage of the Forts," in *Battles and Leaders of the Civil War* (hereafter cited as *B&L*), ed. Robert U. Johnson and Clarence C. Buel (New York: The Century Co., 1884–1888), 2:60n; Edward A. Butler, "Personal Experiences in the Navy, 1862–65," *War Papers*, vol. 2, MOLLUS-Maine (Portland, Me.: LeFavor Tower Co., 1902), 191, accessed at http://suvcw.org/mollus/warpapers/warpapers.htm/; Boston *Journal*, Nov. 8, 1862, accessed at http://www.letterscivilwar.org/11-8-62-uss_con.html/ (Nov. 18, 2009); Kent Packard, ed., "Jottings by the Way: A Sailor's Log—1862–1864," *Pennsylvania Magazine of History and Biography* 71 (April 1947): 143. For whirling capstans, see Charles S. Foltz, *Surgeon of the Seas: The Adventurous Life of Surgeon General Jonathan M. Foltz in the Days of Wooden Ships, Told from his Notes of the Moment* (Indianapolis: Bobbs-Merrill, 1931), 236–37; William C. Holton, *Cruise of the U.S. Flag-Ship Hartford, 1861–1863; being a Narrative of all Her Operations Since Going into Commission, in 1862, until Her Return to New York in 1863*, ed. B. S. Osbon (New York: L. W. Paine, 1863), 21; William B. Gould, IV, ed., *Diary of a Contraband: The Civil War Passage of a Black Sailor* (Stanford, Calif.: Stanford Univ. Press, 2002), 162. For falling objects, see Foltz, *Surgeon*, 271; Josiah P. Higgins, *Yeoman in Farragut's Fleet: The Civil War Diary of Josiah Parker Higgins*, ed. E. C. Herrmann (Carmel, Calif.: Guy Victor Publications, 1999), 52; Keeler, *Aboard the USS Florida*, 175.

16. For exploding cannon, see Benjamin F. Sands, *From Reefer to Rear Admiral: Reminiscences and Journal Jottings of Nearly Half a Century of Naval Life* (New York: Frederic A. Stokes Co., 1899), 259; Robley D. Evans, *A Sailor's Log: Recollections of Forty Years of Naval Life* (New York: D. Appleton and Co., 1901), 74–75; Henry R. Browne and Symmes E. Browne, *From the Fresh-Water Navy* (United States Naval Institute, 1970), 44. For other mishaps, Packard, "Jottings," 130–31; Joseph W. Shively, "The U.S.S. Mississippi at the Capture of New Orleans," *War Papers*, vol. 1, MOLLUS-D.C. (Washington, D.C.: Read before the Commandery, 1853), 231; Vail, *Three Years*, 46; and Bennett, *Union Jacks*, 42, for cigar and powder.

17. Robert W. Daly, "Pay and Prize Money in the Old Navy, 1776–1899," US Naval Institute *Proceedings* 74 (Aug. 1948): 967–71; Frederic Stanhope Hill, *Twenty Years at Sea; Or, Leaves from My Old Logbook* (Boston: Houghton,

Mifflin and Co., 1893), 193. For chicanery, see George Edward Clark, *Seven Years of a Sailor's Life* (Boston: Adams & Co., 1917), 194; Sands, *From Reefer to Rear Admiral*, 257; George H. Perkins, *Letters of Capt. Geo. Hamilton Perkins, U.S.N.* (1886; repr., Freeport, N.Y.; Books for Libraries, 1970), 130.

18. George W. Brown, "The Mortar Flotilla and Its Connection with the Bombardment and Capture of Forts Jackson and St. Philip," in *Personal Recollection*, Ser. 1, MOLLUS-N.Y. (New York: Published by the Commandery, 1891): 175, accessed at http://suvcw.org/mollus/warpapers/warpapers. htm/; Butts, "A Cruise Along the Blockade," 25; Knowles to Loyall Farragut, Dec. 15 [18?], 1878, David G. Farragut Papers, 1815–1964, MS 1887, Special Collections, John C. Hodges Library, University of Tennessee, Knoxville, Tenn. (hereafter cited as Farragut Papers-Tenn.).

19. E. H. Hults, "Aboard the Galena at Mobile," *Civil War Times Illustrated* 10, 2 (May 1971) pt 2:37.

20. Farragut to Assistant Secretary of the Navy G. V. Fox, March 5, 1864, in Thompson and Wainwright, *Confidential Correspondence*, 1:348; James E. Henneberry journal, entry Jan. 1, 1862, Chicago Historical Society, Chicago, Ill. (hereafter cited as Henneberry journal); letter to Cousin, April 10, 1864, in Arthur M. Schlesinger, ed., "A Blue Bluejacket's Letters Home, 1863–1864," *New England Quarterly* 1, 4 (October 1928), 563.

21. G. M. to editor, Worcester *Aegis & Transcipt*, Feb. 28, 1864; letter to Sister Carrie, Oct. 15, 1864, in Daniel Graves, ed., *Civil War Letters from a Gunboat Sailor* (N.p.: Lulu.com, 2006), 33.

22. Ringle, *Life*, 113–14; Geer to wife, Dec. 2, 1863, reporting scurvy on USS *Vermont*, in George S. Geer Papers, Mariners' Museum Library, Newport News, Va. (hereafter cited as Geer Papers); Hill, *Twenty Years*, 220.

23. Guy R. Everson, ed., "Service Afield and Afloat: A Reminiscence of the Civil War," *Indiana Magazine of History* 89, 1 (March 1993): 47, for geese; letter to Rosie, June 2, 1864, in Lester L. Swift, ed., "Letters from a Sailor on a Tinclad," *Civil War History* 7, 1 (March 1961): 55, for raccoons; Rowland Stafford True, "Life Aboard a Gunboat," *Civil War Times Illustrated* 9, 10 (February 1971): 41, for cattle. For fishing examples, see James L. B. Blauvelt to Mother, Oct. 12, 1863, James L. B. Blauvelt Papers, Duke University, Durham, N.C. (hereafter cited as Blauvelt Papers); Van Cleaf to brother, May 4, 1862, Van Cleaf Papers; Clark, *Seven Years*, 208; Oliver A. Batcheller, "The Battle of Mobile Bay: Recollections of One Who Took Part in the Battle," *Scribner's Monthly* 13, 4 (February 1877): 62.

24. George Dewey, *Autobiography of George Dewey, Admiral of the Navy* (New York: Charles Scribner's Sons, 1913), 50; Batcheller, "Battle of Mobile Bay," 62; Leslie G. Morrow, *Journal of Leslie G. Morrow, Captain's Clerk of the U. S. Steamer* Galena, ed. Albert Murrow (Yorba Linda, Calif.: A. P. Morrow, 1988), 54; William F. Hutchinson, "Life on the Texan Blockade," *Personal Narratives*, Ser. 3, Rhode Island Soldiers and Sailors Historical Society (RISSHS) (Providence: RISSHS, 1883), 24–25, accessed at http://

suvcw.org/mollus/warpapers/warpapers.htm/; Edward Blue to Frank L. Stickney, May 19, 1864, Frank L. Stickney Papers (hereafter cited as Blue in Stickney Papers), Library of Congress, Washington, D.C.; for ship drills and duties, see Glenn F. Williams, "Uncle Sam's Webfeet: The Union Navy in the Civil War," *International Journal of Naval History* 1, 1 (April 2002): 1–16, accessed at www.ijnhonline.org (March 15, 2009).

25. Graves, *Civil War Letters*, 41; Charles E. Stedman, *The Civil War Sketchbook of Charles Ellery Stedman, Surgeon, United States Navy*, ed. Jim Dan Hill (San Rafael, Calif.: Presidio Press, 1976), 95, for sketch of skylarking; Clark, *Seven Years*, 208, 213–14; Vail, *Three Years*, 91. For pets, Keeler, *Aboard the USS Florida*, 183; letter to Sallie, Oct. 25, 1864, in Graves, *Civil War Letters*, 41; Evans, *A Sailor's Log*, 48–49. Huch, ed., "Civil War Letters," 18, for officers' balls.

26. Fox to Sen. F. W. Grimes, May 28, 1862, in Thompson and Wainwright, *Confidential Correspondence*, 2:304.

27. "The Grog-Ration in the Navy," *New York Times*, July 29, 1862; Stephen F. Blanding, *Recollections of a Sailor Boy; or, the Cruise of the Gunboat Louisiana* (Providence, R.I.: E. A. Johnson & Co., 1887), 60–61; Sept. 1, 1862, entry, John Simpson diary, William P. Palmer Collection, Western Reserve Historical Society, Cleveland, Ohio (hereafter cited as Simpson diary); Packard, "Jottings," 136, for work needs whisky; Bright to Father, October 25, 1863, Papers of George Adams Bright, 1860–1932, Huntington Library, San Marino, Calif. (hereafter cited as Bright Papers).

28. Geer to wife, March 26, July 31, 1862, Geer Papers; Clark, *Seven Years*, 234.

29. For mail delivery, see letter to Frank, Oct. 13, 1864, in Graves, *Civil War Letters*, 36; William N. Bock to Father, Feb. 5, 1864, William N. Bock Papers. For irregular mail, see Frederic E. Davis to Parents, May 6, 1862, Frederic E. Davis Papers, Manuscript, Archives, and Rare Book Library, Emory University, Atlanta, Ga. (hereafter cited as Davis Papers); William J. Clark to Mother, July 14, 25,1863, William J. Clark Papers, Historical Society of Pennsylvania, Philadelphia, Pa. (hereafter cited as Clark Papers); Morrow, *Journal*, 47, 51.

1. TO THE MISSISSIPPI

1. For Scott's Anaconda plan, see *The War of the Rebellion: A Compilation of the Official Records of the Union and Confederate Armies* (hereafter cited as *OR*) (Washington, D.C.: GPO, 1880–1901) 51, 1:369–70. *OR* citations are from Series 1, unless otherwise noted, and indicate volume, part, and page in that order, using Arabic numerals, rather than the original Roman, for volume and part.

2. Lincoln proclaimed a blockade of southern ports on April 19, 1861. Roy P. Basler, ed., *Collected Works of Abraham Lincoln* (New Brunswick, N.J.: Rutgers Univ. Press, 1955), 4:338–39.

3. David D. Porter, "The Opening of the Lower Mississippi," *B&L*, 2:23–25, 27–28.

4. William T. Meredith, "Farragut's Capture of New Orleans," *B&L*, 2:70; Thompson and Wainwright, *Confidential Correspondence*, 2:93, 323; Lincoln to Simon Cameron, Aug. 2, 1861, Basler, *Collected Works*, 4:468–69.

5. *DANFS*, NHHC.

6. *Hartford* drew 17.2 feet, *DANFS*, NHHC.

7. John A. B. Dahlgren, a naval officer, designed the nine-inch and other muzzle-loading cannon that bore his name. Though dubbed the "soda-bottle" guns for their resemblance to soft drink bottles then in use, Dahlgren guns combined superior performance with safety in firing. Smithsonian Institute, accessed at www.civilwar.si.edu/navies_dahlgrengun.html (4/25/09); Jack Coggins, *Arms and Equipment of the Civil War* (New York: Fairfax Press, 1983), 142; Mark Mays Boatner, *Civil War Dictionary* (New York: David McKay, 1959), 218.

8. Normal complement for the *Hartford* was 302 officers and men, *DANFS*, NHHC. But wartime needs increased her crew, and she may have also carried replacements for other ships.

9. Unknown to Diggins, Farragut had informally inspected the *Hartford* at Philadelphia on Dec. 27, 1861. Charles Lee Lewis, *David Glasgow Farragut: Our First Admiral* (Annapolis, Md.: United States Naval Institute, 1943), 15.

10. Diggins's statement here about his age should resolve any conflict about his birth date and places it in 1844.

11. Ship Island lies about twelve miles from the mainland and about sixty miles from entrances to the Mississippi; after hurricanes struck, beginning in 1969, the island was split in two parts and is now much diminished. See "Ship Island" on National Park Service web site, www.nps.gov. Sailors usually disdained Ship Island. Future Admiral David D. Porter called it "this hole," while a sailmaker on the USS *Vincennes* called it a "most miserable and desolate pile of sand." Porter to Fox May 24, 1862, in Thompson and Wainwright, *Confidential Correspondence*, 2:104; Robert M. Oxley, ed., "The Civil War Gulf Blockade: The Unpublished Journal of a U.S. Navy Warrant Officer Aboard the USS *Vincennes*, 1861–1864," *International Journal of Naval History* 1, 1 (April 2002), 8, accessed at www.ijnhonline. org (March 14, 2009). Note "is now used" is another example of Diggins's using the present tense, suggesting that he relived those days as he recalled them after the war.

12. At this time the Navy split the Gulf Blockading Squadron into East and West Gulf Blockading Squadrons, with Farragut in command of the West group and McKean leading the East unit. *ORN*, 17:187, 18:7–9.

13. Bell, born in North Carolina in 1808 and appointed a midshipman in 1823, served on ships in the Atlantic, Mediterranean, and Caribbean before becoming Farragut's fleet captain. As to his dueling and swordsman abilities,

biographers fail to mention such accomplishments. US-People, NHHC website; J. T. Headley, *Farragut, and Our Naval Commanders* (New York: E. B. Trent, 1867), 523–29.

14. As the name suggests, Pilot Town was and is a base for river pilots, though Farragut's men would have found little dry land to store their stripped equipment. Judith A. Howard, "Home at the Mouth of the Mississippi," *Southern Cultures*, 14, 2 (Summer 2009): 69.

15. The *Brooklyn*, a 2,532-ton screw sloop, drew 16.3 feet, while the *Hartford* drew 17.2; the 3,000-ton *Pensacola*'s draft was 18.7 feet, and the 3,220-ton sidewheel *Mississippi* drew 19 feet; but the *Colorado*, a 3,425-ton screw frigate, drew 23.9 feet, too much to cross the bar. *DANFS*, NHHC; also see Porter, "Opening," *B&L*, 2:33. Capt. Theodorus Bailey, born in 1805, entered the navy as a midshipman in 1818 and became a rear admiral in July 1866. *New York Times*, Feb. 11, 1877, p. 6.

16. Porter placed great store in his mortar boats, but others did not. Thompson and Wainwright, *Confidential Correspondence*, 2:93, 323. Diggins erred— there were 20 mortar schooners, ranging in size from 160 to 250 tons. Each giant 13-inch mortar weighed more than 17,000 pounds, using 20 pounds of powder to fire a 220 pound shell with a 11-pound explosive charge. Firing the mortars caused great concussion and recoil, the downward thrust sinking two mortar boats. One schooner's captain said the concussion "had taken nearly every door off the hinges. The arms chest and round-houses collapsed," and a gunboat sailor declared mortar crews were "deafened for life" after firing the monsters. Brown, "The Mortar Flotilla," 173, 176–77; Graves, *Civil War Letters*, 43; Coggins, *Arms and Equipment*, 96; diary entries April 19, 21, 1862, in Terry Foenander, ed., "Fire and Brimstone— Aboard the USS *Cayuga* ay Forts Jackson & St. Philip: Excerpts from the Journal of Paymaster's Clerk Samuel Massa," accessed at www.tfoenander. com/massa.htm (May 2, 2009). Diary is in Samuel Massa Papers, Special Collections, Syracuse University.

17. Mortar crews normally fired once every ten minutes but that rate varied from five- to thirty-minute intervals, and their bombardment soon set Fort Jackson ablaze. The fort's commander said that they endured a "furious storm of shell" and "this terrible battering." Porter, "Opening," *B&L*, 2:35; report of Lt.-Col. Edward H. Higgins, CSA, April 27, 1862, *OR*, 6:547.

18. That first fire raft, "a huge fiery monster . . . well calculated to strike terror and dismay to any fleet," caused pandemonium. Shively, "The USS Mississippi," 235. In use for centuries, fire ships and rafts were old weapons. In North America, the French used them against a British fleet at Quebec on June 28, 1759; and American revolutionaries also tried them against British warships on the Hudson River, Aug. 16, 1776. See www.sailingwarship. com/french-fire-rafts-attacking-the-english-fleet-off-quebec-28-June-1759. html; Lincoln Diamant, *Chaining the Hudson: The Fight for the River in the American Revolution* (New York: Fordham Univ. Press, 2004), 73, 78–81.

Mississippi flat boats, built to carry freight on one-way trips down the river, drifted with the current. Confederates had readied many fire rafts. Charles Longfellow to father, page before that marked No. 1 and April 4 [1862] in journal letter, Longfellow Papers, Houghton Library, Houghton Library, Harvard University.

19. USS *Sciota* was one of the "ninety-day gunboats" built and launched in a crash program. She and others in her class were 507-ton wooden vessels, 158 feet long with a beam of 28 feet. She operated with a crew of 65 and three cannon. *DANFS*, NHHC. Numbering the ships began a practice that spread to other squadrons and units during the war, making for easy and quick identification.

20. A mortar schooner's captain said he dropped astern to allow a mortar boat shifting from the other side to slip in ahead of him and, not an hour later, an enemy shell hit the boat now in his old place, "sinking her in five minutes." Brown, "The Mortar Flotilla," 179; diary entry April 21, 1862, in Higgins, *Yeoman*, 25. A navy surgeon thought the tree branch camouflage fooled no enemy observers, though the range to the forts was 1½ to 2 miles. Shively, "The USS Mississippi," 235–36. Note that Porter did not become a rear admiral until July 16, 1863, more than a year later.

21. As Diggins explains, sailors stripped their ships from tops to deck of extraneous equipment. They did so to prevent higher pieces, shot away during battle, from falling on men below; small boats and other deck level equipment were removed to reduce the danger of wood splinters, the cause of many wounds and deaths during battle. Winfield Scott Schley, *Forty-five Years Under the Flag* (New York: D. Appleton, 1904), 40. Since there were and are no sky hooks to lift the top masts and spars, this was an arduous task. For illustrations and text of how this was done, see John Harland, *Seamanship in the Age of Sail: An Account of the Shiphandling of the Sailing Man-of-War 1600–1860, Based on Contemporary Sources* (Annapolis, Md.: Naval Institute Press, 1984; rev. ed. 1987).

22. Capstans, upright rotating mechanisms for lifting a ship's anchor, were man-powered by pushing capstan bars, uniform lengths of wood that fitted into the capstan. Pawls, set at regular intervals in the capstan head, allowed rotating movement in one direction only. Another *Hartford* sailor reported the flying capstan bars hit five men, breaking bones, and such capstan accidents were not uncommon. Holton, *Cruise*, 21, 25; Gould, *Diary of a Contraband*, 162.

23. Federals considered several schemes to remove the chain barrier, including the use of a downward exploding petard, but in the end, hammers and cold chisels did the job. Shively, "The USS Mississippi," 233–34; Hill, *Twenty Years*, 169–70; Dewey, *Autobiography*, 59–60; Higgins, *Yeoman*, 25.

24. Farragut's men needed no dire warnings from the Royal Navy. An acting master on the USS *Richmond* recalled, "We were by no . . . means over-confident of success. . . . We were not to meet Indians or Chinese." A mid-

shipman on the USS *Brooklyn* reported that some captains thought that the whole fleet would be annihilated, while others figured that maybe one or two vessels would get by only to be sunk by enemy rams. Farragut himself told USS *Mississippi* officers that he expected to lose four or five ships in passing the forts. Hill, *Twenty Years*, 165; Bartlett, "The *Brooklyn*,"*B&L* 2:60; Shively,"The USS *Mississippi*," 237.

25. Crews hoisted light (760-pound) 12-pounder (4.6 inch bore) howitzers to the fighting tops, protecting the gunners from sharpshooters with metal shields. This enabled the gunners to send plunging fire into opposing ships or shore batteries. Thomas Harris to editor, Chelsea (Mass.) *Telegraph and Pioneer*, April 10, 1862, accessed at www.letterscivilwar.org/4–28–62a.html (February 7, 2008); Coggins, *Arms and Equipment*, 131, 145.

26. Founded in 1807, the Coast Survey later became the Coast and Geodetic Survey, the forerunner of today's National Oceanic and Atmospheric Administration (NOAA). John Cloud, "The 200th Anniversary of the Survey of the Coast," National Archives *Prologue* 39, 1 (Spring 2007): 1–2 of 16, accessed at www.archives.gov/publications/prologue/2007/spring/cosast-survey.html (June 26, 2009). The navy turned over the small gunboat USS *Sachem* to the Coast Survey in March 1862 to conduct triangulations for range-finding. Confederates nightly removed *Sachem*'s survey stakes and flags, but the Coast Survey men repeated the work, enabling the mortars to fire accurately. *Sachem* (2), *DANFS*, NHHC; James Parton, *General Butler in New Orleans: History of the Administration in the Department of the Gulf in the Year 1862*, 5th ed. (New York: Mason Brothers, 1864), 226–27.

27. Note that Farragut did not receive promotion to rear admiral until July 16, 1862. Lewis, *Farragut*, 116. Bell left the *Hartford* for the *Sciota*, taking command of the fleet's 2nd division; Thornton, promoted to Lt.-Cmdr. in July 1862, left to command the gunboat USS *Winona*. People–United States, NHHC. Here Diggins first exhibits his dissatisfaction with Farragut.

28. Fascinated, many men watched the parabolic flight of the mortar shells, their paths marked by the clearly visible burning fuses. Sailors counted the "enormous shells with their trains of fire" in the sky, and one said they were "like large burning meteors." Diary of Albert D. Bache, April 18, 1862, American Philosophical Society, Philadelphia, Pa. (hereafter cited as Bache diary); Hill, *Twenty Years*, 169, 237; John D. Milligan, ed., *From the Fresh-Water Navy, 1861–64: The Letters of Acting Master's Mate Henry R. Browne and Acting Ensign Symmes E. Browne* (Annapolis, Md.: Naval Institute Press, 1970), 52.

29. Hard tack, a thick long-lasting baked cracker made of flour, water, and salt, was issued to both sailors and soldiers and sometimes was so hard that men broke teeth on it; grog, a whisky and water mixture, went to sailors as a small twice daily ration, and extra servings occurred on special occasions. John A. Grier, "A Sketch of Naval Life," in *Military Essays and Recollections*, vol. 3, MOLLUS-Ill. (Chicago: Dial Press, 1899): 318–19; Clark, *Seven Years*,

234. However, pressure mounted to abolish the grog ration, and it officially ended as of Sept. 1, 1862, to sailors' anguish and wrath. George A. Bright to Father, Oct. 25, 1863, Bright Papers; Simpson diary, Sept. 1, 1862; US Naval Institute Staff, "A Hundred Years Dry: The U.S. Navy's End of Alcohol at Sea," USNI News, electronic, http://news.usn.org/2014/07/01/hundred-years-dry-u-s-navys-end-alcohol-sea (accessed June 1, 2015); "The Grog-Ration in the Navy," New York *Times*, July 29, 1862; Ringle, *Life*, 4–5, 70–73. Still, ship captains sometimes ignored the ban. Journal of William Wainwright, July 4, 1864, G. W. Blunt White Library, Mystic Seaport Museum, Mystic, Conn. (hereafter cited as Wainwright Journal); Ringle, *Life*, 72–73. Apparently Farragut was indeed opposed to serving grog before battle. See Ringle, *Life*, 73n44.

30. Note that the nurses were male assistants; *cats*, as used here, were a swiveling davit, a device to lower or hoist casualties.

31. A cathead was a strong piece of wood, with a cat's face carved on the end, projecting over the bows on each side, used to raise or drop an anchor. John V. Noel and Edward L. Beach, *Naval Terms Dictionary*, 4th ed. (Annapolis, Md.: Naval Institute Press, 1985), 60.

32. Others also noted the silence just before battle. A paymaster wrote, "The ship was stiller than a church. I noticed sounds of ropes cheeping, steam soughing and water washing alongside which I had never observed before." Calvin G. Hutchinson journal, Pt. 2, Dec. 24, 1864, Papers of Calvin Gibbs Hutchinson, Huntington Library, San Marino, Calif. (hereafter cited as Hutchinson Papers).

2. Fighting the Forts: "The Nois was Teroble"

1. J. G. Randall, *The Civil War and Reconstruction* (Boston: D. C. Heath, 1937; reprint 1953), 18; "The Opposing Forces," *B&L*, 2:74.

2. "The Opposing Forces," *B&L*, 2:75.

3. Ramming dates from antiquity and persists to this day. Two noteworthy examples from World War II were the ramming of the German heavy cruiser *Admiral Hipper* by the British destroyer *Glowworm* in 1940 in the North Atlantic off Norway and the sinking of future president John F. Kennedy's PT-109 by a Japanese destroyer in 1943 in the Pacific. Geoffrey B. Mason, *Service Histories of Royal Navy Warships in World War 2*, accessed at www.naval-history.net/xGM-Chrono-10DD-250-Glowworm.htm (June 28, 1009); *DANFS*, NHHC.

4. Charles W. Read, "Reminiscences of the Confederate States Navy," *Southern Historical Society Papers* 1,5 (May 1876): 341; Beverley Kennon, "Fighting Farragut Below New Orleans," *B&L*, 2:78–80; "Proceedings of the Court" and Lovell's report, *OR*, 6:588, 590–91, and 832; William B. Robertson, "The Water-Battery at Fort Jackson," *B&L*, 2:100; William J. Seymour, *Civil War Memoirs of Captain William J. Seymour: Reminiscences of a Louisiana*

Tiger, ed. Terry L. Jones (Baton Rouge: Louisiana State Univ. Press, 1991), 12, 18, 20, 24.

5. Porter, "Opening," *B&L*, 2:33; Simpson diary, April 24, 1862.

6. Confederates first saw "several black, shapeless masses, barely distinguishable from the surrounding darkness, moving silently, but steadily, up the river," while another Fort Jackson officer reported they saw the *Hartford*'s "dim outline" at 3:30 A.M. Robertson, "The Water-Battery," *B&L*, 2:100; Seymour, *Civil War Memoirs*, 25.

7. Many voiced similar sentiments during the tense wait while under fire. A sailor aboard the sidewheel gunboat USS *Tyler* called it "trying in the extreme," and a future admiral said that the "wait before action is the period of self-consciousness," while a mortar schooner's captain confessed that it "took more courage to dodge than to stand and take my chances." S. B. Coleman, "A July Morning with the Rebel Ram 'Arkansas,'" *War Papers*, vol. 1, MOLLUS-Mich. (Detroit: Winn & Hammond, 1890): 8; Dewey, *Autobiography*, 62; Brown, "The Mortar Flotilla," 178. More pragmatically, one sailor believed "it is no use to bid the devel good morning till you meet him," and another wryly noted that there was no place to run and next time he would join the army. Schlesinger, "A Blue Bluejacket's Letters," 559; Campbell, "The Mississippi Squadron," 61.

8. Probably the "best sustained rate of fire was 2 2/3 minutes per projectile" for the 13-inch mortars. Eugene B. Canfield, *Civil War Naval Ordnance* (Washington, D.C.: Naval History Division, Navy Dept., GPO, 1969), 12. USS *Cayuga*, launched in October 1861, was a 507-ton screw steamer with four guns; the navy bought the 1300-ton screw-driven *Varuna*, originally intended for merchant service, in December 1861, shortly after she was launched; and the *Oneida* was a three-masted screw sloop of almost 1500 tons of 10 guns, with a crew of 186, also launched in 1861. *DANFS*, NHHC.

9. Confederate artillerymen also could not clearly see their targets because of the thick, low-hanging smoke generated by the black powder used by both sides. Seymour, *Civil War Memoirs*, 25.

10. Anti-personnel ammunition, grape rounds held iron balls about 1½ inches in diameter, while canister held musket balls or any scrap metal, and both acted like giant shotgun blasts. Coggins, *Arms and Equipment*, 67. A Fort Jackson officer said they survived "a perfect storm" of missiles, including grape and canister. Seymour, *Civil War Memoirs*, 25. While grape is now outmoded, canister is still used in field artillery and tank guns.

11. In passing the forts, Paymaster's Clerk Samuel Massa on the *Cayuga* said that "now all is confusion with plenty of hell fire and brimstone." Samuel Massa diary, April 24, 1862, in Foenander, ed., "Fire and Brimstone." Describing the noise level, a Federal officer wrote that "the very heavens seemed to be rent in twain . . . I did not think mortal man could invent such ear splitting thunder." Shively, "The USS *Mississippi*," 239.

165

12. Diggins was in good company when he mistakenly thought the ironclad CSS *Manassas*, a ram of radical design, had nudged the fire raft against the *Hartford*—Farragut himself so reported. Instead, the little tug *Mosher* had guided the fire raft, and Federals quickly sank her. *ORN* 18:157; Albert Kautz, "Letter to Editors," *B&L*, 2:64; James R. Soley, "Letter to Editors," *B&L*, 2:90; W. Crane, *Encyclopedia of Civil War Shipwrecks* (Baton Rouge: Louisiana State Univ. Press, 2008), 70. The "water battery" was doubtless Fort St. Philip's lower battery.

13. Many echoed Diggins's words. Aboard the *Cayuga*, an officer recalled, "There was the wildest excitement all round," and a master's mate on the *Richmond* wrote that "it is all madness." Perkins, *Letters*, 68; Hill, *Twenty Years*, 176.

14. Farragut reported, "Our ship was soon on fire half way up to her tops. . . ." and, watching the flames racing up tarred ropes, he exclaimed, "My God, is it to end in this way!" *ORN* 18:157; Kautz, "Letter to Editors," *B&L*, 2:64.

15. The wooden gratings were impromptu life preservers.

16. Reducing the water would increase steam pressure; Albert Kautz, then a lieutenant, said one man climbed the mizzen rigging with a fire hose and "the sheet of flame succumbed to a sheet of water." Kautz, "Letter to Editors," *B&L*, 2:64.

17. CSS *McRae* passed USS *Brooklyn*'s starboard side "not 10 feet" away and in the sights of Midshipman John R. Bartlett's 9-inch gun when superior officers, mistaking her for the USS *Iroquois*, ordered, "Don't fire!" Bartlett, "The 'Brooklyn,'" *B&L*, 2:67.

18. USS *Richmond* also encountered a riverboat "crowded with rebel troops," but an officer stopped a gunner from firing, sparing the "trembling wretches" from "an awful fate." Hill, *Twenty Years*, 177.

19. CSS *Louisiana* was 1400 tons, 262 feet in length, with a beam of 62 feet. She had four engines, one for each of two center mounted paddle wheels and one for each of two steering propellers. Her engines lacked sufficient thrust, however, and she could be used only as a floating battery. Still, she punched holes in some Federal ships. *DANFS*, NHHC; Bartlett, "The 'Brooklyn,'" 65.

20. Here Diggins relied on secondhand reports, some with minor errors. George H. Perkins, the *USS Cayuga*'s executive officer, said that after passing the forts he saw "eleven of the enemy's gunboats coming down upon us, and it seemed as if we were 'gone' sure." *Cayuga* fought two gunboats and escaped a ramming, Perkins reported, adding that the USS *Varuna* "fired a broadside into us." Perkins, *Letters*, 68; Massa diary, April 24, 1862, in Foenander, ed., "Fire and Brimstone." Charles S. Boggs, *Varuna*'s captain, said two Confederate rams ripped into his port side, putting the *Varuna* in sinking condition, and his executive officer said the rams *Governor Moore* and *Stonewall Jackson* both took a fatal battering from *Varuna*'s guns and those of the USS *Oneida*. *ORN* 18:210–13; Read, "Reminiscences," 343–44. The *Governor Moore*'s captain said that of his ninety-three man crew, sixty-

one were killed or mortally wounded and thirteen were wounded, leaving nineteen unscathed. Kennon, "Fighting Farragut," *B&L*, 2:85.

21. Ramming efforts by the *Manassas* were not "harmless." The *Brooklyn*'s captain called her a "black, whale-like looking beast," and she struck the *Brooklyn* at a coal bunker and serious leaking soon developed. She also tore a "big hole" in the *Mississippi* just abaft the port paddle wheel. Disabled and "helpless," the *Manassas*'s captain ordered her grounded near Fort St. Philip, where her crew abandoned her and where federal sailors set her afire. Thomas T. Craven to wife, May 16, 1862, *ORN* 18:198; Bartlett, "The 'Brooklyn,'" *B&L*, 2:67, 69; Dewey, *Autobiography*, 65; W. H. Robert to wife, April 28, 1962, in Nina Silber and Mary Beth Stevens, eds., *Yankee Correspondence: Civil War Letters between New England Soldiers and the Home Front* (Charlottesville: Univ. Press of Virginia, 1996), 32; A. F. Warley, "The Ram 'Manassas' at the Passage of the New Orleans Forts," *B&L*, 2:90–91.

22. *Manassas*, the "dreaded Monster," exploded and then sank. Porter, "Opening," *B&L*, 2:48; Dewey, *Autobiography*, 77. It was a double joke on the steamers because the sailing vessels salvaged much floating cotton and, rightfully, only they would share in the prize money for the cotton.

23. The top gallant forecastle was a raised and lengthened structure on a ship's stem or bow, illustrated in E. Keble Chatterton, *Steamships and Their Story* (London: Cassell and Co., 1910), 284, accessed at catalog.hathitrust.org/ Record/006249126/ (July 14, 2009).

24. Daylight arrived as *Winona* and *Kennebec* neared the forts, forcing them to drop back; *Itasca*, a 507-ton screw steamer "completely riddled" by the forts and with a 42-pound shot through her boiler, had to run aground to avoid sinking but listed only 4 wounded in her 70-man crew. Porter, "Opening," *B&L*, 2:46; *DANFS*, NHHC; "The Opposing Forces," *B&L*, 2:73.

25. The 600-ton, two-gun sidewheeler *Harriet Lane*, a Treasury Department revenue cutter before transfer to the navy, was named for President James Buchanan's niece, his White House hostess. *DANFS*, NHHC.

26. Established six miles above Fort St. Philip in 1855 at a cost of $50,000, the Quarantine Station inspected for yellow fever and other infectious diseases possibly carried by ships' crews or passengers. Henry Rightor, ed., *Standard History of New Orleans, Louisiana* (Chicago: Lewis Publishing, 1900), 211, accessed at https://archive.org/details/standardhistory00righgoog/ (July 14, 2009). After the Chalmette Regiment, the militia unit posted to the Quarantine Station, surrendered, Farragut paroled the lot because he did not know what to do with them. Arthur W. Bergeron, *Guide to Louisiana Confederate Military Units, 1861–1865* (Baton Rouge: Louisiana State Univ. Press, 1989), 181; Hill, *Twenty Years*, 189–82; Perkins, *Letters*, 68–69; Farragut's report, *ORN*, 18:157. The few roster records extant do not show many German names.

27. In September 1699, an English corvette's captain sailed up the Mississippi to a "point just below modern New Orleans," near a wide bend in the river.

There, French officials told the English to go back because they already controlled the area. The English obligingly turned around and left, and ever since the spot has borne the name "English Turn." Light T. Cummins, "English Spoken Here: Great Britain and Louisiana," *Historic New Orleans Collection Quarterly* 22, no. 4 (Fall 2004): 1.

28. A *Cayuga* officer reported the Chalmette batteries initially appeared deserted, though "there were a lot of treacherous rascals concealed in those batteries." However rascally, the Confederate gunners proved good shots, battering the *Cayuga*, hitting her fourteen times. Perkins, *Letters*, 69–70; Massa diary, April 25, 1862, in Foenander, ed., "Fire and Brimstone."

29. Federals fired broadsides of shell, shrapnel, and grape "in spiteful revenge for their [Confederate] ill treatment of the little *Cayuga*," Farragut's report, *ORN*, 18:158. To spike or disable a cannon, they hammered an iron spike into the gun's vent or firing hole, then broke it off flush with the surface and clinched it inside the bore with a rammer. Board of Artillery Officers, *Instruction for Field Artillery* (Philadelphia, Pa.: J. B. Lippincott & Co., 1861), 128, 139, accessed at catalog.hathitrus.org/Record/002021314/ (July 14, 2009).

30. Farragut called the burning wreckage a "floating conflagration" that sorely taxed their ingenuity to avoid. *ORN*, 18:158. A USS *Mississippi* bandsman thought that "almost everything afloat of value was set on fire" from spite or to prevent Federals from using any of it. Thomas Harris to Editor, Chelsea (Mass.) *Telegraph and Pioneer*, April 28, 1862.

31. CSS *Mississippi*, the promised "terror of the seas," was the unfinished, burning ironclad Diggins saw. Her captain, Comdr. Arthur Sinclair, CSN, had tried to take her up river at the last minute and set her afire to prevent capture when withdrawal became impossible. Farragut's report, *ORN*, 18:158; *DANFS*, NHHC. Stocks were the frame or cradle to hold a ship during construction.

32. Maj. Gen. Mansfield Lovell, West Point graduate and former New York City deputy street commissioner, was held responsible for New Orleans's fall and relieved of command in December 1862, though a court of inquiry had cleared him. Ezra J. Warner, *Generals in Gray: Lives of the Confederate Commanders* (Baton Rouge: Louisiana State Univ. Press, 1959), 194–95.

3. NEW ORLEANS FALLS

1. For more on the stalling, see Albert Kautz, "Incidents of the Occupation of New Orleans," *B&L*, 2:93.

2. Elizabeth Blair Lee, *Wartime Washington: The Civil War Letters of Elizabeth Blair Lee*, ed. Virginia Jeans Laas (Urbana: Univ. of Illinois Press, 1991),139; Clara Soloman, *The Civil War Diary of Clara Solomon: Growing Up in New Orleans, 1861–1862*, ed. Elliott Ashkenazi (Baton Rouge: Louisiana State Univ. Press, 1995), 345; Russell E. Belous, ed., "The Diary of Ann Quigley," *Gulf Coast Historical Review* 4, 2 (Spring 1998): 93.

3. Soloman, *Civil War Diary*, 351.
4. Foltz, *Surgeon*, 258–59, for spitting incident; for Butler's notorious "Woman Order," see Benjamin Franklin Butler, *Autobiography and Personal Reminiscences of Major General Benj. F. Butler: Butler's Book* (Boston: A. M. Thayer, 1892), 414–20.
5. With Bailey on the trek to city hall was Lt. George H. Perkins. Perkins, *Letters*, 70; Abstract of Log of USS *Cayuga*, *ORN*, 18:755.
6. Perkins reported, "They were all shouting and hooting as we stepped on shore . . . the mob followed us in a very excited state . . . Then they began to throw things at us and shout, 'Hang them!' 'Hang them!' We both thought we were in a *bad fix*. . . ." Perkins, *Letters*, 70.
7. Observing the scene, one naval officer saw a "seething mass of human beings" on shore, "a mob of frenzied madness" waving pistols and knives at Farragut's men. Shively, "The USS Mississippi," 242.
8. Mayor John T. Monroe said he could not surrender because the Confederate Army had control; Maj. Gen. Mansfield Lovell said he was leaving town and so now the civil leaders must decide; Monroe then declared he had to consult with city councilmen. Kautz, "Incidents," *B&L*, 2:291–94; Marion A. Baker, "Farragut's Demands for the Surrender of New Orleans," *B&L*, 2:95–99.
9. *Pensacola* sailors raised the flag over the mint on the morning of April 27, when gambler William B. Mumford tore down the flag and thereby lost his life. Butler had him hanged for the offense on June 7, 1862. *ORN*, 18:154; Kautz, "Incidents," *B&L*, 2:92–93; Seymour, *Civil War Memoirs*, 37. Subsequently, Confederate president Jefferson Davis branded Butler an outlaw, subject to prompt hanging upon capture, and Butler, sorry for the woman he had widowed, aided Mrs. Mumford with money and jobs. "A Proclamation" by Jefferson Davis, *ORN*, Ser. 2, 5:795–97; Jefferson Davis, "Beast Butler Outlawed," *Southern Historical Society Papers* (*SHSP*) 14 (1886):470–75; Louis Taylor Merrill, "General Benjamin F. Butler and the Widow Mumford," *Louisiana Historical Quarterly* 29, 2 (April 1946): 341–54.
10. Ashore, the 12-pounder or 24-pounder boat howitzers were pushed or pulled on their wheels, often aided by a third small wheel at the end of the trail. Canfield, *Civil War Naval Ordnance*, 12. Naval landing parties carried pistols and the short, slightly curved cutlass in leather scabbard, a weapon still on some ships up to World War II. Richard Meckel, "The Cutlass Carved its Niche in Our Navy's Annals," NHHC, accessed at www.history. navy.mil/browse-by-topic/heritage/uniforms-and-personal-equipment/ Swords.html (July 21, 2009). Mayor Monroe declared no citizen would dare remove the state flag, and Farragut believed that any civilian doing so would be "assassinated." *ORN*, 18:159.
11. The flag-waver also drew fire from the USS *Cayuga*. Massa diary, April 26, 1862, in Foenander, ed., "Fire and Brimstone."

12. *McRae* carried sick and wounded Confederates to New Orleans but never returned to the forts, sinking on the Algiers side from battle damage. Read, "Reminiscences," 344–46. She sank at night, perhaps explaining why Diggins did not see it and thought she had steamed back to the forts.

13. Farragut said the boom or raft consisted of sections of "three immense logs . . . 3 and 4 feet in diameter and some 30 feet long" chained together, with 96 such sections stretched 3/4 of a mile across the river, "one of the most herculean labors I have ever seen." *ORN*, 18:159.

14. "Picayune Butler" aimed a double slur at Butler and an early use appeared in the *Mobile Register and Advertiser*, as copied by the *New York Times* on Jan. 16, 1862 [p. 2], long before Butler arrived in New Orleans. A picayune was a coin of small value, and John "Picayune" Butler was a popular black French singer and banjo player from the French West Indies. Parton, *General Butler*, 73; James Gill, *Lords of Misrule: Mardi Gras and the Politics of Race in New Orleans* (Jackson: Univ. Press of Mississippi, 1997), 61–62. Southerners applied the "Beast" pejorative to Butler for his harsh rule in New Orleans. Soon irreverent Federals adopted it, for which see Henry G. Marshall to Folks at Home, Oct. 2, 1864, Henry Grimes Marshall Papers, 1861–1865, James S. Schoff Civil War Collection, William L. Clements Library, University of Michigan, Ann Arbor, Mich. (hereafter cited as Marshall Papers); Harry F. Jackson and Thomas F. O'Donnell, eds., *Back Home in Oneida: Hermon Clarke and His Letters* (Syracuse, NY: Syracuse Univ. Press, 1965), 174; Edward W. Bacon, *Double Duty in the Civil War: The Letters of Sailor and Soldier Edward W. Bacon*, ed. George S. Burkhardt (Carbondale: Southern Illinois Univ. Press, 2009), 143. Yellow jack is another name for yellow fever, a virus transmitted by mosquitoes, often fatal in those days. "Yellow Fever," www.cdc.gov/yellowfever (June 5, 2015).

15. Cutters were small boats, manned by oarsmen, as was the dinghy, an even smaller boat. Though "Boy" was the lowest rank in the navy at the time, here Diggins refers to age.

16. Officers paid a certain sum to their mess fund and their stewards shopped for fresh foods when in port. Shinplasters were privately issued, unsecured paper currencies, varying in worth, usually in small denominations, common during the war because metal for coins was in short supply. Diggins was lucky to get coffee and a roll for 75 cents—as the blockade of southern ports tightened, a cup of coffee might cost $5 and a pound of coffee $25, when available. See Albert Theodore Goodloe, *Confederate Echoes: A Soldier's Personal Story of Life in the Confederate Army from the Mississippi to the Carolinas* (Nashville: For the Author by Smith & Lamar, 1907; reprint, Washington, D.C.: Zenger, 1983), 122; and Wirt Armistead Cate, ed., *Two Soldiers: The Campaign Diaries of Thomas J. Key, C.S.A., and Robert J. Campbell, U.S.A.* (Chapel Hill: Univ. of North Carolina Press, 1938), 70.

17. Fort Jackson's garrison mutinied, and that helped persuade the forts' officers to surrender. Porter, "Opening," *B&L*, 2:50–51; report of Brig. Gen. Johnson K. Duncan, CSA, *ORN*, 18:272–74. Then, the St. Charles Hotel was "a grand establishment and one of the first luxury hotels in the world." John T. Magill, curator, Historic New Orleans Collection, email to editor, Feb. 16, 2006, in editor's possession.

18. Hoarding and inflation spurred the scarcity of gold and silver, affected all southerners, and caused many to exhibit a "ravenous appetite" for Federal greenbacks, the gold-secured northern paper currency. Bacon, *Double Duty*, 39; Homer B. Sprague, *Lights and Shadows in Confederate Prisons: A Personal Experience, 1864–65* (New York: G. P. Putnam's Sons, 1915), 43.

19. Before Butler recruited blacks, Brig. Gen. John W. Phelps sought to arm and equip them as soldiers at a camp near the city, a move Butler quashed. Then Butler did the same thing in New Orleans, in direct opposition to prevailing administration policy. See Dudley T. Cornish, *The Sable Arm: Negro Troops in the Union Army, 1861–1865* (New York: Longmans, Green, 1956; repr., New York: W. W. Norton, 1966), 58–66; George S. Burkhardt, *Confederate Rage, Yankee Wrath: No Quarter During the Civil War* (Carbondale: Southern Illinois Univ. Press, 2007), 15; Howard C. Westwood, "Benjamin Butler's Enlistment of Black Troops in New Orleans in 1862," *Louisiana History* 26, 1 (Winter 1985), 5–22. The "unacclimated" were the white troops.

20. Civil War generals frequently closed a newspaper they did not like, but Butler suspended six in one fell swoop, reopening the *True Delta* as an organ for his military rule. Seymour, *Civil War Memoirs*, 30n70; William Winthrop, *Military Law and Precedents* (Boston: Little, Brown, 1896), 2:815; Butler, *Autobiography*, 895.

21. Loyal southerners used many stratagems to aid their cause. For instance, women concealed quinine beneath their dresses and so carried the medicine to Confederate forces outside the city. Perkins, *Letters*, 109. Diggins's examples elude verification.

22. This was the famous (or infamous) "Women Order" that also generated protests abroad. Butler, *Autobiography*, 414–20.

23. "Bonnie Blue Flag," written in 1861, was a very popular Confederate patriotic song. Jonathan M. Foltz, Farragut's fleet surgeon, retaliated by calling for Ireland's independence when he met the *Rinaldo*'s captain ashore. Foltz, *Surgeon*, 254–55.

24. That English captain was Comdr W. N. W. Hewett, who, according to one report, himself halted the provocative behavior. Lewis, *Farragut*, 147.

25. Andrew H. Foote, promoted to rear admiral June 1862, led the river flotilla above Vicksburg, but about the time Farragut steamed upriver, Foote had left his post because of wounds suffered in the fight at Fort Donelson. Flag Officer Charles H. Davis replaced Foote. Michael, "The Mississippi Flotilla," 21–33; William W. Van Cleaf to Mother, May 10, 1862, Van Cleaf Papers.

4. SHIPS BATTLE "TO NO PURPOSE"

1. Fox to Farragut, May 12, 17, 1862, in Thompson and Wainwright, *Confidential Correspondence*, 1:313, 315; Craig L. Symonds, *Lincoln and His Admirals* (New York: Oxford University Press, 2008), 128.

2. For Baton Rouge's surrender, see Bacon, *Double Duty*, 41; *ORN*, 18:473–76. Built in 1838, the arsenal manufactured gunpowder. See Louisiana Secretary of State, accessed at http://www.sos.louisiana.gov/tabid/244/Default.asps (July 27, 2009).

3. Natchez yielded to the USS *Iroquois*, but Grand Gulf's submission proved temporary, prompting Federals to bombard and torch the place in early June. Bacon, *Double Duty*, 42–44; *ORN*, 18:545–47.

4. For Lee's report and the correspondence, see *ORN*, 18:491–93.

5. Another *Hartford* man described Vicksburg as a "pleasant" place about twenty feet above the river with 4,000–5,000 inhabitants, many buildings having slate roofs. Holton, *Cruise*, 26. Vicksburg's mayor declared that "no defenses . . . are within the corporative limits of the city." *ORN*, 18:492.

6. Farragut believed neither he or nor the commander of the army's small force, Brig. Gen. Thomas Williams, could "be of any service" at Vicksburg, but ships would continue to blockade the city and occasionally harass the defenders with naval gunfire. Farragut to Butler and to Comdr. S. P. Lee, May 22, 21, 1862, *ORN*, 18:507, 509.

7. Farragut called it a "wanton attack" by "thirty or forty guerrillas," rather than a regiment of cavalry. *ORN*, 18:515, 520. Comdr. Henry H. Bell, Farragut's fleet captain, related that "some 30 or 50 horsemen" fired on the dinghy with buckshot [which indicates the irregulars used shotguns], severely wounding Kimball, Diggins, and Thomas George, another young sailor. Bell's private diary, May 28, 1862, *ORN*, 18:706; Foltz, *Surgeon*, 239–40, also reports Kimball and "two boys wounded"; Holton, *Cruise*, 39–40; Higgins, *Yeoman*, 31. This occurred May 28, 1862. *Hartford* log entry, *ORN*, 18:725.

8. Apparently Diggins soon recovered from his wounds, never again mentioning the episode. *Headgear* refers to the schooner's bowsprit and attached rigging, while the *cutwater* is the part of the bow that "cuts" the water as the ship moves forward.

9. Watching the angry gunners, Comdr. Henry H. Bell thought that "most of the sailors blazed away right into the houses without regard to the position of the foe." Bell's diary, *ORN*, 18:707.

10. "This style of fighting" continued well into 1863. For a critique, see Perkins, *Letters*, 108, 115.

11. Farragut warned Confederate civil and military authorities along the river that, when they fired upon any Union vessels, his warships would return fire. *ORN*, 18:515, 564–65.

12. Here Diggins apparently repeated an unfounded report about the transport's loss with all hands; however, Federals did bombard and burn Donaldsonville. Foltz, *Surgeon*, 252.

13. Diggins here confuses times and places. Farragut's ships and sailors shelled and torched part of Donaldsonville on Aug. 9, 10, 1862. *ORN*, 19:140–43; Grand Gulf suffered a two-hour bombardment and some burning on June 9, 1862. *ORN*, 18:545–47, 821. Maj. Gen. Mansfield Lovell's complaint and Farragut's reply are at *ORN*, 18:562–63, 564–65.

14. Farragut's threat to bombard towns along the river if fired upon from those towns did inspire some civic leaders to try to safeguard their homes against destruction, but sporadic shore battery attacks continued. Letter home, June 22, 1862, in Loyall Farragut, *The Life of David Glasgow Farragut, First Admiral of the United States Navy: Embodying His Journal and Letters* (New York: D. Appleton & Co., 1879), 272; and see again Perkins, *Letters*, 108, 115.

15. This was not a one-way fight—Confederate artillery hulled one Federal ship twenty-five times, another seventeen, and, while casualty reports differ, one or two sailors were killed and five or six wounded in the hours-long clashes. *ORN*, 18:545–47, 821; Bacon, *Double Duty*, 43–44.

16. Rear Adm. David D. Porter assailed Grand Gulf on April 29, 1863, with seven ironclads, smashing the lower batteries, but could not elevate his guns enough to silence the upper batteries. Then Grant landed troops below Grand Gulf, and that move forced Confederates to abandon the place by May 3. Porter to Fox, May 1, 1863, in Thompson and Wainwright, *Confidential Correspondence*, 2:178–82; George W. Brown, "Service in the Mississippi Squadron, and Its Connection with the Siege and Capture of Vicksburg," *Personal Recollections*, Ser. 2, MOLLUS-N.Y. (New York: G. P. Putnam's Sons, 1897): 310; "The Capture of Grand Gulf . . . ," *New York Times*, May 9, 1863.

17. Ships' officers often enlisted able-bodied contrabands or blacks in the lowest ranks, authorized and urged to do so by Navy Department officials. Thompson and Wainwright, *Confidential Correspondence*, 2:152–53; Thomas O. Selfridge, *What Finer Tradition: The Memoirs of Thomas O. Selfridge, Jr., Rear Admiral, U.S.N.* (New York: Knickerbocker Press, 1924; repr., Columbia: South Carolina Univ. Press, 1987), 87–88. Butler was nowhere near Vicksburg, but busy in New Orleans; Brig. Gen. Thomas Williams used black laborers on the canal project, an effort to bypass Vicksburg by digging across a narrow loop in the river, *ORN*, 18:582; Bacon, *Double Duty*, 48–49, 54.

18. After one severe grounding, Farragut feared the *Hartford* might spend the summer stuck in the mud. Private letter, June 22, 1862, in Loyall Farragut, *Life*, 273.

19. Sickness killed and disabled more sailors than all the Confederate metal fired at them, just as disease likewise felled more soldiers during the war than did battle. In particular, malaria, dengue or break-bone fever, dysentery, diarrhea, and yellow fever, even mumps and sunstroke, took a terrible toll on northern forces during the riverine warfare, sometimes disabling a quarter to a half or more of a ship's crew. USS *Richmond*'s log, June 26,

1862, *ORN*, 18:634, 750; Thompson and Wainwright, *Confidential Correspondence*, 2:112–13, 125, 188; Frederic E. Davis to Parents, May 6, 1862, Davis Papers; Edward M. Galligan diary entries, Aug. 5, 7, 1862, Papers of Edward M. Galligan, Montana Historical Society, Helena, Mont. (hereafter cited as Galligan Papers); James L. B. Blauvelt to Mother, Aug. 24, 1862, Blauvelt Papers; Bacon, *Double Duty*, 199n19.

20. Unless black laborers were included in Williams's force, he had nowhere near 6,000 men; Farragut thought he had "about 3,000." *ORN*, 18:610. That "vigorous" mortar and artillery fire had little effect because they were poorly aimed, according to another sailor. Bacon, *Double Duty*, 45.

21. Ships' crews intently watched the 220-pound mortar shells arch through the sky, one sailor saying they were "like large burning meteors," Everson, "Service Afield," 49; Milligan, ed., *Fresh-Water Navy*, 52. However, a Confederate observer thought it deplorable that the Federals targeted the city, though he said actual damage was minimal and indifferent citizens scarcely glanced skyward at the exploding shells. Edward S. Gregory, "Vicksburg During the Siege," in *Annals of the War*, by Philadelphia Weekly Times (Philadelphia, Pa.: Times Publishing, 1879; repr., Gettysburg, Pa.: Civil War Times Illustrated, 1974), 111–33. In counterpoint, a captain's clerk on the *Hartford* thought they would have to destroy the city to save it from the rebels. Bache diary, May 21, 22, 1862.

22. Of Porter's gunboats, the sidewheelers *Clifton* and *Westfield* were originally ferry boats, then acquired by the rapidly expanding navy; while *DANFS* does not list any *Jackson*, a *J. P. Jackson* was there and took part in the bombardment, for which see *ORN*, 18:639–43, 644, 646.

23. A water battery was an artillery emplacement on shore at water level or slightly above, enabling the gunners to aim at ship waterlines or to sweep their decks with canister. Ships returned the favor with grape and canister.

24. Farragut reported nothing about hospital artillery, but others did. These included the *USS Oneida*'s captain and a clerk on the USS *Iroquois*. Loyall Farragut, *Life*, 276; *ORN*, 18:608–11, 612; Bacon, *Double Duty*, 47. Vicksburg's mayor had carefully declared that "municipal authorities . . . have erected no defenses and none are within the corporative limits of the city," but the *Iroquois*'s captain even reported "cannon planted in the streets." *ORN*, 18:492, 619.

25. Rather than a Machiavellian plot, a simpler cause existed for the failure of several ships to complete the passage, as became evident.

26. Here Diggins outpaces his narrative. Congress voted Farragut its thanks on July 11, and he won promotion to rear admiral on July 16, 1862. But Diggins could have seen northern newspapers hailing Farragut's capture of New Orleans. J. Cutler Andrews, *The North Reports the Civil War* (Pittsburgh, Pa.: Univ. of Pittsburgh Press, 1955), 242.

27. Diggins's esprit de corps and fervor clashed with reality. Unlike New Orleans, Vicksburg the city and Vicksburg the fortress were one and the same;

to seize and hold the fortress city required many ground troops. But there were no such troops at hand.

28. Apparently Diggins thought Vicksburg's capture was the fleet's immediate objective. By "big Rifle," Diggins refers to a large caliber cannon firing spherical shells through a barrel with lands and grooves and so giving the projectile a spin, making it much more accurate at longer ranges than a smooth bore cannon firing round balls. Coggins, *Arms and Equipment*, 76–77.

5. "Ships . . . Can not Crawl Up Hills"

1. *ORN*, 18:619–20, 751; Zeno P. Elwell to dear friend [John Hay], July 10, 1862, Lincoln Presidential Library.

2. Holton, *Cruise*, 31–32; *ORN*, 18:588; Thompson and Wainwright, *Confidential Correspondence*, 2:122.

3. *ORN*, 18:641.

4. *ORN*, 18:588, 590, 636. Note that, in the end, at least 77,000 Federal soldiers besieged Vicksburg, more than six times Farragut's figure of 12,000 men. Michael B. Ballard, *Vicksburg: The Campaign that Opened the Mississippi* (Chapel Hill: Univ. of North Carolina Press, 2004), 394.

5. *ORN*, 18:502.

6. See *ORN*, 18:675 for Farragut's cogent argument of July 10, 1862, for Washington's permission to return to salt water with his ocean-going fleet.

7. Bache diary, May 19, 1862; Bacon, *Double Duty*, 58; *ORN*, 18:675.

8. Bell Irvin Wiley, "Billy Yank and the Black Folk," *Journal of Negro History* 36 (Spring 1951): 35–41; True, "Life Aboard a Gunboat," 38; Gould, *Diary of a Contraband*, 188, 190.

9. Horace Montgomery, *Johnny Cobb: Confederate Aristocrat* (Athens: Univ. of Georgia Press, 1964), 64, where Cobb declares the "negro affiliates with the monkey race"; W. H. Price to Sir, May 2, 1864 (W. H. Price Papers); William W. Van Cleaf to Brother April 14, 1862, Van Cleaf Papers; letter to Cousin, May 15, 1864, in Schlesinger, ed., "A Blue Bluejacket's Letters," 565.

10. Davis and his ships did not arrive until July 1. Loyall Farragut, *Life*, 282.

11. In his official report, Fleet Surgeon J. M. Foltz listed Farragut as among the wounded with a "slight contusion," but Farragut said that when a shot cut away mizzen mast rigging above him, he "escaped with only a touch on the head." *ORN*, 18:620; letter home, June 29, 1862, in Loyall Farragut, *Life*, 276.

12. Porter told Assistant Secretary Fox, "The squadron is chock full of niggers, including women and children . . . I take all that come." Jan 16, 1862, Thompson and Wainwright, *Confidential Correspondence*, 2:155.

13. Incidents and reactions described by Diggins occurred throughout the navy; for some, see Charles A. Poole journal entry, Dec. 8, 1862, G. W. Blunt White Library, Mystic Seaport Museum, Mystic, Conn. (hereafter cited as Poole journal); Clark, *Seven Years*, 212; William N. Bock to brother, Feb. 17, 1864 (William N. Bock Papers).

6. A REBEL RAM MORTIFIES FEDERALS

1. Acting Master's Mate John A. Wilson, CSS *Arkansas*, *ORN*, 18:675, 19:133; Bache diary, May 19, 1862; Bacon, *Double Duty*, 59–60; Milligan, ed., *Fresh-Water Navy*, 107–8.

2. The ignored warning story came from both sides. See *ORN*, 19:56; Isaac N. Brown, "The Confederate Gun-Boat 'Arkansas,'" *B&L*, 3:573; Bacon, *Double Duty*, 62.

3. *ORN*, 19:3; *DANFS*, NHHC, for ship particulars.

4. Brown, "Arkansas," 572; Read, "Reminiscences," 349.

5. *ORN*, 19:37–41, 68–69; Brown, "Arkansas," 574–75, and Note, 580; Coleman, "A July Morning," 9–10.

6. Brown, "Arkansas," 576.

7. Bacon, *Double Duty*, 60.

8. Ibid.; Edward M. Galligan diary, July 15, 1862, Galligan Papers; Brown, "Arkansas," 576; from papers of Acting Master's Mate J. A. Wilson, C. S. Navy, *ORN*, 19:133.

9. *ORN*, 19:69, 747; Brown, "Arkansas," 576; Sylvester Doss to W. D. Crandall, Oct. 8, 1894, Warren D. Crandall Collection, State Historical of Missouri, Columbia, MO.

10. *ORN*, 19:69, 5, 39, 41.

11. Ibid., 4, 15, 36.

12. Charles H. Davis, commanding the Western Flotilla, had six ironclads at that time: the *Benton*, *Carondelet*, *Cincinnati*, *Essex*, *Louisville*, and *Indianola*. *ORN*, 19:xvi.

13. Why Diggins sometimes referred to the Confederate ram as the *Arkansas Traveler* is uncertain. Perhaps it was a play on words, perhaps he mixed up fancy and fact. "Arkansas Traveler" was the name of a humorous, well-known song, the title of a play, and in the twentieth century, Arkansas's official state song, for a while. As noted, *Queen of the West*, *Carondelet*, and *Tyler* had steamed up the Yazoo to find the *Arkansas* and during their fighting retreat, the *Tyler*, a 575-ton sidewheeler, listed 57 casualties, or 85 percent of her 67-man crew. *ORN*, 19:39.

14. No "transports and other vessels" blew up or sank because of friendly cross fire.

15. *Scaling* is removing unwanted deposits from inside a water boiler.

16. The *Benton*, a curious affair, was originally a catamaran snagboat, then converted into a 1,000-ton ironclad river gunboat, commissioned in February 1862. *DANFS*, NHHC. Sailors used a kedge anchor to free a grounded ship or to move one by dropping the anchor, then pulling the vessel to the kedge anchor. Noel and Beach, *Naval Terms*, 169.

17. The *Arkansas* was painted a dull brown and so blended with the river bank where she lay in the growing darkness. Wilson papers, *ORN*, 19:133.

18. Fleet Surgeon J. M. Foltz reported three killed and six wounded on the *Hartford* and five killed and sixteen wounded in the fleet. *ORN*, 19:5; Richard

Wainwright, the *Hartford*'s captain, said it was a 9-inch shell. *ORN*, 19:20; *bitts* were paired posts or horns used to tie lines; Diggins's "colored man" was probably Charles Jackson, an officer's cook, for which see *ORN*, 19:20, 21.

19. Watson's luck held, as he survived other battles and the war. Lewis R. Hamersly, *The Records of Living Officers of the U.S. Navy and Marine Corps* (Philadelphia, Pa.: J. B. Lippincott, 1870).

20. Built in 1856 as a civilian ferry, the War Department bought the *Essex* in September 1861. James B. Eads of St. Louis converted her into a timberclad. After fighting service on western waters, she underwent further conversion to a broader beamed ironclad with a crew of 124. *DANFS*, NHHC.

21. Also joining the attack was the army ram *Queen of the West*, which struck the *Arkansas* a glancing blow; afterward, Lt.-Col. Alfred W. Ellet, the *Queen*'s commander, complained that the navy failed to cooperate with him, exposing the *Queen* to the "undivided attention" of enemy batteries and sharpshooters, severely damaging the *Queen* and forcing her to the north for repairs. *ORN*, 19:46. Subsequently, William D. Porter, commanding the *Essex*, was criticized by Farragut and got a letter of censure from Navy Secretary Gideon Welles for misstatements regarding the *Arkansas*. *ORN*, 19:62, 122.

22. On July 20, 1862, Farragut reported sixty to eighty men sick on each ship, and on July 29 he said some ships had as many as one hundred on the sick list and, in addition to the infectious diseases, scurvy had also appeared. *ORN*, 19:80, 98. However, a sailor aboard the USS *Essex* found a remedy when "swamp fever" laid him low, writing that he "got ahold of a demijohn of whiskey and soon got well again. Edward M. Galligan diary entry, Aug. 7, 1862, Galligan Papers. Often short of quinine and other medicines, Confederates suffered as much or more than Union forces, impelling patriotic southern women to hide quinine under their skirts and so smuggle the medicine out of New Orleans. *ORN*, 19:80; S. W. Farrow, 19th Texas Infantry, to Josephine Farrow, from hospital at Monroe, La., July 4, 1863, Sam W. Farrow Papers, 1852–1865, Center for American History, University of Texas at Austin, Austin, Tex.; Perkins, *Letters*, 109.

23. Autocratic institutions such as the army or navy usually do not hold democratic discussions about operations, so this consulting the crew was indeed a novelty.

7. BACK DOWN RIVER

1. Farragut to Fox, June 12, 1862, in Thompson and Wainwright, *Confidential Correspondence*, 1:316.

2. Loyall Farragut, *Life*, 287, for falling water and other factors.

3. Butler had won election to Massachusetts's lower house in 1853 and to the state's senate in 1858; postwar, he served in Congress as a Republican from 1867 to 1875. *Biographical Directory of the United States Congress, 1774–Present*, accessed at bioguide.congress.gov/biosearch/biosearch.asp (August 16, 2010).

4. Richard Wainwright, 45, joined the navy in 1831 when he was 13. When the war began, he was promoted to commander and to command of Farragut's flagship, the USS *Hartford*. He had fallen ill two weeks before dying of malaria on August 10, 1862. *ORN*, 19:144; NHHC; Foltz, *Surgeon*, 251.
5. Wainwright belonged to a prominent family, and they did not need such aid.
6. James S. Palmer, 51, was another regular navy officer who had entered service as a 13-year-old boy. Earlier, he had commanded the USS *Iroquois* when the Confederate commerce raider CSS *Sumter* had eluded him when tracked to a Caribbean port. That brought Palmer much criticism, including some from subordinate officers, and a formal inquiry, though he was exonerated of any fault. Promoted to rear admiral in 1866, he died of yellow fever the next year at St. Thomas, Virgin Islands. NHHC; Bacon, *Double Duty*, 24–32.
7. Sharp distinctions obtained between officers and enlisted men, and as one sailor wrote, "The discipline in the navy is very strick." True, "Life Aboard a Gunboat," 37. But much depended upon the ship's captain, who might rule as a benign ruler, harsh king, or unpredictable autocrat. For instance, George Yost, 14, a First Class Boy, reported that Commander Thomas O. Selfridge forbid his sailors from using profane language. George Yost diary, entry Sept. 12, 1862, Lincoln Presidential Library.
8. To Farragut's chagrin, officers also deserted at this time. *ORN*, 19:634, 645. The 1st Louisiana Cavalry was indeed organized early on, in August 1862, but the 2nd was not formed until Nov. 25, 1863. The 1st was not the first white Union regiment in the South—that was the 1st North Carolina Union Volunteers, formed on June 27, 1862. Frederick H. Dyer, *A Compendium of the War of the Rebellion* (Des Moines, IA: Dyer, 1908); reprint, Dayton, OH: Morningside Bookshop, 1978, 1212–13, 1472.
9. The navy rewarded police for returning deserters, whether in the United States or abroad. Packard, "Jottings," 150, 151; Schlesinger, ed., "A Blue Bluejacket's Letters," 557; Morrow, *Journal*, 24.
10. This dramatic affray is not mentioned in the abstract from *Hartford*'s log, but such omissions are not unusual. *ORN*, 19:705–10.
11. Lewis, *Farragut*, 116n65; *ORN*, 19:661.
12. While Brig. Gen. Thomas Williams's troops repulsed the Confederates, he fell during the battle. Some sailors heard that Williams was shot from his horse; others that friendly fire had "riddled" him. *ORN* 19:771; Edward M. Galligan diary entry, Aug. 5, 1862, Galligan Papers. Though soldiers reported Williams killed by a rifle shot to his chest, they also said the 7th Vermont fired upon another nearby Federal regiment, a place where Williams had been, so Galligan's version is possible. *OR*, 15:52, 54, 42, 49.
13. Thornton, a midshipman at 14, advanced from lieutenant to lieutenant commander in July 1862 and assumed command of the USS *Winona*, a 607-ton sidewheel gunboat. In April 1863, he became executive officer of the *Kearsarge* under John A. Winslow and helped sink the raider CSS *Alabama* off Cherbourg, France, on June 20, 1864. *DANFS*, NHHC.

14. The *Potomac,* a sail frigate launched in 1822, served as a stores ship for the West Gulf Squadron, as it was useless against fast steam blockade runners. *DANFS,* NHHC.

15. They built clipper ships long and lean, so probably Shaw is saying, "you *skinny* s-o-b."

16. Born in Virginia in 1811, Thornton A. Jenkins joined the navy as a midshipmen in 1828. During the Civil War, he commanded the USS *Oneida* and then became Farragut's chief of staff, rising to rear admiral in 1870. *DANFS,* NHHC. Loyall Farragut, the admiral's only child, was born in 1844 and died in 1916. He served as his father's secretary on the *Hartford* in 1863, entered West Point the same year, and graduated in 1868, serving three years in the 5th Artillery. He wrote a well-regarded biography of his father, published in 1879, and also wrote for the Military Order of the Loyal Legion of the United States (MOLLUS), a postwar organization for officers. Farragut Papers-Tenn., accessed at http://dlc.lib.utk.edu/f/fa/fulltext/1887. html (September 8, 2010); *New York Times* obituaries, Oct. 2, 1916.

17. Their troops needed elsewhere, Confederates withdrew from Pensacola in May 1862. "Florida's Role in the Civil War—Fort Pickens," accessed at http://fcit.usf.edu/florida/lessons/cvl_war/cvl_war1.htm (September 8, 2010); and also see George F. Pearce, *Pensacola During the Civil War: A Thorn in the Side of the Confederacy* (Gainesville: Univ. Press of Florida, 2000). Diggins uses the word "wrecking" in the sense then more current and which he explains: dismantling or raising sunken ships, cleaning up wreckage and rubble.

8. Hard Times

1. CSS *Alabama* sank the USS *Hatteras,* an iron-hulled steamer, on Jan. 11, 1863. Now the *Hatteras* is one of the few sunken ships on the nation's Register of Historic Places, resting under sixty feet of water about twenty miles south of Galveston, Texas. *ORN,* 19:510; *DANFS,* NHHC; John M. Kell, "Cruise and Combats of the 'Alabama,'" *B&L,* 4:605; Arnold, "Hatteras," in *The Handbook of Texas Online,* Texas Historical Association, https://TSHaonline.org/handbook/online/articles/qTh04 (accessed June 5, 2015). Two Federal sailing ships, the *Morning Light* and the schooner *Velocity,* fell into enemy hands at Sabine Pass when winds failed on Jan. 21, 1863, and the pair became easy prey for Confederate steamers, though only the *Morning Light* was burned. *ORN,* 19:558–60; *DANFS,* NHHC. Fleet Surgeon Foltz said that "[w]e are still in amazement at our defeat at Galveston," and Farragut said the affair on Jan. 1, 1863, was a "disaster." Foltz, *Surgeon,* 256; *ORN,* 19:447; James R. Soley, "Gulf Operations in 1862 and 1863," *B&L,* 3:571.

2. Comdr. Jonathan M. Wainwright, born in 1821, entered the navy as a midshipman in 1837 and was the grandfather of General Jonathan M. Wainwright, who led the doomed last struggle against the Japanese

invaders in the Philippines during World War II. Charles E. Cumberland, "The Confederate Loss and Recapture of Galveston," Southwestern Historical Quarterly 51, no. 2 (October 1947): 122–30; *DANFS*, NHHC; and also see Edward T. Cotham Jr., *Battle on the Bay: The Civil War Struggle for Galveston* (Austin: Univ. of Texas Press, 1998).

3. Confederates did not destroy the *Harriet Lane*, but instead put her to use. Later, she was sold, converted into a blockade runner, and interned in Havana. After the war, Spain returned the *Harriet Lane* to the United States, where it became a freighter, but was lost off Brazil in 1884. *DANFS*, NHHC; "Harriet Lane" in *Handbook of Texas Online*. A commissioned vessel of the Confederate States Navy and never a privateer, CSS *Alabama* always served as a commerce raider. John M. Kell, *Beneath the Stainless Banner*, ed. R. Thomas Campbell (Shippensburg, Pa.: Burd Street Press, 1999), 79–86; Raphael Semmes, *Rebel Raider; Being an Account of Raphael Semmes's Cruise in the C.S.S.* Sumter, ed. Harpur A Gosnell (Chapel Hill: Univ. of North Carolina Press, 1948), 195–200.

4. Federal and Confederate reports of the *Hatteras—Alabama* fight, *ORN*, 2:18–23, 684. Homer C. Blake, who joined the navy as a midshipman at 18, returned to the North after his capture and assumed command of James River naval forces, defeating a Confederate squadron in early 1864. He achieved commodore rank after the war, dying of malaria in New York in 1880. *New York Times* obit, Jan. 22, 1880.

5. Whether wood- or iron-hulled, ships sank when cannon fire holed them in vital places.

6. Both sidewheels and propellers powered the broad-beamed ironclad USS *Indianola*. Launched in early September 1862, Confederate ships rammed her from both sides in the Red River on Feb. 24, 1863, ending her fighting career. *Queen of the West*, pressed into service by her captors, was one of two ships that rammed the *Indianola*. *DANFS*, NHHC.

9. DISASTER

1. Andre H. Beauchamp to Margaret, March 6, 1863, Special Collections, Louisiana State University, Baton Rouge, La. .

2. *Harper's Weekly*, March 28, 1863, 196–97; James R. Soley, "Naval Operations in the Vicksburg Campaign," *B&L*, 3:565; Foltz, *Surgeon*, 259.

3. Thompson and Wainwright, *Confidential Correspondence*, 2:164; Loyall Farragut, "Passing the Port Hudson Batteries," *Personal Recollections*, Ser. 1, MOLLUS-N.Y. (New York: By the Commandery, 1891): 314–15.

4. Robert Weir, "Some War Remembrances," 6, Robert Weir Papers, G. W. Blunt White Library, Mystic Seaport Museum, Mystic, Conn. (hereafter cited as Weir, "Remembrances"); Loyal Farragut, "Passing," 315; John C. Parker, "With Farragut at Port Hudson," *Civil War Times Illustrated* 7, 7 (November 1968): 45.

5. William T. Meredith, "Admiral Farragut's Passage of Port Hudson," *Personal Recollections*, Ser. 2, MOLLUS-N.Y. (New York: G. P. Putnam's Sons, 1897): 121; Henneberry journal, March 15, 1863; Weir, "Remembrances," 1–5.

6. Nathaniel P. Banks was one of Lincoln's political generals, appointed because he could attract recruits, money, and support for the cause. Banks, with no military experience, was even more incompetent as a field commander than Benjamin F. Butler, his predecessor and another political general. Ezra J. Warner, *Generals in Blue: Lives of the Union Commanders* (Baton Rouge: Louisiana State Univ. Press, 1964), 17–18. For testimonials to Banks's incompetence, see Welles, *Diary*, 2:18–19; Marcus M. Spiegel, *Your True Marcus: The Civil War Letters of a Jewish Colonel*, ed. Fran L. Byrne and Jean P. Soman (Kent, Ohio: Kant State Univ. Press, 1985), 334, Banks "not worth a pinch of snuff as a soldier"; Lucius F. Hubbard, "Letters of a Union Officer: L. F. Hubbard and the Civil War," ed. N. B. Martin, *Minnesota History* 35 (1957): 316, Banks is a "miserable failure as a military man."

7. Union ships had "no chance with their broadside guns" because they could not be elevated enough to hit Confederate artillery emplaced high on the river bluffs.

8. The USS *Sachem*, a small (197-ton) screw steamer, had a crew of fifty-two and five guns—one 20-pounder and four 32-pounders.

9. For Farragut's son, it was an "unnatural quiet." Loyall Farragut, "Passing," 317. Banks did not provide supporting fire, as Farragut had started earlier than planned, so others in the fleet thought the army had failed the navy, with one officer calling it Banks's usual "masterly inactivity." Parker, "With Farragut," 45.

10. Others said they steamed against a 4-knot current. Meredith, "Admiral Farragut's Passage," 121; Holton, *Cruise*, 58.

11. An engineer on the *Richmond* said the furious cannonading "made a grand Wagnerian effect of sound," while a paymaster on the *Hartford* recalled that the "roar of guns stuns the ear." Weir, "Remembrances," 7; Meredith, "Admiral Farragut's Passage," 122. A Confederate artilleryman said that "[i]t was the greatest sight I ever saw or ever expect to see." Anon. to Julia, March 22, 1863, National Underwater and Marine Agency, accessed at www.numa.net/expeditions/mississippi_letter.html (accessed June 6, 2015).

12. A *New York Herald* correspondent on the USS *Richmond* wrote that "clouds of smoke envelope the river." It was so thick that ships lost sight of each other, and a *Hartford* pilot in the mizzen top yelled for ship gunners to cease fire because he could not see his way. Andrews, *North Reports*, 390; Meredith, "Admiral Farragut's Passage," 123; Loyall Farragut, "Passing," 318.

13. James S. Palmer, *Hartford*'s captain, agreed peril was "imminent" at this juncture, but credited the pilot with extricating the ship from the dangerous situation and praised Kimberly for his "industry, zeal and ingenuity." *ORN*, 19:671.

14. Of the seven ships attempting the passage, only *Albatross* and *Hartford* succeeded. The others, crippled by Confederate fire, could not continue.

15. Last in line, the *Mississippi* had suffered from the improved marksmanship of Confederate gunners. Then, with the ship firmly stuck, they concentrated their fire upon her, furiously pounding the stationary target. After the captain ordered her set afire, *Mississippi*'s crew abandoned ship by small boat and by jumping overboard. Of the 297-man crew, 64 became casualties. George Dewey, then a 24-year-old lieutenant on the *Mississippi* and later a famous admiral during the Spanish-American War, said that "in this action I lived about five years in one hour." *ORN*, 19:682; Dewey, *Autobiography*, 81.

16. Ships below Port Hudson hastened to avoid the drifting, blazing *Mississippi* as her loaded guns fired, mostly fearing her magazine might explode. Henneberry journal, March 15, 1863; Harrie Webster, "Some Personal Recollections and Reminiscences of the Battle of Port Hudson," *War Papers* 16, MOLLUS-D.C. (Washington, D.C.: Read Jan. 3, 1894): 263. When she did blow up, it was with a roar that "reverberated over the hills," while another sailor reported the blast was heard a hundred miles away. Loyall Farragut, "Passing," 318; Meredith, "Admiral Farragut's Passage," 125.

17. Quite simply, Farragut called it a "disaster." *ORN*, 19:665.

18. The ironclad *Indianola* (not a monitor, as Diggins wrote), rammed seven times by Confederate ships and "in an almost powerless condition," ran her bow on the river bank and surrendered on Feb. 24, 1863. *DANFS*, NHHC. The bottle message system worked. Henneberry journal, March 16, 1863.

19. A quick pull on the lock string fired the loaded cannon's powder charge. "Artillery Glossary," accessed at http://www.civilwarartillery.com/glossary/glossarygz.htm (September 20, 2010).

20. Yards are wooden spars, attached to the masts at right angles, to hold and to set *Hartford*'s square sails.

21. The netting supposedly stopped Confederates from boarding and capturing the ship. But Diggins has confused the chronology of events—the *Hartford*'s log shows the crew still working on the anti-boarder netting on March 18, 1863. *ORN*, 20:763.

22. Captured Confederate mails, recounting plans "to attack and capture this ship [the *Hartford*] and her consorts by ramming and boarding," made Federals more vigilant. Foltz, *Surgeon*, 275. *Hartford* began steaming up river at 5 a.m., March 18, 1863. *ORN*, 20:763.

23. Butler called escaped slaves "contraband of war" in 1861, and the name stuck, though the USS *Resolute*'s captain had used the term a bit earlier. *OR*, 2:52; *ORN*, 4:604. Lincoln, incidentally, disliked the term, preferring "freeman" or "freed people." John Y. Simon, ed., *The Papers of Ulysses S. Grant* (Carbondale: Southern Illinois Univ. Press, 1979), 8:342.

24. Intended for slashing rather than thrusting, the model 1860 navy cutlass was a short, slightly curved weapon with a single sharp edged 26-inch-long

blade, measuring 32-inches in length overall, encased in a black leather scabbord. Sailors used the cutlass to repel boarders and for boarding and landing parties, and the weapons remained in cutlass racks on some ships until World War II. "Swords US Navy," NHHC, accessed at "http://www. history.navy.mil/library/online/uniform_sword.htm".htm (September 23, 2010).

25. *Hartford*'s log records this wire-cutting foray taking place on March 17, 1863. *ORN*, 20:763.

26. This letter, with "guerrilla" spelled correctly, is at *ORN*, 20:4.

27. A "masked" battery is hidden until the artillerymen open fire.

28. Confederates moved the *Vicksburg*'s machinery overland to Mobile for use there, and it was they who set her afire. *ORN*, 20:735, 36, 47, 765.

29. Grant sent down the drifting coal barge, *ORN*, 20:7.

30. *Albatross* engaged the Warrenton guns in the forenoon of March 22, 1863. *ORN*, 20:764.

31. While it may have looked that way to some shipboard observers, the "greatest portion" of Warrenton was not destroyed at this time.

32. William T. Sherman commanded in the West after Grant moved to the East as the Union's army leader; Maj. Gen. John A. McClernand of Illinois was another of Lincoln's inept political generals who led the 13th Army Corps during the Vicksburg campaign. Warner, *Generals in Blue*, 444, 293–94.

33. For this complex effort, which ended in failure, as Diggins notes, see Ballard, *Vicksburg*, 101–90.

34. Exactly what action or inaction of Grant's sparked Diggins's indignation is uncertain. Perhaps it was because Grant did not name Farragut as his secretary of the navy, but that is only speculation.

35. The admiral's son left the ship on March 25, 1863. Loyall Farragut, *Life*, 344, 355; abstract of *Hartford* log, *ORN*, 20:764.

36. Col. Charles Ellet, Jr., organized and led the ram fleet, but died in June 1862, whereupon his brother, Brig. Gen. Alfred Ellet, assumed command. Col. Charles Rivers Ellet, the organizer's son, commanded ram fleet ships. A nephew of Charles Ellet, Jr., Lt. Col. John A. Ellet, commanded the *Lancaster* until Confederates sank her in March 1863, while Lt. Edward C. Ellet served on the *Switzerland* when the two ships ran the Vicksburg batteries. Jeanette Cabell Coley, ["Charles Ellet, Jr."], *Smithsonian Associates Civil War E-Mail Newsletter,* Vol. 5, No. 5 (n.d.), accessed at http://civilwar studies.org/articles/Vol_5/charles-ellet.shtm (September 29, 2010); *DANFS*, NHHC. See also Warren D. Crandall and Isaac D. Newell, *History of the Ram Fleet and the Mississippi Marine Brigade . . . the Ellets and their Men* (St. Louis, Mo.: Buschart Bros., 1907) and Chester G. Hearn, *Ellet's Brigade: The Strangest Outfit of All* (Baton Rouge: Louisiana State Univ. Press, 2000). Some recruits may have come from the western frontier, but the Ellets recruited others from hospitals, and they also used black troops. Many held a less flattering view of Marine Brigade soldiers, calling them rascals,

pillagers, and cotton thieves. Hearn, *Ellet's Brigade*, 143; Allan McNeal to Father, Jan. 15, 1863, in Allan McNeal, "Hospital Letters," accessed at www.alaska.net/~design/civilwar/jan15/letter.html (December 19, 2010); William N. Bock to Father, April 19, 1864, Lincoln Presidential Library.

37. The two ships, both sidewheel former towboats, were the 413-ton *Switzerland* and the 257-ton *Lancaster*. They began their perilous run with skeleton crews about 5 a.m. on March 25, exposing them to more accurate daylight fire. *Switzerland*, in the lead, took hits but escaped; *Lancaster*, following, sank when Vicksburg's gunners sent a plunging shot through her bottom. *DANFS*, NHHC; *ORN*, 20:19–24; John E. Hart, "Commanding the USS Albatross," *Civil War Times Illustrated* 15, 4 (July 1976): 133.

10. BLOCKING THE RIVERS

1. Farragut worried about Warrenton, calling the fortifications there so "formidable" that it was "hazardous for the vessels to pass up by that place." *ORN*, 20:35.

2. Keel up or not, the navy sought to salvage the *Indianola* while Confederates tried to destroy her, with the navy succeeding in January 1865. *ORN*, 26:624, 715, 738; 27:53; *DANFS*, NHHC.

3. Effective hand grenades exceeded the era's mechanical, technological, and material ability. Federals threw one, the finned Ketcham, like a heavy dart; another, the Hayne's Excelsior, a round grenade, was very dangerous to use. But rolling, dropping, or tossing a short-fused 6-pounder artillery shell proved a good substitute for one of the war's patented grenades. Coggins, *Arms and Equipment*, 97–98, 66–67.

4. As noted in *Hartford*'s log, *ORN*, 20:765.

5. Apparently the refugees repeated rumors spawned by wishful thinking. In any event, no attempt to capture the *Hartford* and the other ships ever occurred.

6. Diggins refers to Pointe Coupee Parish, Louisiana. One naval officer called the Marine Brigade men, who manned the *Switzerland*, a lot of "rascals" who also stole cotton and charged that "Gen. Ellet . . . is making it pay." William N. Bock to Father, April 19, 1864, Lincoln Presidential Library.

7. Note that if the *Switzerland*'s crew stowed stolen pianos aboard ship, then the captain would likely know about the musical loot. Scanning the *New York Times* for April–May 1863 revealed no articles crediting the *Hartford* with piano plundering or pillage in general, but perhaps such credit came at a later date.

8. Farragut's fleet surgeon reported that ships below Port Hudson sent up two rockets to signal that Gabaudan had arrived safely and gave slightly different times. Foltz, *Surgeon*, 276. Gabaudan's down-river trip was widely reported. Loyall Farragut, "Passing," 320–21; Schley, *Forty-five Years*, 50; *ORN*, 20:49, 54, 67; *OR*, 15:294–95, 303.

9. The *J. D. Clarke* was a sidewheel steamer used by the Confederate army as a transport on the Red River and the captured officer was Major George T. Howard. *ORN*, 20:54; 765; Arthur Wyllie, *The Confederate States Navy* (Raleigh, N.C.: Lulu.com, 2007), 87; *DANFS*, NHHC.

10. Diggins's 100-pound catfish is not a fishy tale—in 2005, an angler caught a record 124-pound catfish in the Mississippi. *AP* story, "DOA Catfish," accessed at www.msnbc.com (October 12, 2010).

11. "The health of the officers and men is generally good," Farragut reported on April 6, 1863. *ORN*, 20:48.

12. Diggins leaps ahead to recount the Red River campaign of 1864 and errs when he casts it as a Federal victory. It was another disaster for the North, albeit a successful cotton raid. On May 7, Banks reached Alexandria, La. Richard S. Irwin, "The Red River Campaign," *B&L*, 4:345–66.

13. Official accounts and army commendations are at *ORN*, 20:256–59.

14. Diggins probably meant the USS *Tyler*, a 575-ton sidewheel gunboat. *DANFS*, NHHC.

15. *Arizona* first carried cargo and passengers from New Orleans until Confederates seized her in January 1862 and turned the iron-hulled sidewheel steamer into a blockade runner. That career ended in late October 1862 when a Federal gunboat captured her, and she became a six-gun Union warship. *DANFS*, NHHC. A distributary of both the Mississippi and Red rivers, the 170-mile course of the Atchafalaya is now a National Heritage Area. See www.atchafalaya.org.

16. Originally an army ship, the 5-gun, 438-ton sidewheel USS *Estrella* transferred to the navy in late 1862. *DANFS*, NHHC.

17. Disabled by shore batteries in mid-February 1863, the *Queen of the West* was captured by Confederates and used against the Union. Two months later, Federal gunboats USS *Arizona*, *Estrella*, and *Calhoun* converged on the *Queen* on Grand Lake or Berwick Bay and set her afire and adrift on the Atchafalaya River, where she grounded and exploded. *ORN*, 20:134–36; *DANFS*, NHHC.

18. *Hartford*'s log shows Farragut leaving at 4:40 a.m. on May 8. See also Foltz, *Surgeon*, 283.

19. Virginia-born Thomas Green had moved to Texas in 1835, fought in the War for Texas Independence, and began the Civil War as the 5th Texas Cavalry's colonel. Warner, *Generals in Gray*, 117. After Port Hudson's fall, Banks said that Green and his superior, Maj. Gen. Richard Taylor, led "12,000 men . . . between Port Hudson and Donaldsonville" who had placed artillery batteries on the river's west banks. *ORN*, 20:265.

20. Abner Read commanded the USS *Monongahela* when a shell from Confederate shore batteries about ten miles below Donaldsonville hit the ship on July 7, 1863, mortally wounding Read. *ORN*, 20:333–35. On July 4, 1863, while steaming down river from Donaldsonville, the USS *New London*'s captain wrote that "the river is now in possession of the rebels and they fire

on all our vessels and destroy our transports," noting that a shore battery opened fire and "we were struck several times." Perkins, *Letters*, 115.

21. Banks ordered his first major flawed, senseless, and unsuccessful attack on May 27, 1863, promising Grant that Port Hudson's fall "will be *instant and certain.*" Burkhardt, *Confederate Rage*, 52n21.

22. *Hartford*'s log reports learning of Vicksburg's fall on July 7.

23. Confederates said the siege reduced them to eating mules, horses, and rats. John S. Kendall, ed., "Recollections of a Confederate Officer," *Louisiana Historical Quarterly* 29, 4 (October 1946): 1112; Howard C. Wright, *Port Hudson: Its History from an Interior Point of View as Sketched from the Diary of an Officer* (1863–1866; 1937; repr., Baton Rouge: Committee for the Preservation of the Port Hudson Battlefield, 1961), 43. A slave in Vicksburg said people there also ate cats and dogs. See Isaac Stier in George P. Rawick, ed., *The American Slave: A Composite Autobiography*, ser. 1 (1941; repr. Westport, Conn.: Greenwood, 1972), 7:14748.

24. Diggins and the *Hartford* departed New Orleans on Aug. 1, arriving at the navy yard in New York on Aug. 12, 1863. *Hartford* log, *ORN*, 20:775. As the ship left New Orleans, Surgeon Foltz exulted, "The river is open from end to end . . . and Rebeldom is down." Foltz, *Surgeon*, 290.

11. WAITING GAME

1. As noted earlier, Lincoln declared a blockade of southern ports on April 19, 1861. Basler, *Lincoln*, 4:338–39; Philip Whitlock, "Life of Philip Whitlock," memoir manuscript, Beth Ahabah Museum and Archives Trust, Richmond, Va., accessed at http://www.jewish-history.com/philip_whitlock.html (October 27, 2010). Shortages of ordinary manufactured items, such as toothbrushes, grew worse, for which see Jan. 7, 1863 entry in George W. Cable, ed., "A Woman's Diary of the Siege of Vicksburg," *Century Illustrated Magazine*, new series 8 (September 1885): 768–74.

2. John Dragoo to parents, Dec. 18, 1862, in John Dragoo file, Indiana Historical Society, Indianapolis, Ind.; Marcus B. Toney, *Privations of a Private*, 2nd ed. (Nashville, Tenn.: M. E. Church, South, 1907), 76–77; William W. Goldsborough, *The Maryland Line in the Confederate States Army* (Baltimore, Md.: Kelly, Piet & Co., 1869), 346; Jesse C. Dormon, 2nd Louisiana Infantry, letter, Dec. 5, 1863, where he writes, "I dont think I shall Rob the dead" in William H. Davidson, ed., "War Was the Place," Chattahoochee Valley Historical Society Bulletin 5 (November 1961): 94; Jill K. Garrett and Marise P. Lightfoot, *The Civil War in Maury County, Tennessee* (n.p.: privately published by authors, 1966), 113; Richard M. McMurry, ed., "A Mississippian at Nashville," *Civil War Times Illustrated* 12 (May 1973): 9, 14, 15.

3. For "precious crystals," see Virginia Clay-Copton, *A Belle of the Fifties* (New York: Doubleday, Page & Co., 1905; electronic ed., Chapel Hill: Univ.

of North Carolina, 1998), 223–24, accessed at http://docsouth.unc.edu/fpn/clay/clay.html (June 27, 2007); Cable, "A Woman's Diary," Jan. 7, 1863; for inflationary prices , Whitlock,, "The Life of Philip Whitlock."

4. James J. Heslin, ed., "Two New Yorkers in the Union Navy," *New-York Historical Quarterly* 43, 2 (April 1959): 174; letter to Mother, Nov. 15, 1863, in Elizabeth W. Roberson, *Weep Not For Me Dear Mother* (Gretna, La.: Pelican, 1996), 147; Walter L. Fleming, *Civil War and Reconstruction in Alabama* (New York: Columbia Univ. Press, 1905; repr., New York: Peter Smith, 1949), 201; for salt $1 a pint at salt mine, see J. Stoddard Johnston, "Sketches of Operations of General John C. Breckenridge," *Southern Historical Society Papers* 7, 8 (August 1879): 386. See Ella Lonn, *Salt as a Factor in the Confederacy* (New York: Walter Neale, 1933) for the humble mineral's importance, not only as a condiment but also as a war material. For coffee at $25 or $30 a pound, $5 a cup, see Cate, ed., *Two Soldiers*, 70; Whitlock, "Life of Philip Whitlock"; Goodloe, *Confederate Echoes*, 122.

5. Thompson and Wainwright, *Confidential Correspondence*, 1:318; letter to Anna, April 11, 1863, in William E. Keeler and Robert W. Daly, eds., *Aboard USS Florida: 1863–65* (Annapolis, Md.: United States Naval Institute, 1968), 20; Joseph M. Simms, "Personal Experiences in the Volunteer Navy during the Civil War," MOLLUS-D.C., *War Papers* 50 (December 1903), accessed at http://openlibrary.org/works/OL7746517W/personal_experiences_in_the_volunteer_navy_during_the_civil_war/ (December 9, 2010), noting blockaders at Wilmington, N.C., had caught fifty-two ocean-going blockade runners in fourteen months; James M. McPherson and Patricia R. McPherson, eds., *The Civil War Letters of Lieutenant Rowell H. Lamson* (New York: Oxford Univ. Press, 1997), 172, 211; Archer Jones, *Civil War Command and Strategy* (New York: Free Press, 1992), 142. For a good look at the blockade, see Anderson, *By Sea and By River*, 215–32.

6. G. T. Beauregard, "Torpedo Service in Charleston Harbor," in Philadelphia Weekly Times, *Annals of the War*, 520; Milton F. Perry, *Infernal Machines: The Story of Confederate Submarines and Mine Warfare* (Baton Rouge: Louisiana State Univ. Press, 1965), 82–86, 105–7; *DANFS*, NHHC; Alvah E. Hunter, *A Year on a Monitor and the Destruction of Fort Sumter*, ed. Craig L. Symonds (Columbia: Univ. of South Carolina Press, 1987), 139–42. See Coggins, *Arms and Equipment*, 150, for drawings of *Hunley* and *David*.

7. I. N. Shannon, "Infernal machines described," *Confederate Veteran* 13, 10 (October 1905): 458; Heslin, "Two New Yorkers," 179; Calvin G. Hutchinson to William Hill, May 19, 1864, Hutchinson Papers, for both "devilish" and "cowardly"; Paul H. Kendricken, *Memoirs of Paul Henry Kendricken* (Boston: privately printed, 1910), 254, for "treacherous"; Farragut to Welles, *ORN*, 21:298; McPherson and McPherson, *Lamson of the* Gettysburg, 164.

8. Oliver W. Farenholt, "The Monitor 'Catskill': A Year's Reminiscences, 1863–1864," *War Papers*, MOLLUS-Calif. (San Francisco, Calif.: Shannon-Commy Printing, 1912): 5, accessed at MOLLUS War Papers, http://suvcw.

org/mollus/warpapers/warpapers.htm; Hunter, *A Year on a Monitor*, 49; William F. Hutchinson, "The Bay Fight, a Sketch of the Battle of Mobile Bay," *Personal Narratives*, ser. 1 RISSHS (Providence, R.I.: Sidney S. Rider, 1878), 6, accessed at MOLLUS War Papers, http://suvcw.org/mollus/warpapers/warpapers.htm (April 4, 2008); True, "Life Aboard a Gunboat," 39; Benjamin Heath journal, May 6, 1864, Benjamin Heath Papers, 1864–1865, Archibald L. Alexander Library, Rutgers, The State Univ. of New Jersey, New Brunswick, N.J. (hereafter cited as Heath Papers); John M. Batten, *Reminiscences of Two Years in the United States Navy* (Lancaster, Pa.: Inquirer Printing and Publishing, 1881), 67, 305; Levi Hayden diaries, June 2, 1864, New York Public Library, New York, N.Y. (hereafter cited as Levi Hayden diaries); Calvin G. Hutchinson to William Hill, May 19, 1864, Hutchinson Papers; Brown, "Service in the Mississippi Squadron," 305. For a mine-sweeping device, see *OR*, 1, 14:254, for "Sketch of the Devil, or Torpedo Searcher. . . ."

9. Levi Hayden diaries, May 29, 1864.

10. Perry, *Infernal Machines*, 199–201, 195–97; Batten, *Reminiscences*, 68; Frank R. Butts, "A Cruise Along the Blockade," *Personal Narratives*, ser. 2, RISSHS (Providence, R.I.: Read Nov. 13, 1898): 13–14; Levi Hayden diaries, June 2, 1864; George A. Bright to Father, March 17, 1863, Birght Papers. Also see Gabriel J. Rains and Peter S. Michie, *Confederate Torpedoes*, ed. Herbert M. Schiller (Jefferson, N.C.: McFarland & Co., 2011), 139–67, for a detailed account of Federal ships and boats sunk or damaged by mines.

11. "Spare boats" refers to the small lifeboats, cutters, and dinghies carried aboard the warships.

12. For months, blockaders feared the CSS *Tennessee* would steam out some dark night and attack wooden Federal ships. Confederates planned such an attack, but unfavorable conditions for the low freeboard, slow-moving *Tennessee* always prevented a sortie. Thompson and Wainwright, *Confidential Correspondence*, 2:341; Batcheller, "The Battle of Mobile Bay," 63; Weir, "Personal Recollections," 1, in Weir Papers; C. Carter Smith, Jr., ed., *Two Naval Journals, 1864: The Journal of Mr. John C. O'Connell, CSN, on the C.S.S.* Tennessee *and the Journal of Pvt. Charles Brother, USMC, on the USS* Hartford *at the Battle of Mobile Bay* (Birmingham, Ala.: Southern University Pres by Birmingham Publishing Co., 1964), 2.

13. Most of the mines thickly seeded in Mobile Bay required a ship to jar a percussion cap to detonate the explosive charge. Perry, *Infernal Machines*, 44, 181. The word torpedo derives from a species of electric ray, but the first self-propelled weapon was the Whitehead torpedo, introduced in 1866 and powered by compressed air. Patrick McSherry, "Whitehead Torpedo," accessed at www.spanamwar.com/torpedo.htm (November 6, 2010).

14. As noted above, Diggins was correct in declaring Mobile "the greatest and only stronghold remaining to the enemy in the west Gulf." Smaller harbors in Texas and western Florida remained in southern hands, but they could

not move goods across the Mississippi River from Texas or easily northward from Florida.

15. *Tennessee*'s exact cost is unknown, but Confederates began building a slightly smaller version in 1861–62 at a fixed contract price of $76,920. *DANFS*, NHHC. The second *Tennessee* was launched in February 1863 at Selma, Ala. *DANFS*, NHHC; George M. Brooke, Jr., ed., *Ironclads and Big Guns of the Confederacy: The Journal and Letters of John M. Brooke* (Columbia: Univ. of South Carolina Press, 2002), 149, 152. Her six rifles, designed by Confederate naval officer John M. Brooke, came from foundries in Richmond and Selma; her weak engines came from the large sidewheel Mississippi river steamer *Alonzo Child*. "John Mercer Brooke," accessed at www.civilwarartillery.com/inventors/Brooke.htm (November 7, 2009); J[ames] D. Johnston, "The Battle of Mobile Bay." *Southern Historical Society Papers* 9 (1881):471, accessed at www.csnavy.org/shsp.mob.bay.johnston. htm (November 18, 2010); *Alonzo Child*, *DANFS*, NHHC.

16. Born in 1800 in Maryland, Franklin Buchanan joined the navy in 1815, served in the Mexican-American War, but resigned when he thought Maryland would secede from the Union. When that did not happen, he tried to regain his commission, but the Navy rejected him, probably nervous about his loyalties. Confederates gladly accepted him, and he commanded the ironclad CSS *Virginia* (the former USS *Merrimack*) when she sank the USS *Cumberland* and destroyed the USS *Congress* at Hampton Roads on March 8, 1862. He and Farragut had served together in the old navy. Jack Friend, *West Wind, Flood Tide: The Battle of Mobile Bay* (Annapolis, Md.: Naval Institute Press, 2004), 45, 129.

17. Diggins was not alone—most who endured blockade duty called it stultifying, a "dull" or "dreary" or "dreadful" experience of unending monotony. Edward Blue to Frank L. Stickney, May 19, 1864, Stickney Papers, Library of Congress; Butler, "Personal Experiences," 189; Batcheller, "The Battle of Mobile Bay," 62. Some thought it smacked of prison, Milligan, ed., *Fresh-Water Navy*, 153; Hutchinson, "Life on the Texan Blockade," 24.

18. A loose cannon, such as *Hartford*'s 9200-pound broadside guns, could cause much damage and injury while rolling about a ship's deck, but that a wayward cannon would cause the ship's "certain destruction" is uncertain. Coggins, *Arms and Equipment*, 145; for an example, see Kendricken, *Memoirs*, 249.

19. Diggins' "terrific storms" might cause some ships to heel over, almost on beam's end, so that the lower yards on masts would touch the high waves. A USS *Gemsbok* sailor reported that they removed yards to make their sailing ship lighter aloft during a storm. Clark, *Seven Years*, 180.

20. For weeks Rear Admiral David D. Porter delayed before sending two monitors to Farragut, arguing that the *Winnebago* and *Chickasaw* were not seagoing vessels, would "break to pieces in the least swell," and, besides, were "unfit" to fight fortifications or an enemy with heavy guns. *ORN*, 26:388.

This caused one of Farragut's biographers to wonder if Porter sought to sabotage Farragut's Mobile operation from jealousy or spite. Lewis, *Farragut*, 246. Farragut scorned iron ships, writing, "I never thought much of Iron Clads but my opinion of them is declining daily." Farragut to Fox, March 7, 1863, Thompson and Wainwright, *Confidential Correspondence*, 1:328. Yet he wanted monitors on hand before he would attack at Mobile Bay.

12. THE *IVANHOE* SAGA

1. The grounded blockade runner was the *Ivanhoe*. Hults, "Aboard the Galena," Pt. 1:17; George S. Waterman, "Afloat–Afield–Afloat," *Confederate Veteran* 9, 11 (November 1902), accessed at www.adp.fus.edu/ivanhoe.html (November 12, 2010); Farragut to Welles, *ORN*, 21:357.

2. Farragut to Welles, July 2, 1864, *ORN*, 21:353–54; Waterman, "Afloat"; Stephen R. Wise, *Lifeline of the Confederacy: Blockade Running During the Civil War* (Columbia: Univ. of South Carolina Press, 1988), 178–79.

3. Drayton to Capt. Thornton A. Jenkins, journal of John B. Marchand, USS *Lackawanna*'s captain, and log of CSS *Tennessee*, all in *ORN*, 21:354, 817, 936; Richard D. Duncan, "The Storming of Mobile Bay," *Alabama Historical Quarterly* 40, 1 and 2 (Spring and Summer 1978): 8; Morrow, *Journal*, 28; Colby Chester, "Showing the Way," *War Papers* 4, 79 MOLLUS-D.C. (Washington, D.C.: By the Commandery, 1910): 166–68; Charles Brother, "The Journal of Private Charles Brother, USMC," *Civil War Naval Chronology, 1861–1865* (Washington, D.C.: Government Printing Office, 1961–1966), 72; Higgins, *Yeoman in Farragut's Fleet*, 76.

4. Waterman, "Afloat"; Hults, "Aboard the Galena," 19; USS *Cowslip* log, July 4 entry, *ORN*, 21:793.

5. *ORN*, 21:354–56; Percival Drayton, "Naval Letters from Captain Percival Drayton, 1861–1865," *New York Public Library Bulletin* 10 (1906): 61.

6. *ORN*, 21:353–54, 905; Waterman, "Afloat," where he asserts, "Nearly three-quarters of her cargo . . . was saved" on the first night.

7. Waterman, "Afloat," where he writes, "How they managed to exist in that fearful place for so many minutes is a mystery."

8. Only two to four small boat crews sought and failed to find the *Ivanhoe*. Drayton to Jenkins, *ORN*, 21:354; Brother, "Journal," 72.

9. "Barge" is a flag officer's small boat, and a "gig" is the one designated for the captain's use.

10. This raid began on the night of Tuesday, July 5, 1864. USS *Metacomet* log, *ORN*, 21:827.

11. Shipboard and Confederate observers saw the fire erupt on the *Ivanhoe* and burn the woodwork in the iron-hulled steamer for a couple of hours with the sailor-arsonists returning "by 2:30 a.m." Farragut's report, *ORN*, 21:354–55; Brother, "Journal," 74; Morrow, *Journal*, 29; Higgins, *Yeoman in Farragut's Fleet*, 77; Waterman, "Afloat," where Confederates discover fire at 12:40 a.m. and fight the flames.

12. Leslie G. Morrow, a captain's clerk on the USS *Galena*, thought that she was "hardly worth blowing up now." Morrow, *Journal*, 30. This raid set out on the night of July 7.

13. Towed in by the USS *Pinola* on the night of July 7, the sailors met a hail of bullets from considerably less than a thousand Confederate soldiers and blasts from a boat howitzer. Drayton's report, July 8, 1864, *ORN*, 21:356; Waterman, "Afloat," where he writes that "our soldiers gave them several volleys of musketry"; Robert Tarleton to Sallie Lightfoot, July 7, 1864, Sallie Lightfoot Tarleton Papers, 1861–1868, MS Collection #71, Joyner Library, East Carolina University, Greenville, N.C. (hereafter cited as Tarleton Papers).

14. Confederates also gave up on the stranded ship when a fierce gale snapped her foretopmast and rolled her far over, and heavy seas flooded her hold, whereupon Confederate midshipman Waterman wrote that "the *Ivanhoe* was abandoned to her fate." Waterman, "Afloat." Yet on July 20, Admiral Franklin Buchanan still hoped to salvage her and ordered the *Tennessee*'s captain to "do all you can to save her." *ORN*, 21:907. But all efforts were for naught, and the bones of the *Ivanhoe* remain today near where she grounded in 1864. National Underwater and Marine Agency (NUMA), "Survey of Civil War Ships," accessed at www.numa.net/expeditions/survey_of_civil_war_ships.html (January 4, 2011).

13. "DAMN THE TORPEDOES"

1. Farragut to Wife, July 31, 1864, Naval Historical Collection, United States Naval War College, Newport, R.I.

2. Thompson and Wainwright, *Confidential Correspondence*, 1:320, 328; Andrews, *North Reports*, 392; David P. Jones, "Something About Our Navy," *Military Essays and Recollections*, vol. 3, MOLLUS-Ill. (Chicago: Dial Press, 1897): 335, 328–29; Drayton, "Naval Letters," 58–60.

3. Mobile fell on April 12, 1865. Dabney H. Maury, "The Defence of Mobile in 1865," *Southern Historical Society Papers* 3, 1 (January 1877): 1–13; James R. Soley, "Closing Operations in the Gulf and Western Waters," B&L, 4:412.

4. OR, 34, 3:491–92; 4:240, 406.

5. Order to Canby, dated June 24, received July 1, 1864, OR, 34, 4:528; Canby to Farragut, July 1, 1864, *ORN*, 21:357.

6. Canby to Farragut, July 18 and 26, 1864, *ORN*, 21:379, 388.

7. Welles to Porter, June 9, 1864, and Porter to Welles, June 13, 1864, *ORN*, 26:379–80, 387–88.

8. Lewis, *Farragut*, 246; Welles to Porter, June 25, 1864, *ORN*, 26:438.

9. *DANFS*, NHHC, for monitor descriptions; Welles to Farragut, *ORN*, 21:344; Friend, *West Wind*, 78–79. "Capes of Delaware" were Cape Henlopen and Cape May where Delaware Bay meets the Atlantic Ocean.

10. Perkins, *Letters*, 127–29, 125, 130; *ORN*, 21:389, 399–401, 351, 390; Harrie Webster, "An August Morning with Farragut at Mobile Bay," *Civil War*

Naval Chronology, 1861–1865, US Navy Historical Division (Washington, D.C.: Government Printing Office, 1961–1966), 6:93; Robert B. Ely, "'this filthy ironpot,'" *American Heritage* 19, 2 (February 1968): 47–49, 51, 109.

11. D. B. Conrad, "With Buchanan on the Tennessee" in *Behind the Guns with American Heroes,* ed. James W. Buel (Chicago, Ill.: International Publishing Co., 1899): 405–6; Smith, *Two Naval Journals,* 2–3. For examples of Federal fears, see Weir, "Personal Recollections," 1; Hults, "Aboard the Galena," Pt. 1:14; Drayton, "Naval Letters," 57; Batcheller, "The Battle of Mobile Bay," 63. On living conditions aboard the *Tennessee,* a Confederate nurse who toured the ironclad declared, "I certainly felt I should not like to be one of the crew." Richard B. Harwell, ed., *Kate: The Journal of a Confederate Nurse* (Baton Rouge: Louisiana State Univ. Press, 1959), 123.

12. John C. Watson, "Farragut and Mobile Bay—Personal Reminiscences," *War Papers* 98, MOLLUS-D.C. (Washington, D.C.: Read before the Commandery, 1916), 2, accessed at http://www.archive.org/stream/farragutmobile ba00wats/farragutmobileba00watts_djvu.txt (November 12, 2010).

13. Drayton, *Naval Letters,* 46; a spy reports torpedo boat construction, April 12, 1864, and CSS *Tennessee* log notes arrival of a torpedo boat at Mobile, June 12, 1864, *ORN,* 21:187, 936; NHHC for *Octorara* and *St. Patrick;* Paul H. Silverstone, *Civil War Navies, 1855–1883* (Annapolis, Md.: Naval Institute Press, 2001), 167, for *St. Patrick.*

14. James E. Jouett recollections (handscript), Alfred Pirtle Collection, The Filson Historical Society, Louisville, Ky. (hereafter cited as Pirtle Collection).

15. An abstract of the *Hartford's* log shows all hands were called at 3 a.m., rather than Diggins's 2 a.m., and the general movement signal came at 5:30, although the *Hartford* did not begin to move until 5:40 a.m. *ORN,* 21:799.

16. Hutchinson, "The Bay Fight," 6, and William T. Meredith to Mollie [Mary Watson], August 4, 1864, William Tuckey Meredith Papers, Rare Books and Special Collections, Princeton University Library, Princeton University (hereafter cited as Meredith Papers), for description of *Brooklyn's* mine-sweeping apparatus.

17. *Hartford's* log reported "at 6:25 vessels reasonably in line." *ORN,* 21:799.

18. Diggins, busy at his gun, gives times that again conflict with those entered in the *Hartford's* log, which has the *Tecumseh* firing earlier, at 6:22, and Fort Morgan firing first at 7:06, whereupon the *Brooklyn* replied at 7:07.

19. Accounts of the *Tecumseh's* sinking vary slightly, though most agree that she very quickly plunged to the bottom. Confederate 2nd Lt. F. S. Barrett said she sank "almost instantly," asserting that the monitor went down in less than 25 seconds. *ORN* 21:569. But a *New York Tribune* reporter with the fleet said she first went up into the air "about 20 feet" before dropping beneath the waves after hitting a torpedo loaded with *ten tons* of powder (his italics), all of which made for good reading of bad facts. Andrews, *North Reports,* 573. Robert Weir, an engineer on the USS *Richmond,* said the *Tecumseh's* bow "seemed to go under and her stern raise so that the

propeller was seen churning the water into foam—a lurch to port and then sinking, so that as the turret went under, the waters rushed together and with a spray dashing high into the air, the vessel disappeared." Weir, "Personal Recollections," [p. 7]. At this writing, the *Tecumseh* lies beneath thirty feet of water in excellent condition, for which see W. Wilson West, Jr., "USS *Tecumseh* Shipwreck Management Plan," joint project of Department of Defense Legacy Resource Management Program, et al., accessed at www.denix.osd.mil/cr/upload/94-1704_hi-res.pdf (November 24, 2010).

20. The usual wording for this famous command is "Damn the torpedoes, full speed ahead." However, Farragut's son said his father ordered, "Damn the torpedoes! Four bells! Captain Drayton, go ahead!" while John J. Almy, then a commander, recalled that Farragut said, "Torpedoes hell, go ahead full speed." Loyall Farragut, *Life*, 416–17; John J. Almy to Rev. and dear Sis, May 24, 1887, John J. Almy Papers, Navarro College, Corsicana, Tex.

21. "[T]o lap her port quarter" means that the *Hartford* neared the port, or left, side of the *Brooklyn*'s stern.

22. Diggins here exaggerates the number of mines, perhaps for effect. In any event, "thousands of torpedoes" did not clog that one small area or even the whole bay. Viktor von Scheliha, who oversaw Confederate mine-laying at Mobile, reported seeding the channel opposite Fort Morgan with 180 torpedoes in three lines. Viktor Ernst K. R. von Scheliha, *A Treatise on Coast-Defence* (London: E. & F. N. Spon, 1868), 105. Later, during clean-up operations, a Federal soldier said they had swept 700 mines from the bay. Rufus Kinsley, *Diary of a Christian Soldier: Rufus Kinsley and the Civil War*, ed. David C. Rankin (Cambridge, Eng.: Cambridge Univ. Press, 2004), 163.

23. The crew's outcry, as reported here, is confusing. On June 28, 1862, while the fleet steamed upriver, the *Brooklyn* lagged behind and did not pass Vicksburg's batteries. For that failure, Farragut censured and relieved her captain. But James Alden, the *Brooklyn*'s captain at Mobile, then commanded the *Richmond* and did pass Vicksburg's guns. So Alden had nothing to do with his ship's timid conduct at Vicksburg, for which see *ORN*, 18: 597–600, 602–6. 613.

24. Ensign Nields and his boat crew rescued ten *Tecumseh* survivors, including John Collins, her pilot, while seven escaped in one of the monitor's boats and another four survivors swam to shore and into captivity. Nields earned the fleet's praise and a recommendation for promotion from Farragut for his action. *ORN*, 21:419, 442, 490. Brig. Gen. Richard L. Page, Fort Morgan's commander, also respected Nields's effort, ordering his gunners not to fire upon the rescue boat. *B&L*, 4:408. When the *Tecumseh* hit the torpedo or mine, her captain, Tunis A. M. Craven, who had earlier said that he did not "care the snap of my fingers" about torpedoes, and Collins were in the pilot house above the turret. Both hurried to the exit ladder to below and escape. Craven reportedly drew back and said, "After you, Sir." But, as the naval strategist Alfred T. Mahan dryly noted, "There was no afterward for him,"

and Craven went down with his ship. A. T. Mahan, *The Navy in the Civil War*, vol. III: *The Gulf and Inland Waters* (New York: Charles Scribner's Sons, 1883), 231, 234.

25. Others echoed Diggins's account of the carnage. For the *Hartford*, see John C. Kinney, "Farragut at Mobile Bay," *B&L*, 4:389; on the *Lackawanna*, see Myron Adams to Cousin Eliza, Aug. 19, 1864, Pearce Civil War Collection, Navarro College, Corsicana, Tex.; and Jesse to Sister, Aug. 7, 1864, "The Battle of Mobile Bay," *Brooklyn Journal*, Brooklyn Institute of Arts and Sciences, Children's Museum, Occasional Papers in Cultural History, No. 5 (1964). Afterward, a soldier described the *Hartford* as "riddled . . . from stem to stern." Kinsley, *Diary*, 160. A *cat* was a swiveling davit to which a cot was attached; scuppers were and are for water drainage from decks. For more on cats, see Bartlett, "The 'Brooklyn' at the Passage," *B&L*, 2:58.

26. When the *Brooklyn* blocked the fleet, the ships became easy targets. Army 1st Lt. John C. Kinney, serving as signal officer aboard the *Hartford*, wrote, "It was during these few perilous moments that the most fatal work of the day was done to the fleet." Kinney, "Farragut at Mobile Bay," 389.

14. ONE AGAINST MANY

1. Lt-Cmdr Lewis A. Kimberly, *Hartford*'s executive officer, reported that Confederate raking fire, the length-wise shots, had cut "down our men at the guns fearfully" and damaged gun carriages and material. Kimberly to Captain P. Drayton, Aug. 8, 1864, *ORN*, 21:429. Speaking plainly, a masters mate said that they were "catching hell" from the *Selma*. Joseph J. Pinelli to Loyall Farragut, June 12, 1881, in Farragut Papers-Tenn.

2. Sidewheeler *Metacomet*'s top speed was 12½ knots. *DANFS*, NHHC.

3. USS Metacomet carried nine guns, while the CSS *Selma*, another sidewheeler, had five guns, including a 6.4" rifle. *Selma*'s top speed was nine knots, and she probably had a smaller crew than the *Metacomet*, as desertions had plagued her that year. *DANFS*, NHHC. James E. Jouett, *Metacomet*'s captain, again met a prewar fellow officer when he captured Peter U. Murphy, the *Selma*'s captain. Jouett to Alfred Pirtle, Aug. 12, 1896, Pirtle Collection; Benjamin B. Cox, "Mobile in the War Between the States," *Confederate Veteran*, 24, 5 (May 1816): 211.

4. When they banked the fires underneath boilers, sharply reducing the burn rate, it required extra time to unbank the fires, to spread the coal and bring the fires up to normal burning, thus heating the water for steam to run the engines. In this instance, Federals did not expect Buchanan so quickly to sally forth alone to do battle.

5. Born in 1800 in Maryland, Buchanan joined the navy in 1815 as a midshipman. Imbued with a strong loyalty to his native state, he thought Maryland would secede from the Union. So Capt. Buchanan, with forty-five years of service and commander of the Washington Navy Yard, jumped the

wrong way. He resigned from the navy and, when Maryland stayed with the Union, he tried to recall his resignation. Secretary of the Navy Welles refused, probably doubting Buchanan's fealty. Thereupon, Buchanan went to Richmond and entered the Confederate navy as a captain. Craig L. Symonds, *Confederate Admiral: The Life and Wars of Franklin Buchanan* (Annapolis, Md.: Naval Institute Press, 1999), xv–xvi, 1–2.

6. Buchanan commanded the CSS *Virginia* (ex-USS *Merrimack*) on March 8, 1862, the first day at Hampton Roads, sinking the USS *Cumberland* and running aground the USS *Congress*. Wounded in the thigh, he did not take part in the next day's fight with the *Monitor*, a historic first fight between ironclads.

7. Note that *Hartford*'s full speed was 13½ knots while the *Tennessee*'s was probably less than the 6 knots her captain claimed, for which see *DANFS* for the *Hartford* and for the *Tennessee*; Johnston, "The Battle," 471, and surgeon D. B. Conrad, "With Buchanan," in Buel, *Behind the Guns*, 405. Another Confederate sailor, not on the *Tennessee*, also gave her top speed as 6 knots. J. Thomas Scharf, *History of the Confederate States Navy from its Organization to the Surrender of its Last Vessel* (New York: Rogers & Sherwood, 1887; repr., New York: Fairfax Press, 1977), 554.

8. A *cathead* was a "strong piece of oak projecting over the bows (one on either side) . . . usually with the face of a cat carved on its end" and used to raise or drop an anchor. Noel and Beach, *Naval Terms*, 60. Whether Drayton's field glasses were government issued or his own is unknown, but probably his rage cost him an expensive imported tool, [Scott Watson], "Civil War Optics," 1–2, accessed at www.civilwarmedicalbooks.com/civil_war_optics.html (April 22, 2013).

9. As noted in this chapter's opening, when the opposing ships scraped sides, sailors cursed each other, threw things, thrust bayonets, and fired small arms, for which see J. B. Marchand to Farragut, Aug. 5, 9, 1864, *ORN*, 21:466, 469; Jesse to Sister, Aug. 7, 1864, "Battle of Mobile Bay," *Brooklyn Journal*; Conrad, "With Buchanan," in Buel, *Behind the Guns*, 410.

10. The *Tennessee*'s surgeon described the scene after the cannon ball struck his ironclad's side. He wrote that "all the men whose backs were against the shield were riven into pieces and I saw their limbs and chests, severed and mangled scattered about the deck, their hearts lying near their bodies. All of the gun crew and the admiral were covered from head to foot with blood, flesh and viscera." Conrad, "With Buchanan" in Buel, *Behind the Guns*, 410.

11. After the collision, a paymaster said, "The old *Hartford* is badly injured by the tremendous butt the *Lackawanna* gave her." William T. Meredith to Mollie, Aug. 12, 1864, Meredith Papers; Charles F, a Marine, wrote that the impact raised "the d—1generally." Brother, "Journal," 81. But Percival Drayton, *Hartford*'s captain, reported, as did Diggins, that the blow resulted in "cutting us down to the water line," though there was no serious leak and the ship was in no danger of sinking. *ORN*, 21:426.

12. Sometime during the action Farragut supposedly signaled the *Lackawanna*, "For God's sake get out of our way." Samuel T. Cushing, "The Acting Signal Corps," *War Papers*, MOLLUS-Kans. (n.p., Jan. 4, 1892):4, accessed at www.civilwarsignals.org/lessons/sigmethod/cushing.html (April 22, 2013).

13. Johnston explained that *Tennessee*'s steering chains lay exposed on her after deck and Federal fire shot away those cables, thus rendering her unsteerable. Johnston, "The Battle," 471. Years later, one sailor said the monitor *Chichasaw*'s guns had disabled the steering gear. W. "Some Errors Corrected," *New York Times*, May 19, 1887. While the *Tennessee* absorbed a damaging pounding, her casualties were comparatively light: two killed and nine wounded. Johnston to Buchanan, [Aug. 25, 1864], *ORN*, 21:581–82. A USS *Monongahela* ensign who boarded the *Tennessee* said her gun deck was "flesh and gore" and that her crew threw many dead overboard to conceal their losses. However, his assertions were the only ones found to that effect. Duncan, ed. "The Storming of Mobile Bay," 18.

14. Confirming Diggins's assessment, when D. B. Conrad, the *Tennessee*'s surgeon, boarded the *Hartford*, he saw a scene of "carnage and devastation" and a "long line of grim corpses, dressed in blue, lying side by side." A Federal officer told him that those casualties, members of two gun crews, "were all killed by splinters." Conrad, "With Buchanan," in Buel, *Behind the Guns*, 412.

15. Farragut's final casualty count was as follows, with those killed listed first, then the wounded: *Hartford*, 25, 28; *Brooklyn*, 11, 43; *Oneida*, 8, 30; and *Lackawanna*, 4, 35; the rest of the fleet listed 4 killed and 16 wounded. Grand total was 52 killed and 170 wounded, Farragut to Gideon Welles, Aug. 8, 1864, *ORN*, 21:407. Note the unusual wounded-to-killed ratio of almost one-to-one for the *Hartford*. By comparison, the four Confederate ships listed just 12 killed and 20 wounded, as follows: *Tennessee*, 2, 9; *Selma*, 8, 7; *Gaines*, 2, 3; and *Morgan*, 1 wounded. *ORN*, 21:578–9, 590–91, 585.

16. *Afterguard* sailors, mostly rated as landsmen, which clearly defines their shipboard status, served on the quarter-deck and poop; the *sweepers* among them enjoyed even lower status, consigned to sweeping the decks. See *A Naval Encyclopædia: Comprising a Dictionary of Nautical Words and Phrases; Biographical Notices, and Records of Naval Officers* (Philadelphia, Pa.: L. R. Hamersly, 1881).

17. The 311-ton sidewheeler USS *Philippi*, a captured blockade runner, took a disabling hit from Fort Morgan's guns and ran aground to avoid sinking. Soon CSS *Morgan* sailors set her afire. *DANFS*, NHHC; *ORN*, 21:557, 584.

18. *Metacomet*'s heaviest guns were two 100-pounders. *DANFS*, NHHC.

19. With others, the *Tennessee*'s surgeon and a USS *Monongahela* officer also said that the *Chickasaw* had inflicted the greatest damage to the ram. Conrad, "With Buchanan," in Buel, *Behind the* Guns, 413; Batcheller, "The Battle of Mobile Bay," 71.

20. The "barge" *Ingomar* was a steam-powered lighter used by Confederates to strengthen Fort Powell. Perkins seized her as a prize, leading to a later claim in Congress by her northern owners. Arthur W. Bergeron, *Confederate Mobile* (Baton Rouge: Louisiana State Univ. Press by arrangement with the Univ. of Mississippi Press, 1994), 144; U.S. Congress, Senate Committee on Claims, Report 103, 42nd Congress, 2nd session, April 1, 1872.

21. J. R. Madison Mullany did lose his left forearm to amputation but fiercely disputed that his *Oneida* was completely disabled, since only the starboard boiler had exploded and he had steamed ahead using the port boiler. *ORN*, 21:410, 485–89.

22. A gig is a small boat designated for use by the ship's captain. Noel and Beach, *Naval Terms*, 137. Lt. Cmdr. James C. P. de Krafft, aboard the 955-ton sidewheel USS *Conemaugh*, led five gunboats, including the armed tug USS *Narcissus* with her crew of nineteen, and the 188-ton tinclad USS *Stockdale*. *ORN*, 21:502–3.

23. Earlier, de Krafft's men had discovered thirteen artillery pieces, a large amount of ammunition, a chest of hand grenades, and other materiel, all "mostly in good order." *ORN*, 21:503, 505.

24. Fort Powell's elimination allowed Federal ships to use the Mississippi Sound side passage to the sea and outside world, bypassing formidable Fort Morgan.

15. Fort Morgan Resists

1. Robert Tarleton to Sallie Lightfoot, August 4, 1864, Tarleton Papers.

2. Joseph B. Wilkinson diary of the siege of Fort Morgan, 1864, entry Aug. 5, 1864, Alabama Department of Archives and History, Montgomery, Ala. (hereafter cited as Wilkinson diary).

3. Page to D. H. Maury, Aug. 30, 1864, *ORN*, 21:574.

4. Warner, *Generals in Blue*, 181, for Granger.

5. Robert L. Page, "Defense of Fort Morgan," *B&L*, 4:410; Wilkinson diary, entry Aug. 12, 1864.

6. For comparative strength numbers, see Foxhall Alexander Parker, *The Battle of Mobile Bay, and the Capture of Forts Powell, Gaines and Morgan* (Boston: A. Williams & Co., 1878; repr. Whitefish, Mont.: Kessinger Publishing, 2011), 17, 42, for Federals; Page, "Defense of Fort Morgan," *B&L*, 4:409, where he reports 400 men in the garrison; [Hurieosco Austill], "Fort Morgan in the Confederacy," *Alabama Historical Quarterly* 7, 2 (Summer 1945): 260, who counts 450; Friend, *West Wind*, 240 n36, who estimates 572 men surrendered.

7. [Austill], "Fort Morgan," 262, 263, 266; Kinsley, *Diary*, 162.

8. Anderson's surrender "deeply mortified" Fort Morgan's defenders and brought scorn from some Federals. [Austill], "Fort Morgan," 259; Meredith to Mollie, Aug. 11, 1864, Meredith Papers. Anderson's superiors denounced

him, Brig. Gen. Richard L. Page calling the surrender "inexplicable and disgraceful," while Maj. Gen. Dabney H. Maury, the district commander, said it was "shameful." *ORN*, 21:561, 562.

9. Federals used sixteen mortars with high arching trajectories to drop explosive shells inside the fort. *OR*, 39, 1:414; Kinsley, *Diary*, 160. The bombardment became very personal for Joseph B. Wilkinson, Fort Morgan's post adjutant, when a Federal shell shattered his office and stopped three feet from him, but failed to explode. Wilkinson diary, entry Aug. 9, 1864.

10. Note this is the same Lt. Tyson that Diggins said misbehaved during a foray to destroy the grounded blockade runner *Ivanhoe*.

11. Farragut's ships stood off a distance from the fort, using only their long range rifled cannon. Report of Miles D. McAlester, chief engineer, Military Division of West Mississippi, *OR*, 39, 1:414. Morgan's misnamed "Citadel" was not an inner fortress or stronghold; rather, it was a wooden barracks, so easily and brightly burned. *OR*, 39, 1:413.

12. Confederates hoisted a white flag about 6:30 a.m. *Hartford* log, *ORN*, 21:802.

13. Other Federals also lauded Confederate tenacity. For example, a *Hartford* paymaster said that Page, Morgan's commander, was "a stubborn, brave man," while a *Conemaugh* engineering officer wrote, "Wonderful was the resistance offered by the defenders." Meredith to Mollie, Aug. 12, 1864, Meredith Papers; Kendricken, *Memoirs*, 245. However, Federals charged that Page spiked some of his cannon and destroyed gunpowder after capitulating, thus committing a "base act" in violation of the rules of war, though he was subsequently acquitted. Friend, *West Wind*, 251; *OR*, 39, 1:420; Morrow, *Journal*, 49, for "base act."

14. Perhaps Diggins was unaware that two strong forts with large garrisons defended the upper or inner bay by the city of Mobile and that Federals would need thousands of ground troops to take Mobile.

16. WAR SERVICE ENDS

1. Lewis, *Farragut*, 310; *ORN*, 21:803; "Admiral Farragut in New York," *New York Times*, Dec. 14, 1864.

2. Farragut, *Life*, 478; Lewis, *Farragut*, 315, 482n12; "Farragut: A Handsome New Year Present," *New York Times*, Jan. 1, 1865.

3. Knowles to Loyall Farragut, Dec. 15, 1878, MS 1887, Farragut Papers-Tenn.

4. Ella Lonn, *Foreigners in the Union Army and Navy* (Baton Rouge: Louisiana State Univ. Press, 1951; repr., New York: Greenwood Press, 1969), 637.

5. Bacon, *Double Duty*, 71; Bartlett, "The 'Brooklyn' at the Passage," *B&L*, 2:56; Farragut to Madam [Mary Blauvelt], ca. May 1862, Blauvelt Papers; Knowles to Loyall Farragut, Dec. 15, 1878, David G. Farragut Papers, 1815–1964, Special Collections, Hoskins Library, Univ. of Tennessee, Knoxville, Tenn.

6. Farragut to Gustavus V. Fox, assistant secretary of the navy, Jan. 30, 1862, Thompson and Wainwright, *Confidential Correspondence*, 1:299.

7. The "forrien" man-of-war was a Swedish warship, and the steamer was the revenue cutter *Bronx*. *ORN*, 21:803; Lewis, *Farragut*, 312.
8. Apparently Diggins did not exaggerate much here as Farragut, the seasoned sailor, called the storm a "terrible gale," so that the *Hartford* "labored heavily" during the "furious" gales. Farragut to Welles, Dec. 13, 1864, *ORN*, 21:759. Head rails were the curved ornamental pieces extending from the back of the ship's figure head to the bow or cathead, for which see Lauchlan McKay, "Explanation of Terms," in *The Practical-Ship Builder, 1839*, accessed at www.bruzelius.info/Nautica/Etymology/English/McKay(1839). html/ (May 20, 2013).
9. Here Diggins again misnames the CSS *Arkansas*, perhaps because the tune to the "The Arkansas Traveler" still thrummed in his head. If he quotes Farragut accurately, then the "or worse" probably referred to the possibility of treachery, though it is difficult to fathom how that could have occurred during that particular event.
10. Diggins won the Congressional Medal of Honor for the Mobile Bay action. Probably most of those who received the CMH during the Civil War would not qualify for the award under modern guidelines. At the time, however, it was the only authorized medal, though some generals issued their own decorations, such as the Kearny Cross and the Butler and Gilmore medals. "Medal of Honor Recipients," NHHC.

EPILOGUE

1. Hearings before the Committee on Naval Affairs, House of Representatives, 1908–1909, (p683) Item No. 47 [Diggins file] (hereafter cited as Naval Affairs Hearings).
2. Diggins family information is courtesy of William Boswell of Alexandria, Va., a direct descendant of Diggins.
3. Horace Greeley, *The Tribune Almanac and Political Register* (New York: Tribune Association, 1908), 228; George W. Baird, "Memorials to the Great Men Who Were Masons," *The Builder Magazine* 6, 4 (April 1920): 2–3, accessed at www.phoenixmasonry.org/the_builder_1920_april.htm (June 17, 2013); Benjamin Perley Poore, *Perley's Reminiscences of Sixty Years in the National Metropolis* (Philadelphia: Hubbard Bros., 1886), 409, accessed at catalog.hathitrust.org/Record/008957690 (June 27, 2013); "Dewey Gives Way Before Admirers," *New York Times*, Sept. 29, 1899.
4. Dewey to Diggins, Oct. 16, 1899, Naval Affairs Hearings.
5. Bartholomew Diggins Pension File #SC1657, National Archives and Records Administration, Washington, D.C.
6. Naval Affairs Hearings, 683–84.
7. Hammock-support, Letters, Patent No. 638,174, dated Nov. 28, 1899, United States Patent Office.
8. Email to the editor from Thomas Lannon, Manuscripts and Archives Division, New York Public Library, Nov. 24, 2008, where Lannon says they

are "unable to uncover the specific provenance of the volume of Diggins' Recollections," in editor's possession.

9. For death dates and burial, William Boswell, Diggins geneology, June 20, 2003; Arlington National Cemetery records, accessed at www.arlington cemetery.net/bdiggins.htm (October 20, 2007).

10. Lewis, *Farragut*, 331.

11. Admiral David Glasgow Farragut, "Biographies in Naval History," NHHC; *DANFS*, NHHC, for the *Franklin*; Farragut, *Life*, 485–538.

12. Lewis, *Farragut*, 371–72, 374.

13. Admiral David Dixon Porter, People—United States, NHHC; Richard S. West, Jr., *The Second Admiral: A Life of David Dixon Porter, 1813–1891* (New York: Coward-McCann, 1937), 327–34, 237–38.

14. For Kimberly, see People—United States, NHHC.

15. For Watson, see the ship to be named after him in *DANFS*, NHHC.

16. For Drayton, see People—United States, NHHC.

17. For USS *Philox, DANFS*, NHHC; Knowles to Loyall Farragut, Dec. 15, 1878, Farragut Papers-Tenn. Warner, *Generals in Gray*, 194–99; proceedings of Lovell's court inquiry, *OR*, 6:554–643.

18. Warner, *Generals in Gray*, 232–33.

19. Symonds, *Confederate Admiral*, 220–25, 228–31; Friend, *West Wind*, 248–49.

20. *DANFS*, NHHC.

21. Friend, *West Wind*, 251–52; *DANFS*, NHHC.

22. *ORN*, 21:561, for "inexplicable" surrender; *ORN*, 21:536, 541–42, for Farragut's comments.

23. Friend, *West Wind*, 252–53; William H. Thiesen, "The 1900 Galveston Hurricane," 2–3, accessed at www.uscg.mil/history/articles/Galveston 1900keepersdlog.pdf (June 15, 2013).

24. For Fort Jackson, see Plaquemines Parish government site at www.plaque minesparish.com/tourism.php and for Fort St. Philip, see Fort St. Philip article on the National Park Service's National Historic Landmarks website, at http://tps.cr.nps.gov/nhl/detail.cfm?ResourceId=261&ResourceType= Structure, where the fort is described as in "very dangerous condition (accessed August 16, 2013).

25. Email to editor from John T. McGill, curator and head of Research Services, Historic New Orleans Collection, Feb. 16, 2006.

26. See description of Vicksburg National Military Park and the National Cemetery at www.nps.gov/vick/.

27. Port Hudson State Historic Site, accessed at www.crt.state.la.us/parks/ ipthudson.aspx (July 7, 2013).

28. For the official report, see Farragut to Welles, Aug. 29, 1864, *ORN*, 21:616; for another version, see Hults, "Aboard the Galena," 2:36.

29. Perry, *Infernal Machines*, 200–201.

30. For Yorktown, see ibid., 20–25; Rains and Michie, *Confederate Torpedoes*, 54–60; Burkhardt, *Confederate Rage*, 238.
31. Burkhardt, *Confederate Rage*, 237.
32. *DANFS*, NHHC; Friend, *West Wind*, 253.
33. For provenance of the fragment sold by Crocker Farm Auctions on June 4, 2011, see "Civil War Flag Fragment from Admiral Farragut's USS Hartford" listing at http://www.crockerfarm.com/antiques-auction/2011-06-04/ lot-186/Civil-War-Flag-Fragment-Reportedly-from-Admiral-Farraguts-USS-Hartford/ (accessed April 27, 2015).
34. For gangway board reproduction, see www.mainememory.net/artifact/82 (accessed July 7, 2013); for Naval Museum replicas, see www.portcolumbus. org/exhibits/uss-hartford (accessed July 7, 2013).

BIBLIOGRAPHY

UNPUBLISHED

Abraham Lincoln Presidential Library, Springfield, Ill.
William N. Bock, Zeno P. Elwell, W. H. Price, George Yost

Alabama Department of Archives and History, Montgomery, Ala.
Joseph B. Wilkinson diary of the siege of Fort Morgan, 1864

American Antiquarian Society, Worcester, Mass.
Letters and diary of Edward Woolsey Bacon

American Philosphical Society, Philadelphia, Pa.
Diary of Albert D. Bache

Auburn University, Auburn, Ala.
Alexander Millard

Boston Athenaeum, Boston, Mass.
Edwin [no last name]

Chicago Historical Society, Chicago, Ill.
James E. Henneberry journal

Cincinnati Historical Society, Cincinatti, Ohio
E. W. Goble

Duke University, Durham, N.C.
James L. B. Blauvelt Papers; David G. Farragut; Robert Melvin; William
Read; Hubert Saunders

East Carolina University, Greenville, N.C.
Robert Tarleton, Sallie Lightfoot Tarleton Papers

Emory University, Atlanta, Ga.
Frederic E. Davis Papers

Filson Historical Society, Louisville, Ky.
James E. Jouett in Alfred Pirtle Collection

Harvard University, Houghton Library, Cambridge, Mass.
Charles Longfellow

Historical Society of Pennsylvania, Philadelphia, Pa.
William J. Clark Papers; Charles Alexander Schetky Log

Huntington Library, San Marino, Calif.
    George A. Bright; Calvin G. Hutchinson

Indiana Historical Society, Indianapolis, Ind.
    John Dragoo

Library of Congress, Washington, D.C.
    Asa Beetham, Edward Blue, Joseph B. Osborn, Oscar Smith

Louisiana State University, Baton Rouge, La.
    Andre H. Beauchamp; Freeman Foster, Jr.

Mariners' Museum Library, Newport News, Va.
    George S. Geer Papers

Missouri Historical Society, Columbia, Mo.
    Sylvester Doss in Warren D. Crandall Collection

Montana Historical Society
    Papers of Edward M. Galligan

Mystic Seaport Museum, G. W. Blunt Library, Mystic, Conn.
    Journals of Carston DeWitt, Charles A. Poole and William Wainwright (all
        also available online at Mystic Seaport Library website); recollections of
        Robert Weir

Naval History and Heritage Command, Washington, D.C.
    William J. Francis

Naval War College, Newport, R.I.
    David G. Farragut

Navarro College, Corsicana, Tex.
    Myron Adams, John J. Almy

New York City Public Library, New York, N.Y.
    Charles F. W. Behm, Bartholomew Diggins, Levi Hayden

Nimitz Library, U.S. Naval Academy, Annapolis, Md.
    John E. Hart, Daniel D. T. Nestell

Ohio Historical Society, Columbus, Ohio
    J. McLeod Murphy, David D. Porter

Princeton University
    Samuel P. Lee letter; annotated log of USS *Oneida*; William Tuckey
        Meredith Papers

Rutgers, The State University of New Jersey, Archibald L. Alexander Library,
    New Brunswick, N.J.
    Benjamin Heath Papers, 1864–1865; William W. Van Cleaf Papers, 1861–1897

University of Michigan, Bentley Historical Library, Ann Arbor, Mich.
  Henry C. Bates; Henry Grimes Marshall Papers, 1861–1865, James S. Schoff
  Collection; Preston Family Papers

University of North Carolina, Chapel Hill, Chapel Hill, N.C.
  George W. Harris

University of Tennessee, Knoxville, Knoxville, Tenn.
  John H. Knowles and Joseph J. Pinelli letters in David G. Farragut Papers,
  1815–1964

University of Texas, Austin, Austin, Tex.
  Sam W. Farrow Papers, Center for American History

Western Reserve Historical Society, Cleveland, Ohio
  John Simpson diary, William P. Palmer Collection

ELECTRONIC SOURCES

Anon. to Julia, March 22, 1863. National Underwater and Marine Agency, www.
  numa.net/expeditions/mississippi_letter.html (accessed February 3, 2008).

Associated Press. "DOA Catfish Swimming with the Fishes," www.msnbc.com
  (accessed October 12, 2010).

Atchafalaya National Heritage Area, www.atchafalaya.org (accessed October 15,
  2010).

Baird, George W. "Memorials to Great Men Who Were Masons." *The Builder
  Magazine*, Vol. 6, 4 (April 1920):1–3, www.phoenixmasonry.org/the_
  builder_1920_april.htm (accessed June 27, 2013).

"Ben" to Roxbury City *Gazette*, June 21, 1862. Published July 17, 1862, www.
  letterscivilwar.org/6–21–62a.html (accessed February 3, 2008).

Biographical Directory of the United States Congress, 1774–Present, www.
  bioguide.congress.gove/biosearch/biosearch.asp/ (accessed August 16, 2010).

Board of Artillery Officers. *Instruction for Field Artillery*. Philadelphia: J. B.
  Lippincott & Co., 1861, http://catalog.hathitrust.org/Record/002021314
  (accessed July 16, 2009).

Browning, Robert M., Jr. "Go Ahead, Go Ahead." *Naval History Magazine* 23, 6
  (December 2009): 1–14, www.usni.org/print/4442 (accessed November 13,
  2010).

Chatterton, E. Keble. *Steamships and their Story*. London: Cassell and Co., 1910,
  http://catalog.hathitrust.org/Record/006249126 (accessed July 14, 2009).

Clay-Copton, Virginia. *A Belle of the Fifties*. New York: Doubleday, Page & Co.,
  1905. University of North Carolina electronic edition, 1998, http://doc
  south.unc.edu/fpn/clay/clay.html (accessed June 27, 2007).

Cloud, John. "The 200th Anniversary of the Survey of the Coast." National Archives *Prologue* 39, 1 (Spring 2007): 1–2 of 16, www.archives.gov/public tions/prologue/2007/spring/coast-survey.html (accessed June 26, 2009).

Coley, Jeannette Cabell. ["Charles Ellet, Jr."]. *Smithsonian Associates Civil War E-Mail Newsletter* 5, 5 (n.d.), http://civilwarstudies.org/articles/Vol_5/ charles-ellet.shtm (accessed September 29, 2010).

CSS *Georgia*—History 1862–1872, www.sas.usace.army.mil/CSS/ (accessed February 17, 2013).

Cushing, Samuel T. "The Acting Signal Corps." *War Papers,* MOLLUS-Kans. (n.p., Jan. 4, 1892), www.civilwarsignals.org/lessons/sigmethod/cushing. html (accessed April 22, 2013).

Davis, C. H. "Memoir of Charles Henry Davis, 1807–1877." Read before the National Academy, April 1896. http://books.nap.edu/html/biomems/cdavis04. pdf (accessed November 23, 2013).

Dictionary of American Naval Fighting Ships, Naval History and Heritage Command, http://www.history.navy.mil/ (accessed June 5, 2015).

Dillingham, John M., Papers. Freeport Historical Society, www.mainememory. net (accessed April 4, 2008).

Farenholt, Oscar W. "From Ordinary Seaman to Rear Admiral." *War Papers,* MOLLUS-Calif. (San Francisco: Shannon-Commy Printing, 1910): 1–14, suvcw.org/mollus/warpapers/CAv2p368.htm (accessed March 27, 2008).

———. "The Monitor 'Catskill': A Year's Reminiscences, 1863–1864." *War Papers,* MOLLUS-Calif. (San Francisco: Shannon-Commy Printing, 1912): 1–15, suvcw.org/mollus/warpapers/CAv1p379.htm (accessed March 27, 2008).

Farragut, David G., Papers, 1815–1864. University of Tennessee, Knoxville. Special Collections Library. Knoxville, Tenn. http://dlc.lib.utk.edu/f/fa/full text/1887.html (accessed September 8, 2010).

"Florida's Role in the Civil War—Fort Pickens." http://fcit.usf.edu/florida/ lessons/cvl_war/cvl_war1.htm (accessed September 11, 2010).

Foenander, Terry, ed. "Fire and Brimstone—Aboard the USS *Cayuga* at Forts Jackson & St. Philip: Excerpts from the Journal of Paymaster's Clerk Samuel Massa." www.tfoenander.com/massa.htm (accessed May 2, 2009). Diary is in Sameul Massa Papers, Special Collections, Syracuse University.

Greeley, Horace. *The Tribune Almanac and Political Register* (1908): 228, http:// catalog.hathitrust.org/Record/000682188 (accessed June 27, 2013).

Harris, Thomas to editor Chelsea (Mass.) *Telegraph and Pioneer,* April 28, 1862, www.letterscivilwar.org/4–28–62a.html (accessed February 7, 2008).

Hutchinson, William F. "The Bay Fight, a Sketch of the Battle of Mobile Bay." *Personal Narratives,* series 1, RISSHS. (Providence: Sidney S. Rider, 1878): 217–42, http://www.geocities.ws/generalgreene1770/RIMOLLUS/battleof mobilebay.html (accessed April 4, 2008).

———. "Life on the Texan Blockade." *Personal Narratives,* series 3, RISSHS (Providence: The Society, 1883): 1–31, suvcw.org/mollus/warpapers/RIv4p1. htm (accessed April 4, 2008).

"John Mercer Brooke." www.civilwarartillery.com/inventors/Brooke.htm (accessed November 7, 2009).

Kemp, Daniel F. "Civil War Reminiscences, Aboard the USS *Cincinnati,* 1862–1863." Courtesy Barbara Covello, http://sunsite.utk.edu/civil-war/kemp.html (accessed October 23, 2005).

"Last Day of 'the Tot' in the Royal Navy." *Royal Navy Memories.* http://royal navymemories.co.uk/day-of-mourning/ (accessed November 27, 2013).

McKay, Lauchlan. *The Practical Ship-Builder, 1839.* www.bruzelius.info/Nautica/Etymology/English/McKay(1839).html (accessed July 23, 2013).

McNeal, Allan. "Hospital Letters." www.alaska.net/~design/civilwar/jan15/letter.html (accessed December 19, 2010).

McSherry, Patrick. "Whitehead Torpedo." www.spanamwar.com/torpedo.htm (accessed November 6, 2010).

Mason, Geoffrey B. *Service Histories of Royal Navy Warships in World War 2.* www.naval-history.net/xGM-Chrono-10DD-250-Glowworm.htm (accessed June 28, 2009).

Meckel, Richard. "The Cutlass Carved its Niche in Our Navy's Annals." http://www.history.navy.mil/browse-by-topic/heritage/uniforms-and-personal-equipment/swords.html (accessed July 21, 2009).

Michael, W. H. C. "The Mississippi Flotilla." *War Sketches and Incidents,* vol. 1. MOLLUS-Neb. (Omaha: Burkley Print, 1902): 21–33, suvcw.org/mollus/warpapers/NEv1p21.htm (accessed March 2004): 1–19.

National Underwater and Marine Agency (NUMA). "Survey of Civil War Ships." www.numa.net/expeditions/survey_of_civil_war_ships.html (accessed January 4, 2011).

Oxley, Robert M., ed. "The Civil War Gulf Blockade: The Unpublished Journal of a U. S. Navy Warrant Officer Aboard the USS *Vincennes,* 1861–1864." *International Journal of Naval History* 1, 1 (April 2002): 1–17, in "Archives," www.ijnhonline.org (accessed March 14, 2009).

Poore, Benjamin Perley. *Perley's Reminiscences of Sixty Years in the National Metropolis.* Philadelphia: Hubbard Bros., 1886, 409, http://catalog.hathi trust.org/Record/008957690 (accessed June 27, 2013).

Reidy, Joseph P. "Black Men in Navy Blue During the Civil War." National Archives *Prologue* 33, 3 (Fall 2001), www.archives.gov/publications/prologue/2001/fall/black-sailor-1.html (accessed August 16, 2008).

Rightor, Henry, ed. *Standard History of New Orleans, Louisiana.* Chicago: Lewis Publishing, 1900. https://archive.org/details/standardhistory00 righgoog (accessed July 14, 2009).

Secretary of State, Louisiana. "Old Arsenal Museum." http://www.sos.louisiana. gov/tabid/244/Default.asps (accessed July 27, 2009).

Simms, Joseph M. "Personal Experiences in the Volunteer Navy during the Civil War."https://archive.org/details/personalexperien01simm (accessed August 10, 2015).

Symonds, Craig L. "Damn the Torpedoes: the Battle of Mobile Bay." *Hallowed Ground* 9, 4 (Winter 2008), http://www.civilwar.org/battlefields/mobilebay/ mobile-bay-history-articles/damn-the-torpedoes-the.html?referrer=https:// www.google.com/ (accessed August 8, 2011).

Szkotak, Steve. "Civil War message opened, decoded: No help coming." December 25, 2010. news.yahoo.com/s/ap/20101225/ap_on_re_us/us-message_ in_a_bottle (accessed March 18, 2011).

Texas Historical Association. "Harriet Lane." *The Handbook of Texas Online.* https://tshaonline.org/handbook/online/articles/qth01 (accessed September 13, 2010).

———. "Hatteras." *The Handbook of Texas Online.* https://tshaonline.org/ handbook/online/articles/qth04 (accessed September 11, 2010).

Thiesen, William H. "The 1900 Galveston Hurricane." www.uscg.mil/history/ articles/Galveston1900keepersdlog.pdf (accessed June 15, 2013).

U.S. Naval Institute Staff. "A Hundred Years Dry: The U.S. Navy's End of Alcohol at Sea. USNI News, http://news.usni.org/2014/07/01/hundred-years-dry-u-s-navys-end-alcohol-sea (accessed June 1, 2015).

Waterman, George S. "Afloat–Afield–Afloat." *Confederate Veteran* 9, 11 (November 1902), www.adp.fsu.edu/ivanhoe.html (accessed November 12, 2010).

Watson, John C. "Farragut and Mobile Bay—Personal Reminiscences." *War Papers* 98. MOLLUS-D.C. (Washington, D.C.: Read before the Commandery 1916): 1–19, https://archive.org/details/farragutmobileba00wats (accessed November 13, 2010).

[Watson, Scott]. "Civil War Optics." www.civilwarmedicalbooks.com/civil_ war_optics.html (accessed April 22, 2013).

West, W. Wilson, Jr. "USS *Tecumseh* Shipwreck Management Plan." Joint project of Department of Defense Legacy Resource Management Program, et al. (1996), www.explorersclub.ca/documents/west/tecumseh_report.pdf (accessed November 24, 2010).

Whitlock, Philip. "The Life of Philip Whitlock, Written by Himself." Beth Ahabah Museum and Archives Trust. Richmond, Va. http://www.jewish-history.com/philip_whitlock.html (accessed October 27, 2010).

"Yellow Fever." http://www.cdc.gov/yellowfever/ (accessed June 5, 2015).

PUBLIC DOCUMENTS

National Archives and Records Administration. Enlistment register, pension file and USS *Hartford* muster roll of Dec. 20, 1864, all for Bartholomew Diggins.

Official Records of the Union and Confederate Navies in The War of the Rebellion. 30 vols. Washington, D.C.: GPO, 1894–1922.

Patent by Diggins: Hammock-support, letters, patent no. 638, 174, dated Nov. 28, 1899, United States Patent Office.

"Regulations for the Government of the United States Navy, 1865." Washington, D.C.: GPO, 1865.

U.S. Congress. Senate. Committee on Claims. Report 103, 42d Cong., 2d Sess. (April 1, 1872), claim denial for steam lighter *Ingomar.*

U.S. Navy History Division. *Civil War Naval Chronology, 1861–1865.* Washington, D.C.: GPO, [1961–1966].

The War of the Rebellion: A Compilation of the Official Records of the Union and Confederate Armies. 128 vols. Washington, D.C.: GPO, 1880–1901.

PRIMARY BOOKS

Bacon, Edward W. *Double Duty in the Civil War: The Letters of Sailor and Soldier Edward W. Bacon.* Edited by George S. Burkhardt. Carbondale: Southern Illinois University Press, 2009.

Basler, Roy P., ed. *The Collected Works of Abraham Lincoln.* 9 vols. New Brunswick, N. J.: Rutgers University Press, 1955.

Batten, John M. *Reminiscences of Two Years in the United States Navy.* Lancaster, Pa.: Inquirer Printing and Publishing, 1881.

Blanding, Stephen F. *Recollections of a Sailor Boy; or, the Cruise of the Gunboat Louisiana.* Providence, R. I.: E. A. Johnson & Co., 1887.

Boyer, Samuel P. *Naval Surgeon Blockading the South, 1862–1866: The Diary of Dr. Samuel Pellman Boyer.* Edited by Elinor Barnes and James A. Barnes. Bloomington: Indiana University Press, 1963.

Brooke, George M., Jr., ed. *Ironclads and Big Guns of the Confederacy: The Journal and Letters of John M. Brooke.* Columbia: University of South Carolina, 2002.

Browne, Henry R., and Symmes E. Browne. *The Letters of Acting Master's Mate Henry R. Browne and Acting Ensign Symmes E. Browne.* Edited by John D. Milligan. Annapolis, Md.: Naval Institute Press, 1970.

Buel, James W., ed. *Behind the Guns with American Heroes.* Chicago, Ill.: International Publishing Co., 1899.

Butler, Benjamin Franklin. *Autobiography and Personal Reminiscences of Major General Benj. F. Butler: Butler's Book.* Boston: A. M. Thayer, 1892.

Cate, Wirt Armistead, ed. *Two Soldiers: The Campaign Diaries of Thomas J. Key, C.S.A., and Robert J. Campbell, U.S.A.* Chapel Hill: University of North Carolina Press, 1938.

Clark, Charles E. *My Fifty Years in the Navy.* Boston: Little, Brown and Co., 1917.

Clark, George Edward. *Seven Years of a Sailor's Life.* Boston: Adams & Co., 1867.

Clarke, Hermon. *Back Home in Oneida: Hermon Clarke and His Letters.* Harry F. Jackson and Thomas F. O'Donnell, eds. Syracuse, N.Y.: Syracuse Univ. Press, 1965.

Cotham, Edward T., Jr., ed. *The Southern Journey of a Civil War Marine: The Illustrated Note-Book of Henry O. Gusley.* Austin: University of Texas Press, 2006.

Crandall, Warren D., and Isaac D. Newell. *History of the Ram Fleet and the Mississippi Marine Brigade . . . the Ellets and their Men.* St. Louis, Mo.: Buschart Bros., 1907.

Davidson, William H. *War was the Place.* Chattahoochee Valley Hhistorical Society Bulletin 5 (November 1961). Old Oakbowery, Ala.: Chattahoochee Valley Historical Society, 1961.

Dewey, George. *Autobiography of George Dewey, Admiral of the Navy.* New York: Charles Scribner's Sons, 1913.

Dodson, C. Marion. *Yellow Flag: The Civil War Journal of Surgeon's Steward C. Marion Dodson.* Edited by Charles A. Earp. Baltimore: Maryland Historical Society, 2002.

Evans, Robley D. *A Sailor's Log: Recollections of Forty Years of Naval Life.* New York: D. Appleton and Co., 1901.

Foltz, Charles S. *Surgeon of the Seas: The Adventurous Life of Surgeon General Jonathan M. Foltz in the Days of Wooden Ships, Told from his Notes of the Moment.* Indianapolis: Bobbs-Merrill, 1931.

Garrett, Jill K., and Marise P. Lightfoot. *The Civil War in Maury County, Tennessee.* N.p.: Pub. by the authors, 1966.

Goldsborough, William W. *The Maryland Line in the Confederate States Army.* Baltimore, Md.: Kelly, Piet & Co., 1869.

Goodloe, Albert Theodore. *Confederate Echoes: A Soldier's Personal Story of Life in the Confederate Army from the Mississippi to the Carolinas.* Nashville: For the Author by Smith & Lamar, 1907. Reprint, Washington, D.C.: Zenger, 1983.

Gould, William B., IV, ed. *Diary of a Contraband: The Civil War Passage of a Black Sailor.* Stanford: Stanford University Press, 2002.

Graves, Daniel, ed. *Civil War Letters From a Gunboat Sailor.* N.p.: Lulu.com, 2006.

Gregg, Josiah. *The Diary of a Civil War Marine, Private Josiah Gregg.* Edited by Wesley Moody and Adrienne Sachse. Madison, Wis.: Fairleigh Dickinson University Press, 2013.

Hackett, Frank Warren, ed. *Deck and Field: Addresses before the United States Naval War College and on Commemorative Occasions.* Washington, D.C.: W. H. Lowdermilk, 1909.

Harwell, Richard B., ed. *Kate: The Journal of a Confederate Nurse.* Baton Rouge: Louisiana State University Press, 1959. Originally published as *A Journal of Hospital Life in the Confederate Army of Tennessee from the Battle of Shiloh to the End of the War.* Louisville, Ky.: John P. Morton, 1866.

Higgins, Josiah P. *Yeoman in Farragut's Fleet: The Civil War Diary of Josiah Parker Higgins.* Edited by E. C. Herrmann. Carmel, Calif.: Guy Victor Publications, 1999.

Hill, Frederic Stanhope. *Twenty Years at Sea; Or, Leaves from My Old Logbook.* Boston: Houghton, Mifflin and Co., 1893.

Holton, William C. *Cruise of the U.S. Flag-Ship Hartford, 1861–1863; Being a Narrative of All Her Operations Since Going into Commission, in 1862, until Her Return to New York in 1863.* Edited by B. S. Osbon. New York: L. W. Paine, 1863.

Hunter, Alvah E. *A Year on a Monitor and the Destruction of Fort Sumter.* Edited by Craig L. Symonds. Columbia: University of South Carolina Press, 1987.

Johnson, Robert U., and Clarence C. Buel, eds. *Battles and Leaders of the Civil War.* 4 vols. New York: The Century Co., 1884–1888.

Kell, John M. *Beneath the Stainless Banner.* Edited by R. Thomas Campbell. Shippensburg, Pa.: Burd Street Press, 1999.

Kendricken, Paul H. *Memoirs of Paul Henry Kendricken.* Boston: privately printed, 1910.

Kinsley, Rufus. *Diary of a Christian Soldier: Rufus Kinsley and the Civil War.* Edited by David C. Rankin. New York: Cambridge University Press, 2004.

Lamson, Roswell H. *Lamson of the Gettysburg: The Civil War Letters of Lieutenant Roswell H. Lamson, U. S. Navy.* Edited by James M. McPherson and Patricia R. McPherson. New York: Oxford University Press, 1997.

Lee, Elizabeth Blair. *Wartime Washington: The Civil War Letters of Elizabeth Blair Lee.* Edited by Virginia Jeans Laas. Urbana: University of Illinois Press, 1991.

Morgan, James Morris. *Midshipman in Gray: Selections from Recollections of a Rebel Reefer.* Edited by R. Thomas Campbell. Shippensburg, Pa.: Burd Street

Press, 1997. Originally published as *Recollections of a Rebel Reefer.* Boston: Houghton Mifflin, 1917.

Morgan, James M., and John P. Marquand. *Prince and Boatswain: Sea tales from the recollection of Rear-Admiral Charles E. Clark.* Greenfield, Mass.: S. A. Hall & Co., 1915.

Morrow, Leslie G. *Journal of Leslie G. Morrow, Captain's Clerk of the U. S. Steamer* Galena. Edited by Albert P. Morrow. Yorba Linda, Calif.: A. P. Morrow, 1988.

Osbon, Bradley S. *A Sailor of Fortune; Personal Memoirs of Captain B. S. Osbon.* New York: McClure, Phillips & Co., 1907.

Oviatt, Miles M. *A Civil War Marine at Sea: The Diary of Medal of Honor Recipient Miles M. Oviatt.* Edited by Mary P. Livingston, ed. Shippensburg, Pa.: White Mane Books, 1998.

Perkins, George H. *Letters of Capt. Geo. Hamilton Perkins, U.S.N.* Concord, N.H.: Rumford Press, 1886. Reprint, Freeport, N.Y.: Books for Libraries, 1970.

Philadelphia Weekly Times. *Annals of the War.* Philadelphia: Times Publishing, 1879. Reprint, Gettysburg, Pa.: Civil War Times Illustrated, 1974.

Porter, David D. *Incidents and Anecdotes of the Civil War.* New York: D. Appleton & Co., 1885.

Rains, Gabriel J., and Peter S. Michie. *Confederate Torpedoes.* Edited by Herbert M. Schiller. Jefferson, N. C.: McFarland & Co., 2011.

Rawick, George P., ed. *The American Slave: A Composite Autobiography.* Ser. 1 and 2, 19 vols. Compiled by Federal Writers' Project, WPA, 1936–37. Originally published 1941. Reprint, Westport, Conn.: Greenwood, 1972.

Roberson, Elizabeth W, ed. *Weep Not For Me Dear Mother.* Gretna, La.: Pelican, 1996.

Safford, Moses. *Showing the Flag: The Civil War Naval Diary of Moses Safford, USS* Constellation. Edited by Lawrence J. Bopp and Stephen R. Bockmiller. Charleston, S. C.: History Press, 2004.

Sands, Benjamin F. *From Reefer to Rear Admiral: Reminiscences and Journal Jottings of Nearly Half a Century of Naval Life.* New York: Frederic A. Stokes Co., 1899.

Scheliha, Viktor Ernst K. R. von. *A Treatise on Coast-Defence.* London: E. & F. N. Spon, 1868.

Schley, Winfield Scott. *Forty-five Years Under the Flag.* New York: D. Appleton, 1904.

Selfridge, Thomas O. *What Finer Tradition: The Memoirs of Thomas O. Selfridge, Jr., Rear Admiral, U.S.N.* New York: Knickbocker Press, 1924. Reprint, Columbia: University of South Carolina Press, 1987.

Semmes, Raphael. *Rebel Raider; Being an Account of Raphael Semmes's Cruise in the C.S.S. Sumter.* Edited by Harpur A. Gosnell. Chapel Hill: University of North Carolina Press, 1948.

Seymour, William J. *Civil War Memoirs of Captain William J. Seymour: Reminiscences of a Louisiana Tiger.* Edited by Terry L. Jones. Baton Rouge: Louisiana State University Press, 1991.

Silber, Nina, and Mary Beth Sievens, eds. *Yankee Correspondence: Civil War Letters between New England Soldiers and the Home Front.* Charlottesville: University Press of Virginia, 1996.

Simon, John Y., ed. *The Papers of Ulysses S. Grant.* 31 vols. Carbondale: Southern Illinois University Press, 1967–2009.

Smith, C. Carter, Jr., ed. *Two Naval Journals, 1864: The Journal of Mr. John C. O'Connell, CSN, on the C.S.S. Tennessee and the Journal of Pvt. Charles Brother, USMC, on the U.S.S. Hartford at the Battle of Mobile Bay.* Birmingham, Ala.: Southern University Press by Birmingham Publishing Co., 1964.

Soloman, Clara. *The Civil War Diary of Clara Solomon: Growing Up in New Orleans, 1861–1862.* Edited by Elliott Ashkenazi. Baton Rouge: Louisiana State University Press, 1995.

Spiegel, Marcus M. *Your True Marcus: The Civil War Letters of a Jewish Colonel.* Edited by Fran L. Byrne and Jean P. Soman. Kent, Ohio: Kent State University Press, 1985.

Sprague, Homer B. *Lights and Shadows in Confederate Prisons; A Personal Experience, 1864–65.* New York: G. P. Putnam's Sons, 1915.

Stedman, Charles E. *The Civil War Sketchbook of Charles Ellery Stedman, Surgeon, United States Navy.* Edited by Jim Dan Hill. San Rafael, Calif.: Presidio Press, 1976.

Symonds, Craig L., ed. *A Year on a Monitor and the Destruction of Fort Sumter.* Columbia: University of South Carolina Press, 1987.

Thompson, Robert Means, and Richard Wainwright, eds. *Confidential Correspondence of Gustavus Vasa Fox, Assistant Secretary of the Navy, 1861–1865.* 2 vols. New York: De Vinne Press, 1918.

Tomb, James H. *Engineer in Gray: Memoirs of Chief Engineer James H. Tomb, CSN.* Jefferson, N.C.: McFarland & Co., 2011.

Toney, Marcus B. *The Privations of a Private.* 2nd ed. Nashville, Tenn.: M. E. Church, South, 1907.

U.S. Naval History Division. *Civil War Naval Chronology, 1861–1865.* 6 vols. Washington, D.C.: GPO, [1961–66].

Vail, I. E. *Three Years on the Blockade: A Naval Experience.* New York: Abbey Press, 1902.

Walke, H[enry]. *Naval Scenes and Reminiscences of the Civil War in the United States on the Southern and Western Waters.* New York: F. R. Reed, 1877.

Welles, Gideon. *Diary of Gideon Welles.* 3 vols. Boston: Houghton Mifflin, 1911.

Wright, Howard C. *Port Hudson: Its History from an Interior Point of View as Sketched from the Diary of an Officer.* Originally published in newspapers in 1863 and 1866; in book form by the St. Francisville (La.) *Democrat* in 1937. Reprint, Baton Rouge: Committee for the Preservation of the Port Hudson Battlefield, 1961.

PRIMARY ARTICLES

Ammen, Daniel. "Du Pont and the Port Royal Expedition." In *Battles and Leaders of the Civil War,* 4 vols., edited by Robert U. Johnson and Clarence C. Buel, 1:671–91. New York: The Century Co., 1884–1888.

[Austill, Hurieosco]. "Fort Morgan in the Confederacy." *Alabama Historical Quarterly* 7, 2 (Summer 1945): 254–68.

Bacon, George B. "One Night's Work, April 20, 1862." *Magazine of American History* 15, 3 (March 1886): 305–7.

Baker, Marion A. "Farragut's Demands for the Surrender of New Orleans." In *Battles and Leaders of the Civil War,* 4 vols., edited by Robert U. Johnson and Clarence C. Buel, 2:95–99. New York: The Century Co., 1884–1888.

Baldwin, Henry D. "Farragut in Mobile Bay: Recollections of One Who Took Part in the Battle." *Scribner's Monthly,* 13, 4 (February 1877): 539–44.

Bartlett, John R. "'The 'Brooklyn' at the Passage of the Forts." In *Battles and Leaders of the Civil War,* 4 vols., edited by Robert U. Johnson and Clarence C. Buel, 2:56–69. New York: The Century Co., 1884–1888.

Basile, Leon, ed. "Harry Stanley's Mess Book: Offenses and Punishments Aboard the *Ethan Allen.*" *Civil War History* 23, 1 (March 1977): 69–79.

Batcheller, Oliver A. "The Battle of Mobile Bay, August 5, 1864." In *War Papers* 1, MOLLUS-Maine, 58–72. Portland: Thurston Print, 1898.

Beauregard, G. T. "Torpedo Service in Charleston Harbor." In *Annals of the War,* by Philadelphia Weekly Times, 513–26. Philadelphia, Pa.: Times Publishing, 1879. Reprint, Gettysburg, Pa.: Civil War Times Illustrated, 1974.

Belous, Russell E., ed. "The Diary of Ann Quigley." *Gulf Coast Historical Review* 4, 2 (Spring 1989): 89–99.

Blakeman, Noel A. "Some Personal Reminiscences of the Naval Service." In *Personal Recollections,* Ser. 2, MOLLUS-N.Y., 231–39. New York: G. P. Putnam's Sons, 1897.

Brother, Charles. "The Journal of Private Charles Brother, USMC." In *Civil War Naval Chronology, 1861–1865,* 6 vols., Naval History Division. Washington, D.C.: Government Printing Office, 1965–1966. 6:47–83.

Brown, George W. "The Mortar Flotilla and Its Connection with the Bombardment and Capture of Forts Jackson and St. Philip." In *Personal Recollection*, Ser. 1, MOLLUS-N.Y., 173–82. New York: By the Commandery, 1891.

———. "Service in the Mississippi Squadron, and Its Connection with the Siege and Capture of Vicksburg." In *Personal Recollections*, Ser. 2, MOLLUS-N.Y., 303–13. New York: G. P. Putnam's Sons, 1897.

Brown, Isaac N. "The Confederate Gun-Boat 'Arkansas.'" In *Battles and Leaders of the Civil War*, 4 vols., edited by Robert U. Johnson and Clarence C. Buel, 3:572–80. New York: The Century Co., 1884–1888.

Butler, Edward A. "Personal Experiences in the Navy, 1862–65." In *War Papers*, vol. 2, MOLLUS-Maine, 185–200. Portland: Read before the Commandery Dec. 6, 1899.

Butts, Frank R. "A Cruise Along the Blockade." In *Personal Narratives*, Ser. 2, RISSHS, 5–37. Providence, R.I.: Read Nov. 13, 1878.

Cable, G[eorge] W., ed. "A woman's Diary of the Siege of Vicksburg." *Century Illustrated Magazine*, New Series 8 (September 1885): 768–74.

———. "New Orleans Before the Capture." In *Battles and Leaders of the Civil War*, 4 vols., edited by Robert U. Johnson and Clarence C. Buel, 2:14–21. New York: The Century Co., 1884–1888.

Campbell, James E. "The Mississippi Squadron." *Ohio Archaeological and Historical Quarterly* 34, 1 (January 1925): 56–62.

Chester, Colby. "Showing the Way." In *War Papers* 4, 79, MOLLUS-D.C., 163–71. Washington, D.C.: By the Commandery, 1910.

Coleman, S. B. "A July Morning with the Rebel Ram 'Arkansas.'" In *War Papers*, Vol. 1, MOLLUS-Mich., 3–13. Detroit: Winn & Hammond, 1890.

Conrad, D. B. "What the Fleet Surgeon Saw of the Fight in Mobile Bay, August 1864, whilst on Board the Confederate Ironclad *Tennessee*." *The United Service* 8, 3 (September 1892): 261–70.

———. "With Buchanan on the Tennessee." In *Behind the Guns with American Heroes*, edited by James W. Buel, 403–15. Chicago, Ill.: International Publishing Co., 1899.

Cox, Benjamin B. "Mobile in the War Between the States." *Confederate Veteran* 24, 5 (May 1916): 209–13.

Davis, Jefferson. "Beast Butler Outlawed." *Southern Historical Society Papers* 14 (1886): 470–75.

Drayton, Percival. "Naval Letters from Captain Percival Drayton, 1861–1865." *New York Public Library Bulletin* 10 (1906): 38–81.

Duncan, Richard D., ed. "The Storming of Mobile Bay." *Alabama Historical Quarterly* 40, 1 & 2 (Spring & Summer 1978): 6–19.

Ely, Robert B. "'this filthy ironpot.'" *American Heritage* 19, 2 (February 1968): 46–51, 108–11.

Everson, Guy R., ed. "Service Afield and Afloat: A Reminiscence of the Civil War." *Indiana Magazine of History* 89, 1 (March 1993): 35–56.

Farragut, Loyall. "Passing the Port Hudson Batteries." In *Personal Recollections*, Ser. 1, MOLLUS-N.Y., 314–21. New York: By the Commandery, 1891.

Gift, George W. "The Story of the Arkansas," *Southern Historical Society Papers* 12 (1884):48–54, 115–19, 163–70, 205–12.

Ginder, Henry. "A Louisiana Engineer at the Siege of Vicksburg: Letters of Henry Ginder." Edited by L. Moody Simms, Jr. *Louisiana History* 8, 4 (Fall 1967): 371–78.

Gregory, Edward S. "Vicksburg During the Siege." In *Annals of the War*, by Philadelphia Weekly Times, 111–33. Philadelphia, Pa.: Times Publishing, 1879. Reprint, Gettysburg, Pa.: Civil War Times Illustrated, 1974.

Grier, John A, "A Sketch of Naval Life." In *Military Essays and Recollections*, vol. 3, MOLLUS-Ill., 303–24. Chicago: Dial Press, 1899.

Hart, John E. "Commanding the USS *Albatross.*" *Civil War Times Illustrated* 15, 4 (July 1976): 128–35.

Heslin, James J., ed. "Two New Yorkers in the Union Navy." *New-York Historical Society Quarterly* 43, 2 (April 1959): 160–201.

Hubbard, Lucius F. "Letters of a Union Officer: L. F. Hubbard and the Civil War." Edited by N. B. Martin. *Minnesota History* 35 (1957): 313–19.

Huch, Ronald K., ed. "The Civil War Letters of Herbert Saunders." *Register of the Kentucky Historical Society* 69 (January 1971):17–29.

Hults, E. H. "Aboard the Galena at Mobile." Parts 1 and 2. *Civil War Times Illustrated* 10, 1 (April 1971): 12–21; 10, 2 (May 1971): 28–40.

Irwin, Richard S. "Land Operrations Against Mobile." In *Battles and Leaders of the Civil War*, 4 vols., edited by Robert U. Johnson and Clarence C. Buel, 4:410–11. New York: The Century Co., 1884–1888.

———. The "Red River Campaign" In *Battles and Leaders of the Civil War*, 4 vols., edited by Robert U. Johnson and Clarence C. Buel, 4:345–66. New York: The Century Co., 1884–1888.

"Jesse." "The Battle of Mobile ." In *Brooklyn Journal*, Brooklyn Institute of Arts and Sciences, Children's Museum, Occasional Papers in Cultural History, No. 5 (1964).

Johnston, J[ames] D. "The Battle of Mobile Bay." *Southern Historical Society Papers* 9, (1881):471–76.

Johnston, James D. "The Ram 'Tennessee' at Mobile." In *Battles and Leaders of the Civil War*, 4 vols., edited by Robert U. Johnson and Clarence C. Buel, 4:401–6. New York: The Century Co., 1884–1888.

Johnston, J. Stoddard. "Sketches of Operations of General John C. Breckinridge." *Southern Historical Society Papers* 7, 8 (August 1879): 385–92.

Jones, David P. "Something About Our Navy." In *Military Essays and Recollections*, vol. 3, MOLLUS-Ill., 325–39. Chicago: Dial Press, 1897.

Kautz, Albert. "Incidents of the Occupation of New Orleans." In *Battles and Leaders of the Civil War*, 4 vols., edited by Robert U. Johnson and Clarence C. Buel, 2:91–94. New York: The Century Co., 1884–1888.

———. "Letter to Editors." In *Battles and Leaders of the Civil War*, 4 vols., edited by Robert U. Johnson and Clarence C. Buel, 2:64. New York: The Century Co., 1884–1888.

Kell, John M. "Cruise and Combats of the 'Alabama.'" In *Battles and Leaders of the Civil War*, 4 vols., edited by Robert U. Johnson and Clarence C. Buel, 4:600–14. New York: The Century Co., 1884–1888.

Kendall, John S., ed. "Recollections of a Confederate Officer." *Louisiana Historical Quarterly* 29, 4 (Oct. 1946): 1041–1228.

Kennon, Beverley. "Fighting Farragut Below New Orleans." In *Battles and Leaders of the Civil War*, 4 vols., edited by Robert U. Johnson and Clarence C. Buel, 2:76–89. New York: The Century Co., 1884–1888.

Kinney, John C. "Farragut at Mobile Bay. In *Battles and Leaders of the Civil War*, 4 vols., edited by Robert U. Johnson and Clarence C. Buel, 4:379–400. New York: The Century Co., 1884–1888.

McMurry, Richard M., ed. "A Mississippian at Nashville" *Civil War Times Illustrated* 12 (May 1973): 8–11, 14–15.

Maury, Dabney H. "The Defence of Mobile in 1865." *Southern Historical Society Papers* 3, 1 (January 1877): 113.

Meredith, William T. "Admiral Farragut's Passage of Port Hudson." In *Personal Recollections*, Ser. 2, MOLLUS-N.Y., 118–25. New York: G. P. Putnam's Sons, 1897.

———. "Farragut's Capture of New Orleans." In *Battles and Leaders of the Civil War*, 4 vols., edited by Robert U. Johnson and Clarence C. Buel, 2:70–73. New York: The Century Co., 1884–1888.

"The Opposing Forces in the Operations at New Orleans, La." In *Battles and Leaders of the Civil War*, 4 vols., edited by Robert U. Johnson and Clarence C. Buel, 2:73–75. New York: The Century Co., 1884–1888.

Packard, Kent, ed. "Jottings by the Way: A Sailor's Log—1862–1864." *Pennsylvania Magazine of History and Biography* 71 (April 1947): 121–51.

Page, Robert L. "The Defense of Fort Morgan." In *Battles and Leaders of the Civil War*, 4 vols., edited by Robert U. Johnson and Clarence C. Buel, 4:408–9. New York: The Century Co., 1884–1888.

Parker, John C. "With Farragut at Port Hudson." *Civil War Times Illustrated* 7, 7 (November 1968): 42–9.

Porter, David D. "The Opening of the Lower Mississippi." In *Battles and Leaders of the Civil War*, 4 vols., edited by Robert U. Johnson and Clarence C. Buel, 2:22–54. New York: The Century Co., 1884–1888.

Read, Charles W. "Reminiscences of the Confederate States Navy." *Southern Historical Society Papers* 1, 5 (May 1876): 331–62.

Robertson, William B. "The Water-Battery at Fort Jackson." In *Battles and Leaders of the Civil War*, 4 vols., edited by Robert U. Johnson and Clarence C. Buel, 2:99–100. New York: The Century Co., 1884–1888.

Sands, Francis P. B. "'Lest We Forget': Memories of Service Afloat from 1862 to 1866." In *War Papers*, 73, MOLLUS-D.C., 45–68. Washington, D.C.: By the Commandery, 1908.

Schlesinger, Arthur M., ed. "A Blue Bluejacket's Letters Home, 1863–1864." *New England Quarterly* 1, 4 (October 1928): 554–67.

Shannon, I. N. "Infernal machines described." *Confederate Veteran* 13, 10 (October 1905): 458.

Shively, Joseph W. "The U.S.S. Mississippi at the Capture of New Orleans, 1862." In *War Papers*, 15, MOLLUS-D.C., 229–45. Washington, D.C.: Read before the Commandery 1893.

Simms, L. Moody, Jr. "A Union Volunteer with the Mississippi Ram Fleet." *Lincoln Herald* 70, 4 (Winter 1968): 189–92.

Soley, James R. "Closing Operations in the Gulf and Western Waters." In *Battles and Leaders of the Civil War*, 4 vols., edited by Robert U. Johnson and Clarence C. Buel, 4:412. New York: The Century Co., 1884–1888.

———. "Gulf Operations in 1862 and 1863." In *Battles and Leaders of the Civil War*, 4 vols., edited by Robert U. Johnson and Clarence C. Buel, 3:571. New York: The Century Co., 1884–1888.

———. "Letter to Editors." In *Battles and Leaders of the Civil War*, 4 vols., edited by Robert U. Johnson and Clarence C. Buel, 2:90. New York: The Century Co., 1884–1888.

———. "Naval Operations in the Vicksburg Campaign." In *Battles and Leaders of the Civil War*, 4 vols., edited by Robert U. Johnson and Clarence C. Buel, 3:551–70. New York: The Century Co., 1884–1888.

———. "The Union and Confederate Navies." In *Battles and Leaders of the Civil War*, 4 vols., edited by Robert U. Johnson and Clarence C. Buel, 1:611–31. New York: The Century Co., 1884–1888.

Stanton, O. F. "A Few Yarns of the Early Sixties." In *Personal Recollections*, Ser. 2, MOLLUS-N.Y., 280–89. New York: G. P. Putnam's Sons, 1897.

Swift, Lester L., ed. "Letters from a Sailor on a Tinclad." *Civil War History* 7, 1 (March 1961): 48–62.

True, Rowland Stafford. "Life Aboard a Gunboat." *Civil War Times Illustrated* 9, 10 (February 1971): 37–43.

W. "Some Errors Corrected in Mr. Freeman's Account." *New York Times*, May 19, 1887.

Warley, A. F. "The Ram 'Manassas' at the Passage of the New Orleans Forts." In *Battles and Leaders of the Civil War*, 4 vols., edited by Robert U. Johnson and Clarence C. Buel, 2:89–91. New York: The Century Co., 1884–1888.

Waterman, George S. "Afloat-Afield-Afloat." *Confederate Veteran* 9, 11 (November 1902): 18–21; also available at www.usgennet.org/usa/ga/topic/news/CV/cvmiscpg12.htm (accessed November 25, 2010).

Watson, J. Crittenden, and Joseph Marthon. "The Lashing of Admiral Farragut in the Rigging." In *Battles and Leaders of the Civil War*, 4 vols., edited by Robert U. Johnson and Clarence C. Buel, 4:406–8. New York: The Century Co., 1884–1888.

Webster, Harrie. "An August Morning with Farragut at Mobile Bay." In *Civil War Naval Chronolgy, 1861–1865*, 6 vols. Naval History Division. Washington, D.C.: Government Printing Office, 1961–1966, 6:86–97.

———. "Some Personal Recollections and Reminiscences of the Battle of Port Hudson." In *War Papers*, 16, MOLLUS-D.C., 249–66. Washington, D.C.: Read Jan. 3, 1894.

PERIODICALS

Boston Daily Traveller

Boston Journal

Boston Transcript

Chelsea (Mass.) Telegraph and Pioneer

Harper's Weekly

Hartford Courant

New York Herald

New York Times

Roxbury City Gazette

Worcester Aegis & Transcript

SECONDARY ARTICLES AND BOOKS

A Naval Encyclopædia: Comprising a Dictionary of Nautical Words and Phrases; Biographical Notices, and Records of Naval Officers. Philadelphia: L. R. Hamersly, 1881.

Abbot, Willis J. *Blue Jackets of '61: A History of the Navy in the War of Secession.* New York: Dodd, Mead and Co., 1887.

Anderson, Bern. *By Sea and By River: The Naval History of the Civil War.* New York: Knopf, 1962. Reprint, New York: Da Capo, 1989.

Andrews, J. Cutler. *The North Reports the Civil War.* Pittsburgh, Pa.: University of Pittsburgh, 1955.

Ballard, Michael B. *Vicksburg: The Campaign That Opened the Mississippi.* Chapel Hill: University of North Carolina Press, 2004.

Bennett, Michael J. *Union Jacks: Yankee Sailors in the Civil War.* Chapel Hill: University of North Carolina Press, 2004.

Bergeron, Arthur W. *Confederate Mobile.* Baton Rouge: Louisiana State University Press by arrangement with University of Mississippi Press, 1994.

———. *Guide to Louisiana Confederate Military Units, 1861–1865.* Baton Rouge: Louisiana State University Press, 1989.

Boatner, Mark May, III. *Civil War Dictionary.* New York: David McKay, 1959.

Bradlee, Francis B. C. *Blockade Running During the Civil War and the Effect of Land and Water Transportation on the Confederacy.* Salem, Mass.: The Essex Institute, 1925. Reprint, Philadelphia: Porcupine Press, 1974.

Brodine, Charles E., Jr., Michael J. Crawford, and Christine F. Hughes. *Interpreting Old Ironsides: An Illustrated Guide to USS Constitution.* Washington, D.C.: Navy Historical Center, Navy Department, GPO, 2007.

Burkhardt, George S. *Confederate Rage, Yankee Wrath: No Quarter During the Civil War.* Carbondale: Southern Illinois University Press, 2007.

Butler, John A. *Sailing on Friday: The Perilous Voyage of America's Merchant Marine.* Washington, D.C.: Brassey's, 1997.

Calore, Paul. *Naval Campaigns of the Civil War.* Jefferson, N.C.: McFarland & Co., 2002.

Campbell, R. Thomas. *Sea Hawk of the Confederacy: Lt. Charles W. Read and the Confederate Navy.* Shippensburg, Pa.: Burd Street Press, 2000.

Canfield, Eugene B. *Civil War Naval Ordnance.* Washington, D.C.: Naval History Division, Navy Department, GPO, 1969.

Canney, Donald L. *Lincoln's Navy: The Ships, Men and Organization, 1861–65.* Annapolis, Md.: Naval Institute Press, 1998.

Coggins, Jack. *Arms and Equipment of the Civil War.* New York: Fairfax Press, 1983.

Coombe, Jack D. *Thunder Along the Mississippi: The River Battles That Split the Confederacy.* New York: SARPEDON, 1996. Reprint, Edison, N.J.: Castle Books, 2005.

Cornish, Dudley T. *The Sable Arm: Negro Troops in the Union Army, 1861–1865.* New York: Longmans, Green, 1956. Reprint, New York: W. W. Norton, 1966.

Cornish, Dudley T., and Virginia Jeans Laas. *Lincoln's Lee: The Life of Samuel Phillips Lee, United States Navy, 1812–1897.* Lawrence: University of Kansas Press, 1986.

Cotham, Edward T., Jr. *Battle on the Bay: The Civil War Struggle for Galveston.* Austin: Univ. of Texas Press, 1998.

Crane, W. Craig. *Encyclopedia of Civil War Shipwrecks.* Baton Rouge: Louisiana State Univ. Press, 2008.

Cumberland, Charles C. "The Confederate Loss and Recapture of Galveston." *Southwestern Historical Quarterly* 52, no. 2 (October 1947):122–30.

Cummins, Light T. "English Spoken Here: Great Britain and Louisiana." *Historic New Orleans Collection Quarterly* 22, no. 4 (Fall 2004):1–2.

Dalzell, George W. *Flight from the Flag: The Continuing Effect of the Civil War on the American Carrying Trade.* Chapel Hill: Univ. of North Carolina Press, 1940.

Diamant, Lincoln. *The Fight for the River in the American Revolution.* New York: Fordham Univ. Press, 2004.

Dyer, Frederick H. *A Compendium of the War of the Rebellion.* Des Moines, Iowa: Dyer, 1908. Reprint, Datyon, Ohio: Morningside Bookshop, 1978.

Farragut, Loyall. *The Life of David Glasgow Farragut, First Admiral of the United States Navy: Embodying His Journal and Letters.* New York: D. Appleton & Co., 1879.

Fleming, Walter L. *Civil War and Reconstruction in Alabama.* New York: Columbia University Press, 1905. Reprint, New York: Peter Smith, 1949.

Fowler, William M., Jr. *Under Two Flags: The American Navy in the Civil War.* New York: W. W. Norton, 1990.

Fox, William F. *Regimental Losses in the American Civil War.* Albany, N.Y.: Albany Publishing Co., 1889.

Friend, Jack. *West Wind, Flood Tide: The Battle of Mobile Bay.* Annapolis, Md.: Naval Institute Press, 2004.

Fulton, Robert. *Torpedo War and Submarine Explosions.* New York: William Elliot, 1810. Reprint, Chicago: The Swallow Press, 1971.

Gill, James. *Lords of Misrule: Mardi Gras and the Politics of Race in New Orleans.* Jackson: University Press of Mississippi, 1997.

Gosnell, H. Allen. *Guns on the Western Waters: The Story of River Gunboats in the Civil War.* Baton Rouge: Louisiana State University Press, 1949.

Hamersly, Lewis R. *The Records of Living Officers of the U.S. Navy and Marine Corps.* Philadelphia: J. B. Lippincott, 1870.

Harland, John. *Seamanship in the Age of Sail: An Account of the Shiphandling of the Sailing Man-of-War 1600–1860, Based on Contemporary Sources.* Annapolis, Md.: Naval Institute Press, 1984. Rev. ed., 1987.

Harrod, Frederick S. "Jim Crow in the Navy (1798–1941)." *Proceedings of the United States Naval Institute* 105 (September 1979): 46–53.

Headley, J. T. *Farragut, and Our Naval Commanders.* New York: E. B. Trent, 1867.

Hearn, Chester G. *Ellet's Brigade: The Strangest Outfit of All.* Baton Rouge: Louisiana State University Press, 2000.

Howard, Judith A. "Home at the Mouth of the Mississippi." *Southern Cultures* 14, 2 (Summer 2009): 69–88.

Jameson, Edwin M., and Sanford Sternlicht. *The Black Devil of the Bayous: The Life and Times of the United States Steam Sloop Hartford, 1858–1957.* Upper Saddle River, N.J.: Gregg Press, 1970.

Joiner, Gary D. *Mr. Lincoln's Brown Water Navy: The Mississippi Squadron.* Lanham, Md.: Rowman & Littlefield, 2007.

Jones, Archer. *Civil War Command and Strategy.* New York: The Free Press, 1992.

Kagan, Neil, and Steven G. Hyslop, eds. *Smithsonian Civil War: Inside the National Collection.* Washington, D.C.: Smithsonian Books, 2013.

Lewis, Charles Lee. *David Glasgow Farragut: Our First Admiral.* Annapolis, Md.: United States Naval Institute, 1943.

Lonn, Ella. *Foreigners in the Union Army and Navy.* Baton Rouge: Louisiana State University Press, 1951. Reprint, New York: Greenwood Press, 1969.

———. *Salt as a Factor in the Confederacy.* New York: Walter Neale, 1933.

Mahan, A. T. The *Navy in the Civil War.* Vol. III. *The Gulf and Inland Waters.* New York: Charles Scribner's Sons, 1883.

McEwen, W. A., and A. H. Lewis. *Encyclopedia of Nautical Knowledge.* Centreville, Md.: Cornell Maritime Press, 1953.

McPherson, James M. *War on the Waters: The Union and Confederate Navies, 1861–1865.* Chapel Hill: University of North Carolina, 2012.

Merrill, Louis Taylor. "General Benjamin F. Butler and the Widow Mumford." *Louisiana Historical Quarterly* 29, 2 (April 1946): 341–54.

Miller, Francis T., ed. *The Photographic History of the Civil War.* 10 vols. New York: Review of Reviews, 1911.

Milligan, John D. *Gunboats Down the Mississippi.* Annapolis, Md.: U.S. Naval Institute Press, 1965.

Montgomery, Horace. *Johnny Cobb: Confederate Aristocrat.* Athens: University of Georgia, 1964.

Noel, John V., and Edward L. Beach. *Naval Terms Dictionary.* 4th ed. Annapolis, Md.: U.S. Naval Institute Press, 1985.

Parker, Foxhall Alexander. *The Battle of Mobile Bay, and the Capture of Forts Powell, Gaines and Morgan.* Boston: A. Williams & Co., 1878. Reprint, Whitefish, Mont.: Kessinger Publishing, 2011.

Parton, James. *General Butler in New Orleans: History of the Administration in the Department of the Gulf in the Year 1862.* 5th ed. New York: Mason Brothers, 1864.

Pearce, George F. *Pensacola during the Civil War: A Thorn in the Side of the Confederacy.* Gainesville: University Press of Florida, 2000.

Perry, Milton F. *Infernal Machines: The Story of Confederate Submarines and Mine Warfare.* Baton Rouge: Louisiana State University Press, 1965.

Pirtle, Alfred. "Rear Admiral James Edward Jouett, United States Navy (Retired)." *United Service* 17, 1 (January 1897): 17–43.

Randall, J. G. *The Civil War and Reconstruction.* Boston: D. C. Heath, 1937. Reprint, 1953.

Ringle, Dennis J. *Life in Mr. Lincoln's Navy.* Annapolis, Md.: Naval Institute Press, 1998.

Roberts, William H. *USS New Ironsides in the Civil War.* Annapolis, Md.: Naval Institute Press, 1999.

Ross, David. *Ireland: History of a Nation.* New Lanark, U.K.: Geddes & Grosset, 2002.

Scharf, J. Thomas. *History of the Confederate States Navy from its Organization to the Surrender of its Last Vessel.* New York: Rogers & Sherwood, 1887. Reprint, New York: Fairfax Press, 1977.

Silverstone, Paul H. *Civil War Navies, 1855–1883.* Annapolis, Md.: Naval Institute Press, 2001.

Still, William M., Jr. *Iron Afloat: The Story of the Confederate Ironclads.* Nashville, Tenn.: Vanderbilt University Press, 1971. Reprint, Columbia, S.C.: University of South Carolina Press, 1985.

Surdam, David G. *Northern Naval Superiority and the Economics of the American Civil War.* Columbia: University of South Carolina Press, 2001.

Symonds, Craig L. *Confederate Admiral: The Life and Wars of Franklin Buchanan.* Annapolis, Md.: Naval Institute Press, 1999.

———. *Lincoln and His Admirals.* New York: Oxford University Press, 2008.

Tucker, Spencer C. *Blue and Gray Navies: The Civil War Afloat.* Annapolis, Md.: Naval Institue Press, 2006.

Walker, Carroll. *Norfolk A Pictorial History.* Edited by Linda G. Fales. Norfolk, Va.: Donning Co., 1975.

Warner, Ezra J. *Generals in Blue: Lives of the Union Commanders.* Baton Rouge: Louisiana State University Press, 1964.

———. *Generals in Gray: Lives of the Confederate Commanders.* Baton Rouge: Louisiana State University Press, 1959.

West, Richard S., Jr. *The Second Admiral: A life of David Dixon Porter, 1813–1891.* New York: Coward-McCann, 1937.

Westwood, Howard C. "Benjamin Butler's Enlistment of Black Troops in New Orleans in 1862." *Louisiana History* 26, 1 (Winter 1985): 522.

Wiley, Bell Irvin. "Billy Yank and the Black Folk." *Journal of Negro History* 36 (Spring 1951): 35–52.

Williams, Glenn F. "Uncle Sam's Webfeet: The Union Navy in the Civil War." *International Journal of Naval History* 1, 1 (April 2002): 1–16. Also available in "Archives" at www.ijnhonline.org (accessed March 15, 2009).

Winthrop, William. *Military Law and Precedents.* 2 vols. 2nd ed. Boston: Little, Brown, 1896.

Wise, Stephen R. *Lifeline of the Confederacy: Blockade Running During the Civil War.* Columbia: University of South Carolina Press, 1988.

Wyllie, Arthur. *The Confederate States Navy.* Raleigh, N.C.: Lulu.com, 2007.

INDEX

Page numbers in **boldface** refer to illustrations.

African Americans: attitudes towards, 54–55, 175n9, 175n12; as "contraband" of war, 81, 90, 173n17, 182n23; and enlistment in Navy as laborers, 173n17, 174n20; and illiteracy, xix; and killed and wounded from land mines, 152; as newly freed slaves, 54–55; and New Orleans, 48; and recruitment of by Gen. Butler, 32, 48, 171n19; and slaves taken on board, 81; as soldiers, 183n36; and those killed in fire on board USS *Hartford*, 60; and treatment of by crew of the USS *Hartford*, 55–56; and U.S. army, 55, 138; in U.S. navy, 55, xix; and USS *Hartford*, 48, 177n18; and warnings from about Grand Gulf, 83

Alden, Capt. James, 51, 76, 122, 146, 193n23

Allen, E. J., 5

Anaconda Plan: and blockade of southern ports, 3, **36**; and capture of New Orleans, 3–4; and control of the Mississippi River, 3–4, **36**; scholarship on, 159n1

Anderson, Colonel Charles DeWitt, 151, 197–98n8

Bache, Albert D., 5

Bacon, Edward W., 58, 172n2, 172n3

Bailey, Capt. Theodorus: as commander of the fleet's second division, 9; flag ship of, 16; as a rear admiral, 161n15; and surrender of New Orleans, 28–29

Banks, Maj. Gen. Nathaniel P., 74, 76, 92, 93, 94, 120, 181n6

Baton Rouge, LA: and attack on Gen. Williams, 65; surrender of, 45; and USS *Hartford*, 46, 47, 62, 74

batteries: aboard the USS *Hartford*, 132, 139; and black men, 32; and boom across the river, 29–30, 170n13; in Carrollton, 29; Chalmette Batteries, 23, 168n28; destruction of, 30; enemy's desertion of, 17, 23; and the English Turn, 23; First Alabama Battery, 138; and force of six thousand men erecting, 49; at Grand Gulf, 47, 88; guns of, 17, 29, 30, 45, 49, 78; and light batteries on river banks, 46–47; and locations in cellars or basements, 49; masked batteries, 83, 183n27; of Natchez, MS, 82; at New Orleans, 74; noise from, 77; at Port Hudson, 47, 76, 77–78, 79, 80, 92, **97**, 147; and the Red River, 80; shore batteries, 163n25; and Vicksburg, MS, 45–51, **50**, 54, 58, 60, 61, 62, 73, 79, 83, 92; at Warrenton, MS, 87; water batteries, 15, 49, 60, 174n23; and yellow hospital flag, 46, 49

battles: and Admiral Farragut, 145; and attack on forts outside of New Orleans, 9–14; and attack on Port Hudson, 94, 151–52; and attack on Vicksburg, MS, 49–51; and battle for Port Hudson, 76–82, 85, 92; and battle of Mobile Bay, 119–36, 146; and CSS *Arkansas*, 58, 65; and diagram of Mobile Bay battle, **124**; engagement in Galveston Harbor, Jan. 1, 1863, 69–70; and General

161n15; and fighting with batteries, 23; guns of, 20, 24; and killed and wounded, 134; and medals of honor, 146; and mine sweeping, 123; and passing over a bar, 8; sailors on, 16, 162–63n24; and torpedoes (mines), 146

USS *Cairo*, 151

USS *Carondelet*: and blockade of Yazoo River, 59; as a gunboat, 59; and losses from battle with CSS *Arkansas*, 58; of the U.S. army, 57

USS *Cayuga*, 16, 21, 23, 165n8, 166n20, 168n28

USS *Chickasaw*, 112, 121, 123, 135, 136, 139

USS *Clifton*, 49

USS *Colorado*, 149

USS *Cricket*, xxi–xxii

USS *Essex*: and attempts to hit the CSS *Arkansas*, 58, **97**; and Baton Rouge, LA, 62; description of, 177n20; and goal of destroying the CSS *Arkansas*, 61; killed and wounded on, 61; at Port Hudson, 76, 77, 94; and sailors' meals, xxiii

USS *Estrella*, 93, 185n16

USS *Florida*, xxiv

USS *Franklin*, 148

USS *Harriet Lane*, 9, 22, 49, 69–70, 167n25, 180n3

USS *Hartford*: and Admiral Davis's fleet, 55; and anchoring at the Quarantine ground, 22–23; and attack on Vicksburg, MS, 46–51, **50**, 53, 55, 60; battle damage to, 133, 194n25, 195n11; and battle for New Orleans, 16–25; and battle of Mobile Bay, 122, 123, 125–27, 129–36, 152; and blockade of Mobile Bay, 111–12; and blockade of Red River, 87–88, 93; and broadside from the CSS *McRae*, 20; at the Brooklyn Navy Yard, 94–95, 145; claim of capture of, 82; and Comd. De Krafft, 135–36; and command of Capt. Percival Drayton, 149; and command of

USS *Hartford*, 178n4; and Confederate plans to board and capture, 88–89; and consultation of sailors, 62, 177n23; crew of, 5, 6, 8, 12–14, 46, 48, 51, 55–56, 74, 83, 84, 125, 145; and cruise to China, 4; and damage to ship, 78, 94; description of, 4; and desertions due to Capt. Palmer's discipline, 64–65; and destruction of enemy's property, 92; and dinghy's boys, 30–31; en route to New Orleans, 62; and expedition to destroy English blockade runner, 115; and fear of mortars, 13; and fight with CSS *Tennessee*, 131–33; final resting place of, 152; and fire from pitch from seams, 18–20, 60, 166n14, 166n16; first Rear Admiral Flag on, 65; as a flagship, 5, 122, 143; and foreign-born sailors, 144, xix; guns on, 4–5, 46, 48, 77, 83, 130, 189n18; and heavy fire, 23, 77, 130; and hospital in the main hold, 13, 18, 126; injuries on, 11, 46, 162n22; and killed and wounded, 17–18, 22, 23, 48, 60, 78, 83, 93–94, 126–27, 132, 133–34, 176n18; and killed and wounded from raid on English blockade runner, 116; and Loyall Farragut, 63; and men lost in the battle of Mobile Bay, 146; at Mobile Bay in 1864, **37**; muster roll of, 156n11; and Natchez, MS, 45, 82; and number of crew, 145, 160n8; and objective to capture or destroy CSS *Arkansas*, 60, 62; officers of, 4, 5, 8, 12, 48, 51, 57, 65, 84, 94–95, 125, 145; and passing over a bar, 8; and passing Port Hudson, **75**; and poor health of the crew, 92; and Port Hudson, 74–75, 76, 78, 94; post-Civil War uses of, 152; and preparations for attacks on the enemy, 4, 6, 11–12, 13, 46, 47, 48, 117; and preparations to repel attacks, 80–81; and prize money, xxii–xxiii; and problem with pay and